The Best
AMERICAN
ESSAYS
2010

GUEST EDITORS OF
THE BEST AMERICAN ESSAYS

The Best
AMERICAN
ESSAYS®
2010

Edited and with an Introduction
by CHRISTOPHER HITCHENS

Robert Atwan, Series Editor

A MARINER ORIGINAL
HOUGHTON MIFFLIN HARCOURT
BOSTON • NEW YORK 2010

www.hmhbooks.com

ISSN 0888-3742
ISBN 978-0-547-39451-0

Printed in the United States of America

DOC 10 9 8 7 6 5 4 3

"Who Killed Tolstoy?" from *The Possessed: Adventures with Russian Books and the
People Who Read Them,* by Elif Batuman. Copyright © 2010 by Elif Batuman. Re-
printed by permission of Farrar, Straus and Giroux, LLC. Originally published in
Harper's, February 2009, under the title "The Murder of Leo Tolstoy."
"The Bad Lion" by Toni Bentley. First published in the *New York Review of Books,*
November 5, 2009. Copyright © 2009 by Toni Bentley. Reprinted by permission of
Toni Bentley.
"The Dead Book" by Jane Churchon. First published in *The Sun,* February 2009.
Copyright © 2009 by Jane Churchon. Reprinted by permission of Jane Churchon.
"Irreconcilable Dissonance" by Brian Doyle. First published in *Oregon Humani-
ties,* Fall/Winter 2009. Copyright © 2009 by Brian Doyle. Reprinted by permission
of Brian Doyle.
"The Elegant Eyeball" by John Gamel. First published in *Alaska Quarterly Review,*
Spring/Summer 2009. Copyright © 2009 by Alaska Quarterly Review. Reprinted by
permission of *Alaska Quarterly Review.*
"How Einstein Divided America's Jews" by Walter Isaacson. First published in the
Atlantic, December 2009. Copyright © 2009 by Walter Isaacson. Reprinted by per-
mission of Walter Isaacson. Excerpt from *The Collected Papers of Albert Einstein,* by Al-
bert Einstein. Copyright © 1987–2008 Hebrew University and Princeton University
Press. Reprinted by permission of Princeton University Press.
"Lunching on Olympus" by Steven L. Isenberg. First published in the *American*

Contents

Foreword

AS I WRITE THIS FOREWORD, Apple has just released its iPad to compete with Amazon's popular Kindle, and the news media is once again abuzz over the "death of the book." Although I think that prophesying the end of bound and printed books or magazines is somewhat hyperbolic, there can be little doubt that with each passing year we will be reading more and more electronic texts. And it is possible that in years to come, many years it would seem, ink-and-paper book publishing, short of vanishing, will become something of a craft, like basket weaving, issuing *objets d'art* for a special literary audience — those who enjoy books as physical objects, who love collecting and displaying them, who cherish first editions and autographed copies. It's also possible book lovers will begin collecting first editions of e-books and even autographed e-books, though it's difficult to imagine how. And what will book signings be like when the electronic edition is the only edition?

Earlier generations fetishized printed books just as the younger generation now fetishizes the gadgets that can deliver books electronically. But the book is a hand-held gadget too, a technology that once transformed the world as the new devices are doing today. How much will be sacrificed if e-books eventually become the major product of publishing and the first printings of hardcover books grow smaller and smaller? How many years before authors would prefer to see their books published only in electronic form? At this stage of such momentous publishing upheaval, all we can do, it seems, is ask questions and try to make good guesses about the upsides and downsides, the gains and sacrifices, of moving to a predominately electronic publishing.

I love books as physical objects. They are extremely convenient and user-friendly, and they don't require chargers that are misplaced or forgotten. I treasure my luxuriously calf-bound signed first edition of Laurence Sterne's *Tristram Shandy*, that brilliantly demanding novel in nine volumes that called attention to itself, long before postmodernism, *as* a book. But as we edge closer to the day when books—as we are repeatedly informed, though no one says when—will be a marginalized medium (the prevalence today of actual books appearing in artwork, sculpture, and installations surely signifies some presentiment of obsolescence*), I find myself worrying less about the future of the book in our digital age and more about the fate of reading. The issue, it seems to me, isn't so much about how the books we read are delivered— whether we read on paper or on a screen. The question that needs asking is: What will be the impact of the new media on the art of reading?

[handwritten: traditionally]

[handwritten: essayistic]

Allow me a digression. I can distinctly recall the moment I finally learned to read. The sunny afternoon, the drab apartment, the old faded brown sofa on which I had lazily stretched out, the boisterous tavern that crowded my imagination. This isn't some dubious early childhood memory; I was a graduate student who had been an addicted reader since first grade, devouring books, newspapers, magazines, comics, and whatever printed word came my way. On that day, the book happened to be a small paperback edition of Shakespeare's *Henry IV, Part One*. I was in act 2, scene 4. I still own that edition.

I had of course been exposed to the usual Shakespearean suspects in high school, and then encountered them again in more specialized ways in college, where, in an Introduction to Shakespeare course, we were required to turn in a plot outline for every play assigned. But not until the apprentice tapster, Francis, finds himself the victim of a practical joke staged by the Prince of Wales and can only keep crying "Anon, anon" (colloquially, "Coming, I'll be right there") to the impatient calls of one of the Prince's tavern cronies stationed in another room, did I truly realize how literature works. I had always read for content, main point, theme, the

---

*For a fascinating look at this phenomenon, see "Bookwork as Demediation" by Garrett Stewart (*Critical Inquiry*, Spring 2010).

"big ideas," and I read in a straightforward linear fashion, whatever the genre. This enabled me to test well in certain circumstances, but as I realized after my sudden literary awakening, I had been reading literature for years with proficiency and passion but without aesthetic insight. Though an A student, I had been a B-minus reader. I still feel embarrassed when I return to a novel I read in college and find scrawled in the margin "Man vs. Nature."

Put simply, I hadn't been noticing the intricately layered network of imagery, verbal interconnectivity, conversational echoes, and dominant tropes that could be found on practically every page of Shakespeare. I'm not speaking here of simply observing certain metaphorical strands or symbolic patterns; reading literary genius is more like entering an astonishing zone of sublime verbal complexity in which we seem to encounter—to use Hamlet's words— "thoughts beyond the reaches of our souls." Using the technology of that time, I began to picture a Shakespeare play, with its overarching system of passages "wired" to countless other passages, as a schematic or electronic circuit diagram, the sort of large paper foldout that back then accompanied a new stereo set.

I thought a schematic diagram that would represent graphically the internal circuitry of a play like *Hamlet* or *Othello*—with all its signal paths laid out to show how any single passage connects to and illuminates many others throughout the grid—would be a far more expressive way to imagine what was going on inside the work than the popular blackboard diagram of "Exposition / Rising Action / Climax / Falling Action / Denouement," known officially, after its nineteenth-century German inventor, as the Freytag Pyramid, a model still being used after nearly a century and a half, despite all the years of student yawns, to explain Shakespeare.

When I eventually taught Shakespeare to undergraduates, I would cover the blackboard with my Circuit Diagram. Far less tidy than Freytag's linear model, my artwork had at least the instructional advantage of displaying a play's unique internal wiring. It helped students understand that the language of the play—unlike its action—did not need to be processed sequentially but could be seen as existing simultaneously in different locations and variations throughout the play. If I'd only had PowerPoint back then!

For talented readers nothing I've said here is surprising. Good readers detect the intricate internal wiring in the works of such lit-

erary figures as Jane Austen, John Keats, James Joyce, Vladimir
Nabokov, and David Foster Wallace. These readers, as the critic
and teacher Reuben Brower put it in an influential 1959 essay,
read in "slow motion." A good reader also rereads the great books.
In fact, Nabokov thought that just as there are major and minor
authors, so too are there major and minor readers: "A good reader,
a major reader, an active and creative reader is a rereader." Such
readers know that as they expand their mental and emotional ca-
pacities reading Shakespeare or Joyce—or Nabokov—they too
participate actively in the creative experience. Minor readers,
Nabokov thought, those with restricted imaginations, enjoy a novel
because they merely identify with a situation, a place, an ideological point of view, or one of its characters. Genuine imaginative writing, he suggests, demands readers with broader imaginations.

After my graduate school epiphany, when I realized how a single
comic incident could encapsulate the dramatic tension of an entire play, I became by choice a much slower reader of literature.
Pen in hand, I often paged backward and reread passages when I
noticed connections; I read always on the lookout for patterns and
structures, my inner eye focused on the writing's wiring; the text
absorbed my total attention. But I feel that my generation's style of
slow, patient, and close reading may be a dying art in the age of
YouTube, Facebook, and Twitter. In our multitasking environment,
how many find the leisure to read leisurely? Philip Roth has talked
about the dwindling "core of serious readers," and one can speculate on the impact the new technology is having on our tolerance
for long, demanding literary works. Will the number of serious
readers decline even further, or will the concept of a serious reader
change to accommodate all the new digital formats we are likely to
see?

There can be no doubt that the Internet has dramatically changed
the way we read. People want information delivered faster, in
smaller chunks, and with more visual accompaniment; one needs
only to examine the changes in student textbooks over the past
decade to see the impact Web design has had on reading and learning, and once these print textbooks evolve into e-books the opportunities for more embedded features will further alter reading
skills—creating, I believe, learning patterns that will be less discur-

sive and more discontinuous. In a few years American-literature students may be reading an enhanced e-version of *The Great Gatsby*, with background music from the early 1920s, colorful advertisements for the luxury cars of that era, photographs of mansions along Long Island Sound, clips from various film adaptations, appropriate multimedia links to the book's historical background, and interactive responses from readers eager to exchange insights. The effect would be like reading a novel, enjoying a movie, watching a documentary, and entering a chatroom at the same time. All in all, it would be a far different literary experience than opening the classic Scribner paperback and starting with "In my younger and more vulnerable years . . ."

But will such enhanced classics—a number of them already in the works—attract serious readers? Will they bring readers closer to the details of great books in the way Nabokov encouraged ("caress the details," he would tell his students), or will the audio-visual layering interfere with the imaginative process of turning words into mental pictures? Did readers over a hundred years ago read less creatively because their edition of *Middlemarch* contained engraved plates depicting Dorothea Brooke, or their copy of *Frankenstein* featured illustrations of the monster?

The recent success of e-books depended on finding ways to simulate a book with pages; new media often imitate the old devices at first, which helps explain why early television featured so many puppet shows. But as electronic books evolve, they may not retain the page model but come closer to a multisequential approach that Borges might have appreciated, or to the labyrinth of wired paths I found so exciting in Shakespeare. Writers are already finding various ways to approach literature in more spatial or topographical ways that take advantage of digital productions, and such works can now be read—or perhaps a better word is *seen*—in some of the cutting-edge magazines found online.

What will these changes mean to the essay? I find the cultural climate very encouraging, more so now than twenty-five years ago, when the first volume of this series appeared and the essay was pretty much, as Phillip Lopate aptly put it, living "in disguise." Given its relative brevity, its tendency toward topicality, and its lower budget, the essay seems perfectly suitable for electronic pub-

lishing, if that's where books are indeed headed. Besides, an enormous audience already exists for blogs—and what are blogs but
today's version of essays in disguise?

On the other hand, as I hold a copy of the inaugural *Best American Essays* I can detect little difference in the styles and substance
of the essays then compared to those in the book you are presumably now holding in *your* hand. The collection of 1985 essays, reflecting many of the same sources and subjects as found in this volume, shows how little the periodical essay has changed in twenty-five
years. Here are essays on writing and literature, politics and foreign policy, people and places, the arts and sciences. Almost half of
that collection's contents come from journals also represented in
this collection; in fact, only one periodical from the 1985 book no
longer exists. "1985 was surely a year like any other for the essay,"
Elizabeth Hardwick aptly wrote in her introduction, "that is, a year
filled with gifts that arrived without expectation. In a sense, every
interesting essay is a surprise." The same can be said of this collection, and I expect of all the others in years to come, as they attract
serious readers, whether in print or on a screen.

The Best American Essays features a selection of the year's outstanding essays, essays of literary achievement that show an awareness of
craft and forcefulness of thought. Hundreds of essays are gathered
annually from a wide assortment of national and regional publications. These essays are then screened, and approximately one hundred are turned over to a distinguished guest editor, who may add
a few personal discoveries and who makes the final selections. The
list of Notable Essays appearing in the back of the book is drawn
from a final comprehensive list that includes not only all of the essays submitted to the guest editor but also many that were not submitted.

To qualify for the volume, the essay must be a work of respectable literary quality, intended as a fully developed, independent
essay on a subject of general interest (not specialized scholarship),
originally written in English (or translated by the author) for publication in an American periodical during the calendar year. Today's essay is a highly flexible and shifting form, however, so these
criteria are not carved in stone.

Magazine editors who want to be sure their contributors will be considered each year should submit issues or subscriptions to: Robert Atwan, Series Editor, The Best American Essays, P.O. Box 220, Readville, MA 02137. Writers and editors are welcome to submit published essays from any American periodical for consideration; unpublished work does not qualify for the series and cannot be reviewed or evaluated. Please note: all submissions must be directly from the publication and not in manuscript or printout format. Editors of online magazines and literary bloggers should not assume that appropriate work will be found online; they are invited to submit printed copies of the essays (with full citations) to the address above.

I would like to dedicate this volume to the memory of Richard Poirier, a friend and mentor, a "major reader" and literary critic, a generous man, and a true Emersonian, who died on August 15, 2009. I thank my assistant, Kyle J. Giacomozzi, for all his invaluable help on this edition, from start to finish. As always, the Houghton Mifflin Harcourt staff could not have been more helpful, and I once again appreciate the efforts of Deanne Urmy, Nicole Angeloro, Larry Cooper, and Megan Wilson. It was a privilege and an honor to work on this collection with one of my favorite writers, Christopher Hitchens, who first appeared in the series in 1989. His wit, range of insight, and intellectual gusto have made him one of our nation's outstanding essayists, and those same qualities of mind and spirit can be found in abundance throughout this collection.

R. A.

Introduction

UNUSUALLY DISQUALIFIED AS I am for this high privilege and responsibility (I never wanted to be an editor of anything; no, what I really always wanted to be was . . . a scribbler), I have found extraordinary pleasure in reading through the entries for this, the quarter-centennial of the annual edition of the best essays published in America.

The very word "essay," which I first learned in the most boring of its declensions—a school "composition"—has the power to thrill. When I was very young I lived in a remote village on the edge of an English moorland. Every week, a mobile library would stop near my house, and I would step up through the back door of a large van to find its carpeted interior lined with bookshelves. Anything one borrowed could be kept for seven days and then returned or exchanged for fresh lendings. (If I live to see retirement, I would quite like to be the driver of such a vehicle, bringing books to eager young readers like a Librarian in the Rye.) One day I took a chance on a collection of science-fiction stories. One of these concerned a weary teacher who picked up the scrawled "compositions" of his class after the children had piled them on his desk, and found at the bottom a letter from the future. Bound in luminous green plastic, it was headed in oddly shaped characters: "An Essy. By Jon Grom." I was struck by this simple contrivance and also found myself noticing, as if for the first time, that an "essay" is really a try, an attempt, even an adventure.

It also holds its meaning as a test, as in its cognate "assay"—which is useful, since the assayer's job is to tell base metals from true gold—and as a trial, or a putting to the proof. One could also enfold it with the word "experiment," as when Shakespeare in Sonnet 110 so ruefully says: "These blenches gave my heart another youth / And worse essays proved thee my best of love . . . Mine appetite I never more will grind / On newer proof, to try an older friend." Allowance made for this grimmer version of an acid test or even an arraignment, the jaunty original French word *essai* still connotes a challenge, a good try, an effort, even a first draft (Gouverneur Morris: "I have made an essay of a letter"). The resulting form is agreeably provisional and elastic and invites one to take a chance or, to borrow one of America's most charming idioms, to give something one's best shot.

It's necessarily arbitrary to subdivide these "tries," but some main subcategories would have to include the following. There is the heuristic essay: an attempt to call attention to new information that has been overlooked or ignored or even suppressed, or that perhaps is simply deserving of a larger audience. Then—in no especial order—comes the polemical, or an attempt to persuade, or refute, or explode and debunk, or to mobilize. One has to add the confessional, in which the writer seeks to engage the reader in either an apologia or a revelation, disburdening something (and not, thank heavens, always with the aim of attracting sympathy). No disgrace is the merely descriptive, where the writer paints a scene in the hope of presenting it through his or her eyes. I would want to add the revisionist to the heuristic: an article that approaches familiar material or common assumptions in a fresh light. Then perhaps we could mention the conversational: something composed for pleasure alone or for its own sake, where the "point" is that there is no particular point. A coda is provided by the valedictory, where the writer either bids adieu to someone else or tries to do the near impossible and deliver some last words of his own while the faculties are still intact.

Though the essay form probably originates with Michel de Montaigne, I would still want to suggest that there is something about it that conforms very well with the Anglo-American style. After all, the United States itself—and even its very name, according to some sources—is partly the outcome of the essayistic brilliance of the radical English artisan Thomas Paine. Somewhat like the word "intellectual," the word "essayist," and its cousin "pamphleteer," has a natural kinship with the idea of dissent. Or at least a kinship with its most celebrated practitioners, such as George Orwell—about whom somebody (James Wood this time) writes a decent essay almost every year. May this kinship flourish and bring forth numerous and vigorous descendants. And let us not neglect other sturdy branches of the tradition, such as Lord Macaulay, and John Maynard Keynes's *Essays in Persuasion,* which go to show that this outwardly slight form need not be ephemeral and may have history-altering consequences.

For all that, there are many slighter nonfictional subjects whose proper treatment falls somewhere between the merely anecdotal and the full-length. Perhaps I should already have mentioned the travel piece, relating something from a locale that is (to us) exotic while managing to phrase it in terms that are simultaneously familiar. Elif Batuman's excursion into the topography of classic Russian literature made me envious because of its dry control over the farcical element and also because of its quiddity—an account of a trip gone slightly awry would have been only a tenth as good if it was about a less portentous subject. (She also made the absolute most of an absence of evidence in order to mount a challenge to the evidence of absence.) S. Frederick Starr's learned plea for a closer acquaintance with Central Asia, by contrast, relies not on a traveler's tale but on a distillation of many past travelers' tales, urging a reconsideration of the area adjoining the near-magically named Aral Sea as something far more than *partibus infidelium.*

The year 2009 was not an auspicious one for the American essay—or rather, it was not a healthy one for the sorts of magazines that take the risk of publishing the essay form. Following closely on the contraction of the advertising business and of the inflated boom that had sustained it, publications slashed budgets and pages, newsstand shelves were culled, and editors invited columnists to contribute articles with an accent on brevity. Perhaps not altogether a bad thing in itself in the long run, this meanwhile helped call attention to the smaller magazines which Americans so indefatigably continue to produce. (My colleague and series editor, the no-less-indefatigable Bob Atwan, continues to mine this resource with happy results.) I have been mightily impressed, paging through the submissions and making the final selections, by the staunch way in which publications like *Missouri Review, Wilson Quar-*

terly, American Scholar, Alaska Quarterly Review, and *Oregon Humanities* continue to trust authors to write at length, and readers to take the trouble to repay that trust.

It was also a year in which some great practitioners of the art were lost to us, and appropriately memorialized. Ian McEwan on John Updike and Garry Wills on William F. Buckley represent the retrospective mode at its most skillful—principally in producing with apparent ease what must have been quite exacting to write. The first, though beautifully modulated, is somewhat love-love, and the second makes up with true affection for a certain history of love-hate, but both perform the supreme office of evoking the still-echoing voices of their subjects and of doing so with care and measure.

Perhaps surprisingly, 2009 was not an especially good year for the polemical. Possibly it was felt that the inauguration of a new president would or perhaps should see an end to a decade of rancor and "partisanship," in which case my strong suspicion—and devout hope—is that this was only a twelvemonth of a very brief truce. Even Matt Labash of the vigorously combative *Weekly Standard* found himself looking for a human pulse in one of Washington's notorious rogue figures—albeit a fallen one. The polemical element of the essayist's craft is an essential one: the element that sounds an alarm or calls attention to an injustice or explodes an inflated reputation. John Edgar Wideman's terse and eloquent piece on the background of the Emmett Till murder struck me as exemplary in this respect, not just because its sense of outrage was so well mobilized but because it taught me several things about a famous episode that I felt indignant with myself at not having known before. Walter Isaacson's reconstruction of a neglected episode in the life of Albert Einstein and American Jewry was another instance—in this case heuristic rather than polemical—of a historical controversy with continuing relevance to the present day and the origins of its discontents. Combining a sense of history with a feeling for the environment is John Summers's protest against the denaturing and pseudo-domestication of the Republic's nearest approximation to hallowed ground.

In my own case the inner urge to write an article is usually connected to the desire to inform or to persuade, and when I find myself writing about a general topic or for pleasure alone, it is almost

interesting that he uses article & essays interchangeables

always because somebody else has had the idea for me. Has asked me to "essay" something, in other words, or give something a try: I am fortunate in having editors who can think of things for me to do. Thus I have an inordinate admiration and envy for those who can simply make amusing and enlightening prose out of their own experience. (We continue to miss the lighthearted yet profound work of George Plimpton—a man of whom it might be said that he would essay anything once—in this vineyard.) It was a happy day for me when my younger daughter introduced me to the writing of David Sedaris, and ended up by causing me to wish I could meet "Hugh" as well (the inauguration of their relationship is actually curtain-raised here). The steady development of the individual voice of Zadie Smith has been something to notice every year for several years.

About a decade ago, I published a plea for fiction and nonfiction writers to come up to the new levels of language and metaphor that have been set for us by the extraordinary pace and rhythm of two scientific revolutions. The first of these—the micro, so to speak—has been the unraveling of the skein of our DNA, showing among other things our genetic relationship with our fellow animals but also demonstrating the material basis for considering the evolved human species as one. The second—the macro—is the almost exponential manner, from the Big Bang to the Hubble redshift, in which physics has been both elucidating the origins of our cosmos and mapping the path to its, and our, eventual extinction. One or two novelists have tried to raise and refine language to the point where it recognizes and engages with this new imperative (Richard Powers being one and Ian McEwan being another), and some scientific popularizers have also taken on the hard responsibility, but so far the micro dimension has been largely the province of specialists. So it was a special pleasure to read Steven Pinker's account—at once entertaining and instructive—of the humanistic implications of the genomic. One must hope that this is only the beginning of a new kind of writing on this and kindred subjects, because one of the first principles of essayism is that the proper study of mankind is man.

As one who tries to teach the essay as well as to write it, I hear my share of collegial complaints about the short attention span of the young, the sharp decline of print, the randomness and promiscuity of electronic media, and the prevalence of instant and even grammarless or punctuation-free idioms. This is the familiar complaint, or so I suspect, of every generation that bemoans the decline of standards in the rising one. Yet working with David Eggers, say, on his Valencia Street project, or witnessing the enviably long and eager lines for a David Sedaris reading, I feel relatively confident that neither the demand for nor the supply of the well-wrought *feuilleton* will ever become exhausted. We are not likely to reach a time when the need of such things as curiosity, irony, debunking, disputation, and elegy will become satisfied. For the present, we must resolve to essay, essay, and essay again.

CHRISTOPHER HITCHENS

The Best
AMERICAN
ESSAYS
2010

ELIF BATUMAN

The Murder of Leo Tolstoy

FROM *Harper's Magazine*

THE INTERNATIONAL TOLSTOY CONFERENCE lasts four days and is held on the grounds of Yasnaya Polyana, the estate where Tolstoy was born, lived most of his life, wrote *War and Peace* and *Anna Karenina,* and is buried.

Once, when I was a graduate student, a paper of mine was accepted at the conference. At the time, my department awarded two kinds of travel grants: $1,000 for presenting a paper at an international conference or $2,500 for international field research. My needs clearly fell into the first category, but with an extra $1,500 on the line, I decided to have a go at writing a field-research proposal. Surely there was some mystery that could only be solved at Tolstoy's house?

I rode my bicycle through blinding summer sunshine to the library and spent several hours shut up in my refrigerated, fluorescent-lit carrel, with a copy of Henri Troyat's seven-hundred-page biography *Tolstoy.* I read with particular interest the final chapters, "Last Will and Testament" and "Flight." Then I checked out a treatise on poisonous plants and skimmed through it outside at the coffee stand. Finally, I went back inside and plugged in my laptop.

"Tolstoy died in November 1910 at the provincial train station of Astapovo, under what can only be described as strange circumstances," I typed. "But the strangeness of these circumstances was immediately assimilated into the broader context of Tolstoy's life and work. After all, had anyone really expected the author of *The Death of Ivan Ilyich* to drop dead quietly, in some dark corner? And

so a death was taken for granted that in fact merited closer examination."

I was rather pleased by my proposal, which I titled "Did Tolstoy
Die of Natural Causes or Was He Murdered?: A Forensic Investigation," and which included a survey of individuals who had motive
and opportunity to effect Tolstoy's death:

> Arguably Russia's most controversial public figure, Tolstoy was not with-
> out powerful enemies. "More letters threatening my life," he noted in
> 1897, when his defense of the Dukhobor sect* drew loud protests from
> the Orthodox Church and Tsar Nikolai II, who even had Tolstoy fol-
> lowed by the secret police.
>
> As is often the case, Tolstoy's enemies were no more alarming than
> his so-called friends, for instance, the pilgrims who swarmed Yasnaya
> Polyana: a shifting mass of philosophers, drifters, and desperados, col-
> lectively referred to by the domestic staff as "the Dark Ones." These vol-
> atile characters included a morphine addict who had written a mathe-
> matical proof of Christianity; a barefoot Swedish septuagenarian who
> preached sartorial "simplicity" and who eventually had to be driven away
> "because he was beginning to be indecent"; and a blind Old Believer
> who pursued the sound of Tolstoy's footsteps, shouting, "Liar! Hypo-
> crite!"
>
> Meanwhile, within the family circle, Tolstoy's will was the subject of
> bitter contention . . .

"You are certainly my most entertaining student," said my adviser
when I told her my theory. "Tolstoy—murdered! Ha! Ha! Ha! The
man was eighty-two years old, with a history of stroke!"

"That's exactly what would make it the perfect crime," I explained patiently.

The department was not convinced. They did, however, give me
the $1,000 grant to present my paper.

On the day of my flight to Moscow, I was late to the airport. Check-
in was already closed. Although I was eventually let onto the plane,

---

*The Dukhobors—literally, Spirit Wrestlers—were a Russian peasant religious sect
whose tenets included egalitarianism, pacifism, and the rejection of all written
scripture in favor of an oral body of knowledge called the "Living Book." When they
were persecuted for their refusal to fight in the Russo-Turkish War, Tolstoy donated
all the proceeds from his novel *Resurrection* to finance their emigration to Canada in
1899.

my suitcase was not, and it subsequently vanished altogether from the Aeroflot informational system. Air travel is like death: everything is taken from you.

Because there are no clothing stores in Yasnaya Polyana, I was obliged to wear, for all four days of the conference, the same clothes in which I had traveled: flip-flops, sweatpants, and a flannel shirt. I had hoped to sleep on the plane and had dressed accordingly. Some International Tolstoy Scholars assumed that I was a Tolstoyan — that, like Tolstoy and his followers, I had taken a vow to walk around in sandals and wear the same peasant shirt all day and all night.

We were some twenty-five in number, the International Tolstoy Scholars. Together, between talks on Tolstoy, we wandered through Tolstoy's house and Tolstoy's garden, sat on Tolstoy's favorite bench, admired Tolstoy's beehives, marveled at Tolstoy's favorite hut, and avoided the vitiated descendants of Tolstoy's favorite geese: one of these almost feral creatures had bitten a cultural semiotician.

Every morning I called Aeroflot to ask about my suitcase. "Oh, it's you," sighed the clerk. "Yes, I have your request right here. Address: Yasnaya Polyana, Tolstoy's house. When we find the suitcase we will send it to you. In the meantime, are you familiar with our Russian phrase 'resignation of the soul'?"

On the first morning of talks, a Malevich scholar read a paper about Tolstoy's iconoclasm and Malevich's Red Rectangle. He said that Nikolai Rostov was the Red Rectangle. For the rest of the day he sat with his head buried in his hands in a posture of great suffering. Next an enormous Russian textologist in an enormous gray dress expounded at enormous length upon a new study of early variants of *War and Peace*. Fixing her eyes in the middle distance, consulting no notes, she chanted in a half-pleading, half-declaratory tone, like somebody proposing an hourlong toast.

Just when she seemed about to sit down, she bounced back up and added: "We will hear more about these very interesting editions on Thursday! . . . If we are still alive." It was fashionable among International Tolstoy Scholars to punctuate all statements about the future with this disclaimer, an allusion to Tolstoy's later diaries. After his religious rebirth in 1881, Tolstoy changed his practice of ending each diary entry with a plan for the next day, replacing it with the phrase "if I am alive." It occurred to me that ever since 1881 Tolstoy had *always known he would be murdered.*

At the time of his conversion Tolstoy resolved to give away all his copyrights "to the people." The decision pitted him in "a struggle to the death" against his wife, Sonya, who managed the household finances and who, over the years, bore Tolstoy a total of thirteen children. Tolstoy eventually ceded Sonya the copyrights for all his pre-1881 works but turned the rest over to one of the Dark Ones, Vladimir Chertkov, an aristocrat-turned-Tolstoyan whose name contains the Russian word for "devil" (*chert*).

A doctrinaire known for his "heartless indifference to human contingencies," Chertkov made it his mission to bring Tolstoy's entire life and work into accord with the principles of Tolstoyanism. He became Tolstoy's constant companion and soon gained editorial control over all of his new writings—including the diaries, which treated the Tolstoys' conjugal life in great detail. Sonya never forgave her husband. The Tolstoys began to fight constantly, long into the night. Their shouting and sobbing would make the walls shake. Tolstoy would bellow that he was fleeing to America; Sonya would run screaming into the garden, threatening suicide. According to Tolstoy's secretary, Chertkov was succeeding in his plan: to achieve "the moral destruction of Tolstoy's wife in order to get control of his manuscripts." During this stormy period in his marriage, Tolstoy wrote *The Kreutzer Sonata*—a novella in which a husband resembling Tolstoy brutally murders a wife resembling Sonya. Anyone investigating foul play in the death of Tolstoy would find much to mull over in *The Kreutzer Sonata*.

That evening at the academicians' dormitory, I went out onto my balcony and lit a cigarette. A few minutes later, the door of the adjacent balcony opened. The balconies were extremely close, the railings separated by a mere ten inches of black space. An elderly woman stepped outside and stood very still, gazing sternly into the distance, apparently pursuing her own thoughts about Tolstoy. Abruptly she turned to me. "Would you be so kind as to give me a light?" she asked.

I fished a matchbook from my pocket, lit a match, cupped my hand around it, and held it over her balcony. She leaned over, ignited a Kent Light, and began puffing away. I decided to take advantage of this moment of human contact to ask for shampoo. (There wasn't any in our bathrooms, and mine was lost somewhere with my suitcase.) But when I mentioned shampoo, some strong emotion flickered across the old woman's face. Fear? Annoyance? Hatred? I consoled myself that I was providing her an opportunity to practice resignation of the soul.

"Just a minute," said my neighbor resignedly, as if she had read my thoughts. She set down her cigarette in a glass ashtray. The thread of smoke climbed up into the windless night. I ducked into my room to find a shampoo receptacle, choosing a ceramic mug with a picture of the historic white gates of Yasnaya Polyana. Under the picture was a quotation from L. N. Tolstoy, about how he was unable to imagine a Russia with no Yasnaya Polyana.

I held the mug over the narrow chasm, and my neighbor poured in some sudsy water from a small plastic bottle. I realized then that she was sharing with me literally her last drops of shampoo, which she had mixed with water in order to make them last longer. I thanked her as warmly as I knew how. She responded with a dignified nod. We stood a moment in silence.

"Do you have any cats or dogs?" she asked finally.

"No," I said. "And you?"

"In Moscow, I have a marvelous cat."

"There are no cats at the Tolstoy estate at Yasnaya Polyana," begins Amy Mandelker's well-known study *Framing Anna Karenina:*

> Curled, or rather, coiled in the sunny patches in the Tolstoy house, protecting it from pestilential infestations, instead of the expected feline emblems of domesticity . . . [are] snakes . . . The ancestors of these ophidian house pets were adopted by Tolstoy's ailurophobic wife, Sophia Andreevna [Sonya], to rid the house of rodents.

I was contemplating these lines on the second morning of talks, when I counted a total of four cats actually inside the conference room. That said, in fairness to Mandelker, you couldn't reproach Yasnaya Polyana for a shortage of snakes. At breakfast, one historian had described his experience researching the marginalia in Tolstoy's editions of Kant: he had seen a snake right there in the archive.

"Were there at least any good marginalia?" someone asked.

"No. He didn't write anything in the margins at all," the historian said. He paused, before adding triumphantly, "But the books fell open to certain pages!"

"Oh?"

"Yes! Clearly, those were Tolstoy's favorite pages!"

The morning panel was devoted to comparisons of Tolstoy and Rousseau. I tried to pay attention, but I couldn't stop thinking about snakes. Perhaps Tolstoy had been killed by some kind of venom?

"The French critic Roland Barthes has said that the least productive subject in literary criticism is the dialogue between authors," began the second speaker. "Nonetheless, today I am going to talk about Tolstoy and Rousseau."

I remembered a Sherlock Holmes story in which an heiress in Surrey is found in the throes of a fatal conniption, gasping, "It was the band! The speckled band!" Dr. Watson assumes that she was killed by a *band* of gypsies who were camping on the property and who wore polka-dotted kerchiefs. But Watson is wrong. Her words actually refer to a rare spotted Indian adder, introduced to the heiress's bedroom through a ventilation shaft by her wicked stepfather.

The heiress's dying words, "the speckled band," represent one of the early instances of the "clue" in detective fiction. Often, a clue is a signifier with multiple significations: a band of gypsies, a handkerchief, an adder. *But if the "speckled band" is a clue,* I wondered drowsily, *what is the snake?* There was a loud noise, and I jerked upright. The Tolstoy International Scholars were applauding. The second speaker had finished her talk and was pushing the microphone along the conference table to her neighbor.

"The most important element of nature, for both Tolstoy and Rousseau, was—air."

I walked along the birch-lined alleys of Yasnaya Polyana, looking for clues. Snakes were swimming in the pond, making a rippling pattern. Everything here was a museum. *The snakes are the genetic snake museum. The flies buzz across generations; I know they know, but they won't tell me.* I walked along the winding path to Tolstoy's grave: a grassy lump, resembling a Christmas log. I stared at it for three minutes. I thought I saw it move. Later, near Tolstoy's apiary, I sat on a bench, not Tolstoy's favorite, and looked in the garbage can. It was full of cigarette butts and cucumber peels.

On a tree stump in these very woods in 1909, Tolstoy signed a secret will. He left all his copyrights in the control of Chertkov and of his youngest daughter, Sasha, a fervent Tolstoyan. This had long been Sonya's worst fear—"You want to give all your rights to Chertkov and let your grandchildren starve to death!"—and she addressed it through a rigorous program of espionage and domestic sleuth work. She once spent an entire afternoon lying in a ditch, watching the entrance to the estate with binoculars.

One afternoon in September 1910, Sonya marched into Tolstoy's study with a child's cap pistol and shot Chertkov's picture, which she then tore into pieces and flushed down the toilet. When Tolstoy came into the room, she fired the pistol again, just to frighten him. Another day, Sonya shrieked, "I shall kill Chertkov! I'll have him poisoned! It's either him or me!"

On the afternoon of October 3, Tolstoy fell into a fit. His jaws moved spasmodically, and he uttered mooing noises, interspersed with words from an article he was writing about socialism: "Faith . . . reason . . . religion . . . state." He then suffered convulsions so violent that three grown men were unable to restrain him. After five convulsions, Tolstoy fell asleep. He woke up the next morning, seemingly recovered.

A few days later, Tolstoy received a letter from Chertkov and refused to let Sonya see it. Sonya flew into a rage and renewed her accusations about the secret will. "Not only does her behavior toward me fail to express her love," Tolstoy wrote of Sonya, "but its evident object is to kill me." Tolstoy fled to his study and tried to distract himself by reading *The Brothers Karamazov:* "Which of the two families, Karamazov or Tolstoy, was the more horrible?" he asked. In Tolstoy's view, *The Brothers Karamazov* was "anti-artistic, superficial, attitudinizing, irrelevant to the great problems."

At three in the morning on October 28, Tolstoy woke to the sound of Sonya riffling through his desk drawers. His heart began pounding wildly. It was the last straw. The sun had not yet risen when the great writer, gripping an electric flashlight, left Yasnaya Polyana for good. He was accompanied by his doctor, a Tolstoyan called Makovitsky. After a strenuous twenty-six-hour journey, the two arrived in Shamardino, where Tolstoy's sister Marya was a nun. Tolstoy decided to spend the remainder of his life here, in a rented hut. But the very next day he was joined by Sasha, who, together with Dr. Makovitsky, convinced the feverish writer that he ought to run away to the Caucasus. The little party left on October 31, in a second-class train carriage, purchasing their tickets from station to station to avoid pursuit.

Tolstoy's fever mounted. He shook with chills. By the time they reached Astapovo, he was too ill to travel. A sickroom was made up for him in the stationmaster's house. Here Tolstoy suffered fever, delirium, convulsions, loss of consciousness, shooting head pains, ringing in the ears, delusions, difficulty breathing, hiccups, an irregular and elevated pulse, tormenting thirst, thickening of the tongue, disorientation, and memory loss.

During his last days, Tolstoy frequently announced that he had written something new and wanted to give dictation. Then he would utter either nothing at all or an inarticulate jumble of words. "Read to me what I have said," he would order Sasha. "What did I write?" He once became so angry that he began to wrestle with her, shouting, "Let me go; how dare you hold me! Let me go!"

Dr. Makovitsky's diagnosis was catarrhal pneumonia.

Sonya arrived at Astapovo on November 2. She was not allowed to enter the stationmaster's house and took up residence in a nearby train car. If Tolstoy recovered and tried to flee abroad, she decided, she would pay 5,000 rubles to have him followed by a private detective.

Tolstoy's condition worsened. He breathed with great strain, producing fearsome wheezing sounds. He forgot how to use his pocket watch. In a final period of lucidity on November 6, he said to his daughters, "I advise you to remember this: there are many people on earth besides Lev Nikolayevich."

He died of respiratory failure on November 7.

On the third day of the International Tolstoy Conference, a professor from Yale read a paper on tennis. In *Anna Karenina*, he began, Tolstoy represents lawn tennis in a harshly negative light. Anna and Vronsky swat futilely at the tiny ball, poised on the edge of a vast spiritual and moral abyss. When he wrote that scene, Tolstoy himself had never played tennis, which he only knew of as an English fad. At the age of sixty-eight, Tolstoy was given a tennis racket and taught the rules of the game. He became an instant tennis addict.

"No other writer was as prone to great contradictions." All summer long, Tolstoy played tennis for three hours every day. No opponent could rival Tolstoy's indefatigable thirst for the game; his guests and children would take turns playing against him.

The International Tolstoy Scholars wondered at Tolstoy's athleticism. He should have lived to see eighty-five, ninety, one hundred!

It was also during his sixties that Tolstoy learned how to ride a bicycle. He took his first lesson exactly one month after the death of his and Sonya's beloved youngest son. Both the bicycle and an introductory lesson were a gift from the Moscow Society of Velocipede-Lovers. One can only guess how Sonya felt, in her mourning, to see her husband pedaling along the garden paths. "Tolstoy has learned to ride a bicycle," Chertkov noted at that time. "Is this not inconsistent with Christian ideals?"

On the last day of talks, wearing my Tolstoyan costume and flip-flops, I took my place at the long table and read my paper about the double plot in *Anna Karenina*. It ended with a comparison of Tolstoy's novel to *Alice in Wonderland*, which provoked controversy, since I had no proof that Tolstoy had read *Alice in Wonderland* by the time he wrote *Anna Karenina*.

"Well, *Alice in Wonderland* was published in 1865," I said, trying to ignore a romance that was being enacted, just outside the window, by two of the descendants of Tolstoy's horses. "It's well known that Tolstoy liked to receive all the latest English books by mail."

"Tolstoy had a copy of *Alice in Wonderland* in his personal library," said one of the archivists.

"But it's an 1893 edition," objected the conference organizer. "It's inscribed to his daughter Sasha, and Sasha wasn't born until 1884."

"So Tolstoy *hadn't* read *Alice* in 1873!" an old man called from the back of the room.

"Well, you never know," said the archivist. "He might have read it earlier and then bought a new copy to give to Sasha."

"And there might be mushrooms growing in my mouth — except then it wouldn't be a mouth but a whole garden!" retorted the old man.

One of the Rousseau experts raised her hand. "If Anna represents Alice, and Levin represents the White Rabbit," she said, "then who is Vronsky?"

I tried to explain that I wasn't suggesting a one-to-one correspondence between every character in *Alice in Wonderland* and *Anna Karenina.* The Rousseau expert stared at me. "Anyway," I concluded, "it's Oblonsky whom I was comparing to the White Rabbit—not Levin."

She frowned. "So Vronsky is the White Rabbit?"

"Vronsky is the Mad Hatter!" someone shouted.

The conference organizer rose to her feet. "I think we can continue this interesting discussion over tea."

In the crush at the tea table, I was approached by the archivist, who patted my shoulder. "I'm sure Tolstoy read *Alice in Wonderland* before 1873," she said. "Also, we received a police report today. A certain suitcase was delivered and is being held in security."

She directed me to the security holding area, which was inside one of the historic white gate-towers of Yasnaya Polyana—the very towers depicted on the mug that I had used to solicit shampoo. As the Keebler Elf factory is hidden inside a hollow tree, so was an entire security department concealed within this gatepost. The mug, it seemed, had been a clue. Next to one of the officers' steel desks, under a framed portrait of Tolstoy, sat my suitcase. It had arrived two days earlier, but the officers hadn't known whose it was. I signed a form and dragged the suitcase over moss and tree roots back toward the conference hall. It was a good opportunity to examine the ground. I was looking for *Hyoscyamus niger*, a toxic plant known as henbane or stinking nightshade, which is native to Eurasia.

Henbane contains the toxin atropine, which is associated with nearly all of Tolstoy's symptoms, including fever, intense thirst, delirium, delusions, disorientation, rapid pulse, convulsions, difficulty breathing, combativeness, incoherence, inability to speak, memory loss, disturbances of vision, respiratory failure, and cardiopulmonary arrest. A particularly distinctive feature of atropine poisoning is that it dilates the pupils and causes sensitivity to light. In this context, Chertkov's memoir contains a suggestive observation: "Tolstoy—to the amazement of his doctors—continued to show signs of consciousness to the very end . . . *by turning away from the light that was shining directly into his eyes.*" (Italics mine.)

Nearly anyone might have slipped henbane into Tolstoy's tea (of which he drank large quantities). Chertkov, for example, in concert with Dr. Makovitsky. They, the fanatical Tolstoyans, had motive enough: What if Tolstoy repented and changed his will again? What if, in his dotage, by some new weakness, he contradicted the principles of Tolstoyanism?

Sonya had, in addition to motive, a known interest in poisons. "I have consulted Florinsky's book on medicine to see what the effects of opium poisoning would be," she wrote in her diary in 1910. "First excitement, then lethargy. *No antidote.*" Then there were the Tolstoys' sons. Although the daughters tended to side with Tolstoy, the sons, who were usually short on money, backed their mother. In 1910, Sonya boasted that even if Tolstoy *had* written a secret will she and the boys would have it thrown out: "We shall prove that he had become feeble-minded toward the end and had a series of strokes . . . We will prove that he was forced into writing that will in a moment of mental incapacity."

Perhaps Sonya had used atropine to simulate the effects of a stroke. She might not have intended to kill her husband—just to furnish grounds to invalidate his will. But in his atropine-induced delirium, Tolstoy had embarked on a bizarre and fatal flight.

After Tolstoy's death, Sonya, supported by a pension from the tsar, tried to fight Sasha and Chertkov for the copyrights. History opposed her in the form of the Great War, followed by the 1917 revolution. Sonya and Sasha were finally reconciled during the famine of 1918–19. Of her mother at this time, Sasha later recalled, "She seemed strangely indifferent to money, luxury, things she liked so much before." On her deathbed, Sonya made a strange confession. "'I want to tell you,' she said, breathing heavily and interrupted by spasms of coughing, 'I know that I was the cause of your father's death.'"

Of all the papers at the conference, the most mysterious was about Tolstoy's little-read play *The Living Corpse.* This paper was delivered by a septuagenarian with large, watery gray eyes, an émigré to Canada from somewhere in northern Europe, well liked both for his bombastic sociability and for his generosity with the bottle of single-malt scotch he carried in his suitcase. Everyone called him Vanya, though I believe that wasn't his real name.

The hero of *The Living Corpse* is a man called Fyodor. Fyodor is married, but he keeps running off with the gypsies. He is chastely in love with a gypsy singer. Meanwhile, his wife, Liza, is chastely in love with his best friend, whose name is, oddly, Karenin. (Karenin's mother's name is actually Anna Karenina.) Although Karenin returns Liza's love, the two are unable to act on their feelings unless Fyodor grants Liza a divorce. Fyodor, for his part, cannot file for divorce without besmirching the honor of the gypsy singer. Fyodor resolves to kill himself and even writes a note, but the gypsy girl intercedes at the last minute, and they adopt a different course: Fyodor leaves his clothes on a riverbank, with the suicide note in one pocket. Everyone believes he has drowned, including Liza and Karenin. They get married. But just at the point when a new life should begin for Fyodor as well—nothing happens. Somehow Fyodor doesn't change his name. He and the gypsy girl don't get married. They quarrel and drift apart. Fyodor spends all his time in the tavern. "I am a corpse!" he shouts, slamming his glass on the table. Eventually, Fyodor's identity comes to light, and Liza is arrested for bigamy. In despair, Fyodor shoots himself. The living corpse becomes just an ordinary corpse.

The Living Corpse was based on the true story of an alcoholic named Gimer who had faked his own suicide and been sentenced to Siberia. The Moscow Art Theater wanted to stage it, but Tolstoy kept making excuses. "It has seventeen acts," he said. "It needs a revolving stage." The real reason for Tolstoy's refusal came to light only much later. Gimer, it seems, had somehow learned that a play had been written about him, and, upon his return from Siberia, he presented himself at Yasnaya Polyana. Tolstoy took the unhappy man in hand, persuaded him to give up drink, and found him a job in the very court that had convicted him. In light of Gimer's "resurrection," Tolstoy consigned *The Living Corpse* to a drawer.

This strange story has an even stranger epilogue. As Tolstoy lay in fever in 1908, a visitor brought him news of Gimer's death. "The corpse is now really dead," quipped the visitor—but Tolstoy had completely forgotten not only his former protégé but also the existence of the play. Even when the plot was recounted, Tolstoy had no recollection of having written such a thing: "And I am very, very glad that it escaped my mind to give place to something else."

The central question of Vanya's talk was "Who is the living corpse?" The argument twisted and glinted, like a mobile in the wind. At one moment it seemed that Tolstoy's Fyodor was actually Fyodor Dostoevsky, who had lived through the firing squad and survived the House of the Dead. Then it turned out that Fyodor was really Fyodorov, the Russian mystic philosopher who believed the common task of mankind was to harness the forces of nature and science in order to achieve the universal resurrection of all the dead. Still later, it seemed the living corpse was actually Anna Karenina, who had died an adulteress in *Anna Karenina* and returned a mother-in-law in *The Living Corpse*. Then there was Jesus Christ, whose tomb was found empty after three days and nights: What was Tolstoy's God if not a living corpse? And what was Tolstoy?

I clapped until my palms stung.

The banquet that night lasted until ten or eleven. Yasnaya Polyana is in Tula province—a famous center of accordion production —and entertainment was provided by students from a local accordion school: boys aged six to fifteen, already able to play the accordion with all the mannerisms of genial, nostalgic old men. Even the tiniest of the boys, playing on the tiniest doll-sized accordion, smiled knowingly, nodded, and even winked at the audience.

Before the banquet, I had stopped at the dormitory, where I took a shower and put on a linen dress. Many of the International Tolstoy Scholars congratulated me on my change of costume. Some of them had really thought that I didn't own any other clothes. A White Russian from Paris shook my hand. "You should change three times this evening," he said, "to make up for lost time."

At dinner, many toasts were proposed. An unknown man in a sports jacket recited a particularly long, pointless toast; later, I learned that he was Tolstoy's great-great-grandson.

We had to get up early the next morning for the last event of the International Tolstoy Conference: a field trip to Anton Chekhov's former estate, Melikhovo, which lay directly along the three-hour route from Yasnaya Polyana to Moscow. In this respect, visiting Chekhov's estate made a certain amount of logistical sense. Nonetheless, after four days of total devotion to Tolstoy, master of the Russian novel, it felt strange to drop in so breezily on Chekhov

—master of the Russian short story and an altogether different writer—simply because one happened to be passing through the neighborhood.

And so, after the banquet, when the participants went to their rooms to pack their suitcases—mine, of course, had never been unpacked to begin with—I went onto the balcony to think about Chekhov. The air smelled like plants and cigar smoke, bringing to mind the marvelous story that begins with a young man's arrival, late one spring night, at the country estate of his former tutor, a famous horticulturist. There is the nip of frost in the air, and the horticulturist and his daughter are in a panic that the orchards might freeze. The daughter has resolved to stay up all night, supervising the bonfires. All night long, the young man and the daughter pace, coughing and weeping, through the rows of trees, watching the workers who stoke the smoldering bonfires with manure and damp straw. I tried to remember how the story ends. It does not end well.

Chekhov was nine years old when *War and Peace* was published. He admired Tolstoy tremendously and longed to meet him; at the same time, the prospect of this meeting filled him with such alarm that he once ran out of a bathhouse in Moscow when he learned that Tolstoy was also there. Chekhov did not want to meet Tolstoy in the bath, but this apparently was his inescapable destiny. When at last he worked up the nerve to go to Yasnaya Polyana, Chekhov arrived at the exact moment when Tolstoy was headed to the stream for his daily ablutions. Tolstoy insisted that Chekhov join him; Chekhov later recalled that, as he and Tolstoy sat naked in the chin-deep water, Tolstoy's beard floated majestically before him.

Despite his lifelong hostility toward the medical profession, Tolstoy took an instant liking to Chekhov. "He is full of talent, he undoubtedly has a very good heart," he said, "but thus far he does not seem to have any very definite attitude toward life." Chekhov had only a poorly defined attitude toward life, this strange process that brought one eye-to-eye with the floating beard of the greatest crank in world literature. Today the stream where they bathed is partly obstructed and full of vegetable life. One of the International Tolstoy Scholars who insisted on sitting in it emerged completely green.

Chekhov, grandson of a serf, never saw the point of Tolstoyan-

ism. Why should educated people lower themselves to the level of
peasants? The peasants should be raised to the level of educated
people! Nonetheless, Chekhov remained in awe of Tolstoy to the
end of his days. "He is almost a perfect man," Chekhov observed
once. And, another time: "I am afraid of Tolstoy's death. It would
leave a great void in my life." In fact, Tolstoy outlived Chekhov by
six years.

Ever since he was a medical student, Chekhov had experienced
episodes of coughing blood. He dismissed them as bronchitis or
the flu, but everyone knew the real cause. One night in 1897,
while dining with his editor in Moscow's best restaurant, Chekhov
suffered a severe lung hemorrhage. Blood poured from his mouth
onto the white tablecloth. He was rushed to a private clinic and
diagnosed with advanced tuberculosis in both lungs. He survived
the attack but was, for some days, extremely weak and unable to
speak. Only family members were admitted to see him. Then Tolstoy turned up, wearing an enormous bearskin coat. Nobody had
the nerve to tell him to leave, so he sat at Chekhov's bedside and
talked for a long time about the "immortality of the soul." Chekhov listened silently. Although he did not believe in the immortality of the soul, he was nonetheless touched by Lev Nikolayevich's
solicitude.

The last meetings between Tolstoy and Chekhov took place in
Gaspra, the spa town on the Black Sea that Tolstoy frequented.
One day in Gaspra, Tolstoy put his arm around Chekhov. "My dear
friend, I beg of you," he said, "do stop writing plays!" Another time,
when the two writers were gazing at the sea, Tolstoy demanded,
"Were you very profligate in your youth?" Chekhov was speechless with embarrassment. Tolstoy, glaring out at the horizon, announced, "I was insatiable!" How could Chekhov not have sought
treatment? How could he not have recognized his symptoms—especially when he spent weeks nursing his own brother Nikolai, who
died of tuberculosis in 1889?

I was reminded of a production of *Uncle Vanya*, the first play I
ever saw in Russian, put on some years ago in Moscow. The actor
playing Dr. Astrov had been a television star, famous for playing Dr.
Watson in the Sherlock Holmes series on Soviet TV. Watching Dr.
Astrov smoke a pipe, pore over maps, and rail against deforesta-
tion—watching Dr. Astrov fail to notice the really important thing,
that Sonya was in love with him—I was struck by his similarity to

Dr. Watson. *Doctor,* I thought, *you see but you do not observe! For all your scientific enlightenment, you always misread the signs.*

At six o'clock the next morning, the twenty-five International Tolstoy Scholars boarded a chartered bus to Moscow. Nobody seemed to know how far Melikhovo was from Yasnaya Polyana, how long it would take to get there, or whether there would be any stops along the way. Leena, a keen-eyed young woman writing a dissertation about Tolstoy and Schopenhauer, was particularly concerned about the subject of bathroom breaks. "The bus will bump," she observed. "There is no toilet on this bumping bus."

Leena and I made a pact: if either of us had to go to the bathroom, we would march to the front of the bus together and request a stop.

The bus raced along the highway to Moscow. Through the birch forests that flickered past my window, I glimpsed the same north-south railway line that had carried Tolstoy from Shamardino toward Astapovo.

About an hour north of Tula, Leena slipped into the seat beside me. "It is time," she said. "Remember your promise."

"I remember," I said, preparing to get up, but Leena didn't move. "I just got my period," she said, staring straight ahead. "It's ten days early. It's not the right time." I made some expression of sympathy. "It is the wrong time," she said firmly, and stood up.

We walked to the front of the bus. The driver didn't acknowledge our request in any way, but something about his shiny, shaven head indicated that he had heard us. A few minutes later the bus lurched off the road and skidded to a stop at a gas station.

The women's bathroom was located fifty yards behind the gas pumps, in a little hut on the edge of the woods. The door appeared to have been boarded over, but the boards were decayed and hanging from their nails. The enormous textologist went in first. She reemerged almost immediately, preceded by a kind of muffled splintering sound.

"Into the woods, girls," the textologist announced. We dispersed into the scraggly woods behind the gas station. The woods were full of garbage. *Why am I here?* I thought, looking at a vodka bottle that lay on the ground. *It's because of Chekhov.*

Back on the bus, the driver was cleaning his nails with a pocketknife. Leena came back after a minute or two. She said that she had been bitten by one of God's creatures.

"He made a lot of them," I observed of God and his creatures.

I don't know how long we had been waiting in our seats when it began to seem odd that the bus hadn't moved. I became aware of some external commotion. Just outside my window, the conference organizer—a brisk Canadian, who had written a well-received book about Tolstoy's representation of peasant life—was opening the luggage compartment. Her round, bespectacled face was set in a resolute expression as she dragged out a suitcase and began carrying it away.

Looking around, I suddenly noticed the absence of several International Tolstoy Scholars: a military historian and his wife, the tennis scholar from Yale, and the expert on *The Living Corpse*. Leena and I got off the bus to investigate.

"I told him just to throw them out," the conference organizer was saying. "He insists on taking them with him. I'm at least going to find double bags." She strode off in the direction of the gas station, carrying a big plastic bag that appeared to contain some heavy object.

"It's going to be so awful when he opens the suitcase," said the military historian's wife.

It emerged that Vanya had had an accident and was refusing to throw out his pants. He wanted them to be put into his suitcase, in a plastic bag. The military historian and the tennis scholar were in the men's toilet, trying to reason with him. Leena had turned completely pale. "It's the tyranny of the body," she said.

The conference organizer came back with her double bags.

"We must not go to Melikhovo," Leena told her. "It is not the right time."

The conference organizer looked Leena in the eye. "We planned to go, so we are going to go."

Back on the bus, the driver was complaining about how he was going to be late. Instead of dropping us off in Moscow, he was going to leave us at the outermost metro stop of the outermost suburbs.

"He is a bandit!" someone shouted of the bus driver. There were murmurs of agreement. One by one, the remaining passengers returned to the bus. Last was Vanya, whose pale eyes wandered over

the two aisles of International Tolstoy Scholars. "Ladies and gentlemen," he announced, clinging to the handrail, as if climbing out of
a swimming pool. "Ladies and gentlemen, I must apologize for the
delay. I am an old man, you see. A very old man."

When the bus started again, a wave of sleepiness passed over me. I
had stayed up late the previous night, reading a biography of Chekhov. I had wanted to prepare my soul for the visit to Melikhovo, but
Yasnaya Polyana was like a haunted house: no matter how hard you
tried to think about Chekhov, you kept tripping over Tolstoy. There
was no way around it; it all seemed to have been fated before they
were born. In 1841, Chekhov's serf grandfather purchased his
family's freedom from their master, a nobleman called Chertkov
—who was none other than the future father of *Vladimir* Chertkov,
the Dark One, the beneficiary of Tolstoy's secret will! (Chekhov's
grandfather paid Chertkov's father 220 rubles per soul; Chertkov
père, apparently not a bad guy, threw in one of Chekhov's aunts for
free.) No wonder Chekhov didn't believe in immortality. In the
moment the money changed hands, his own grandfather had become a Gogolian "dead soul": a serf who had been paid for, though
he no longer existed.

I also learned that night that Tolstoy had seen *Uncle Vanya* during its first run in Moscow, when the role of Astrov was played by
Stanislavsky himself. The only positive impression retained by Tolstoy from this production was of the sound of a cricket chirping
in the final act. A well-known actor had spent an entire month
acquiring precisely this skill, from a cricket in the Sandunov public baths. Nevertheless, his masterful chirping was not enough to
counterbalance the overall terrible impression left on Tolstoy by
Uncle Vanya. "Where is the drama?" Tolstoy once shouted when the
play was mentioned. He even harangued the actors, telling them
that Astrov and Vanya had best marry peasant girls and leave the
professor's wife in peace.

Tolstoy's diary entry for January 27, 1900, reads, "I went to see
Uncle Vanya and became incensed. Decided to write a drama,
Corpse." Tolstoy started work on *The Living Corpse* that month.

I dreamed I was playing tennis against Tolstoy. As Alice in Wonderland plays croquet with a flamingo for a mallet, I was playing tennis

with a goose for a racket. Lev Nikolayevich had a normal racket. I served the ball, producing a flurry of fluffy gray down. Tolstoy's mighty backhand projected the ball far beyond the outermost limits of the tennis lawn, into the infinite dimension of total knowledge and human understanding. Match point.

I handed my goose over to Chekhov, who was next in the line of Tolstoy's opponents. Sitting on the edge of the lawn, watching the Tolstoy-Chekhov game, I suddenly realized, with a shiver, the identity of the living corpse. *It was Chekhov.* Tolstoy had written that play about Chekhov, whom he had always intended to outlive.

I woke to the crunching of gravel. We had reached Melikhovo, where we were offered the choice of a full or an abridged tour. "We want the full tour," the conference organizer said grimly, pulling out her video camera. Our tour guide, a pensioner with chemically tangerine-colored hair, took twenty minutes to guide us from the ticket booth to the front door. "Respected guests!" she shouted. "We are now located in the back yard of the neighbor of Anton Pavlovich Chekhov!"

Inside the house, I felt nothing. Yasnaya Polyana was Tolstoy's ancestral estate and the center of his universe; it makes sense to visit Yasnaya Polyana. Chekhov had no ancestral estate. He bought Melikhovo, a house infested at that time by bedbugs and roaches, from a destitute artist. Seven years later, when tuberculosis obliged him to seek a milder climate, he sold the land to a timber merchant and moved to Yalta. Melikhovo was just a stage for Chekhov —almost a stage *set.* The neighboring estates were owned by social outcasts: the bodybuilding grandson of a Decembrist rebel; a fallen countess and her much younger lover.

No single room in Chekhov's house was large enough to contain the entire body of International Tolstoy Scholars. We shuffled along a dark corridor. The guide gestured toward various rooms, too small to enter.

We passed on to a tiny "parloir": "the scene of in-ter-minable, interesting conversations."

"Did Chekhov play the piano?" someone asked.

"No!" the guide exclaimed with great emphasis. "He absolutely did not play!"

I noticed a pocket of space around Vanya, who looked a bit forlorn. I approached him but inadvertently stepped back, because of the smell.

Somewhere in the shadows that lay ahead, the guide was shouting, "Here is the beloved inkwell of the great writer!"

I extricated myself from the dark forest of shoulders, hurried down the narrow hallway, and exited into Chekhov's garden. The garden was empty but for the conference organizer, who was making a video recording of Chekhov's apple trees, and the Malevich scholar, who stooped to pick up an apple, stared at it, and took an enormous, yawning bite.

I walked quickly, trying to recapture the spark of mystery. Perhaps, I thought, Tolstoy had been killed by the "corpse"—by Gimer, who was supposedly dead two years at this time, but had anyone actually seen the body? "*Now* who's the corpse!" I imagined Gimer muttering, setting down the teaspoon—all I had to do was think of a motive. But somehow this time the motive wasn't forthcoming. My heart wasn't in it anymore. I found myself remembering "The Adventure of the Final Problem," the first and last story in which Watson has no trouble and no fun applying Holmes's method: "It was, alas, only too easy to do." Two sets of prints lead to the waterfall, and none lead back; nearby lies the alpenstock of the best and wisest man he has ever known.

Later, of course, Conan Doyle recants. Holmes's death and Watson's bereavement turn out to be a temporary illusion, and real life starts again: the late nights, the hansom rides, the peat bogs, the thrill of the chase.

But can things ever really be the same between the doctor and the "living corpse"? Will there not come a time when Holmes has to tell his friend that all the murderers they apprehended were but the pawns of a far greater force, untouchable by human justice—a force even capable of acting independently, with no human agent?

Watson will be utterly confused. "A criminal act, without a criminal actor—my dear Holmes, surely you cannot have gone over to the supernaturalists!"

Holmes will smile sadly. "Nay, my old friend—I fear that, of all forces, it is the most natural."

Call it Professor Moriarty or Madame la Mort, call it the black monk, or use its Latin name: this killer has infinite means and unfathomable motives.

And still life goes on in Chekhov's garden, where it's always a fine day for hanging yourself, and somebody somewhere is playing the guitar. In a hotel in Kharkov, the old professor is deducing the identity of his future murderer: "I will be killed by . . . that abominable wallpaper!" Interior decoration is so often the Final Problem; Ivan Ilyich was done in by some drapes. Now the samovar has almost gone cold, and frost has touched the cherry blossoms. Dr. Chekhov, loyal custodian of the human body, you who could look in the ear of an idle man and see an entire universe — where are you now?

TONI BENTLEY

The Bad Lion

FROM *The New York Review of Books*

WE SAW HIM on our first game drive. We had left the camp at
about 4 P.M. and it was shortly after that. The vehicle stopped by
a clearing between some small trees and Alfie, the ranger, said,
"Lion." We couldn't see him.

"Where?" Camouflage and jet lag together can be blinding.

Alfie pointed again. "There."

Then we saw him. He was right there, fifteen feet from us, lying flat on his left side, feet toward us, the rangy edges of a mane
farther on. We had arrived at Londolozi, in the Sabi Sands Game
Reserve, 65,000 hectares (160,550 acres) adjacent to Kruger National Park in the northeast of South Africa, only an hour earlier
from Paris.

Bennett, the tracker, who sat on a seat protruding over the front
left of the jeep—he called it his "office"—hopped casually off his
perch and climbed into the vehicle with us, so that it would have
no visual irregularities that might look unusual to the lion. The
jeep is completely open, no roof, exposed on all four sides. There
is a rifle perched across the dashboard, but Alfie says he has never
had to use it. After decades of seeing Land Rovers, with little, chat-
tering, camera-snapping, hat-wearing humans sitting inside, the
animals—lions, leopards, elephants, giraffes, rhinos, hippos, hye-
nas—not only appear entirely unthreatened but hardly seem to
notice us at all. Just don't get out of the jeep and don't stand up in
the jeep. Then you're meat. There are a few deaths every year in
Kruger, Alfie says: someone taking that all-important, final close-
up.

The lion's sandy color matched perfectly the rubble-studded dirt on which he was lying. But once you saw him, you saw nothing else, and immediately felt the joy of safari: one's shrunken significance, one's thin shadow. Five hundred pounds, a great mound of lion muscle, napping. He didn't flick a whisker at the vehicle driving up and stopping. But when Alfie started the motor again he lifted his heavy head slowly and looked our way with drowsy disdain. A mammoth weary warrior, his whole body ticked with scars, his mane many mottled shades from blond to black, punk and jagged on his head. His right nostril appeared bigger and blacker than the left, an old wound. He closed his eyes again, and laid his great head back down. We had been dismissed.

One cannot really see animals in a zoo. The safety provided by the cages and enclosures completely distorts perception. Only in the wild, where the animals are free and man is the curious visitor, caged in his jeep, can one feel the power of their dangerous beauty, the enormity of their dignity, and the frailty—and occasional idiocy—of humans. As with the American we saw in another vehicle photographing, with his twelve-inch lens, a young male lion while wearing a baseball cap topped with a miniature stuffed lion.

We saw the same lion two days later, about 7:30 in the morning. I recognized him because of the scar on his nose. He was with his brother and three females: a mother and her two grown daughters. The mother had no tail. She had lost it along with two of her four cubs in a hyena attack four years ago. The two remaining cubs are the grown daughters with her now. They killed a baby hippo a few hours ago and are feeding, each in turn: the males first, then the females. Their bellies are bulging.

Earlier that morning, in a large pond just outside the camp, we counted twenty-eight hippos in the water. They stay there all day and only exit—single file along their narrow hippo path—to feed at night. They cannot swim, and stand in the shallow water. We watched one baby hippo lying crosswise over its mother's back, stumpy legs draped over each side of her huge slippery body, bobbing up and down in the water as the mother went up and down as hippos do.

We saw this same group of lions a day later on a failed hunt. The females led, spreading out in three directions to surround an impala, the two males languidly following at the rear. They will help only if the prey is so large that the females can't do it alone. But the males always eat first. The impala got wind of them and escaped, and the five lions reassembled at a clearing and took a long nap preceded by plenty of paw- and face-cleaning and licking of each other. And finally, one female rolled over and slept on her back, belly and feet to the sky. It was then, while all was quiet, that Alfie told us that they call the male Satan, the one with the scarred nostril.

The rangers and trackers know the animals—there are about sixty lions in Sabi Sands, and they know each pride, all the males —but they do not appropriate them by naming them. Except for this one lion.

"He is a bad lion," said Alfie with little emotion.

The next afternoon, sometime after five, Bennett pointed to the left, climbed down from his "office," and got in the jeep with us. It was already getting cold. Alfie drove on, then turned left. Running at a good clip straight toward us was a lioness, followed at short range by Satan, with his brother close behind. She made a sharp right in front of the vehicle and the males followed her. Alfie made a sharp left and followed them, mowing down several acacia bushes along the way, as we ducked the two-inch thorns. The three lions had stopped a short space away. Satan, panting, was standing, blood dripping from his nose into his mouth and onto his chin. "They were fighting," said Alfie.

The lioness buried herself on her belly in some tall yellow brush, almost invisible except that the grass about her head grew slowly red. The two males settled about eight feet from her, beside each other. The panting slowed down and all became quiet. What was going on? Our jeep was just behind the lioness, only ten feet from her. We waited in silence. The minutes passed, maybe ten. Satan stands up, turns around, cocks his head up, sniffs the wind, and opens his jaws, showing huge bloody incisors. I wonder if he is in pain.

The violence was so quick, so out of the silence, that I remember only a few flashed images. Satan's brother circled, imperceptibly, around behind the lioness and the two attacked her from both front and back. Incredibly loud growls and roars, she is on her back, paws to her neck, protecting her spine and throat from their jaws. Awful, awful throaty noises and suddenly our vehicle is jolted to one side. Satan has hit the back corner, full force, and we all are knocked sideways to the right. There is blood among the lions but I don't know whose. Alfie turns on the motor and asks if we want to stay or go. "Go."

We drive off, leaving the three lions alone. It is now that Alfie explains about Satan.

"He has been killing lionesses for years. He has killed many lionesses."

Male lions kill other male lions over territory, females, food. And they will kill the cubs of another male lion. But very rarely do they kill lionesses. It does not serve them genetically. Satan is not, now, in his own territory, which belongs to the pride of the lioness we just saw him attack. With his brother—who Alfie says is not "bad," just a "follower"—he tries to mate with a lioness, and when she refuses him, as she almost always will since she doesn't know him and he is not of her pride, he tries, often with success, to kill her. He had attacked another one only two days ago but she got away.

Once, Alfie says, they watched him mate for two days straight with a lioness he had killed. "We have never seen this before." Satan's behavior—a serial rapist, necrophiliac, killer—is deviant, the need to dominate gone awry, even for a lion. But in a conservation reserve like Sabi Sands, humans do not interfere, even with a criminal animal. It is the lions who must deal with their own, and Satan remains at large.

If he is deviant, crazy, I ask Alfie, how does he know that Satan won't jump in the jeep and attack us? Alfie shakes his head and says, "He won't. He's not interested in us."

We drive on and see the pride of the lioness, about a half mile away. I count thirteen lions, including the dominant male with a scraggly dark mane and a handsome young male whose thick reddish mane is just filling in around his neck. He is about three and a half years old, and the son, Alfie tells us, of the lioness Satan just attacked. She separated herself from her pride, he explains, to divert Satan and his brother from them, her family, as it were. The females in a lion pride are related: mothers, daughters, sisters, aunts. I watch the young lion, beautiful and alert, watching, seeming to look in her direction. But it is probably just the wind.

We follow the pride on a hunt. They have spotted a baby wart-hog. Too late for the capture, we arrive in time to see the still squealing animal in four mouths: those of the alpha male, the handsome young male, an even younger male, and the female who made the kill. All four growl and pull simultaneously and the ani-mal is literally torn into four rather unequal pieces. Each settles down to eat, blood, meat, skin, and bones, crunch-crunch. The en-tire pride had eaten earlier and the other females wait patiently. The little warthog was a chance snack. Finished, the pride strolls down to a small watering hole and drinks, nuzzling and licking one another. We watch them for a while and then head back to camp. As the sky darkens, the Southern Cross appears above us. I wonder how the lioness is.

The next day we hear that she was wounded badly in the attack, her back broken, her spinal cord gouged, paralyzed. She had been seen by some rangers but they weren't encouraging guests to go that way anymore.

The morning we were leaving Sabi Sands I asked Alfie about the lioness.

"She died yesterday," he said.

I thought of her lying by the small brush bush where she was last seen, with her broken back, taking two days to die. Alfie says that Satan has two more years to rampage before he gets too old to keep killing other lions. Unless, I think, the young lion challenges him. But it would not be to avenge his murdered mother. It would be to protect his pride.

[handwritten annotations: - Questions body/mortality - The Absurd or almost Grotesque]

JANE CHURCHON

[handwritten annotations: - matter-of-fact tone that conveys great emotion - Insider POV w/ idioms + usages of occupation / tools / hierarchies → almost a process analysis = internal language helps w/ necessary detachment to survive this world]

The Dead Book

FROM *The Sun*

I LIKE TO TAKE MY TIME when I pronounce someone dead. *[handwritten: idioms]* The bare-minimum requirement is one minute with a stethoscope pressed to someone's chest, listening for a sound that is not there; with my fingers bearing down on the side of someone's neck, feeling for an absent pulse; with a flashlight beamed into someone's fixed and dilated pupils, waiting for the constriction that will not come. If I'm in a hurry, I can do all of these in sixty seconds, but when I have the time, I like to take a minute with each task.

I talk to the patients I'm about to pronounce, even though they're dead. "Mrs. Jones," I might say, "I'm just going to listen to your heart," before I touch the plastic stethoscope to her chest. Because I don't provide direct nursing care to patients anymore, I don't carry my own stethoscope. When I pronounce someone dead, I use one of the disposable stethoscopes designed for listening to the chests of patients with infectious illnesses. They are made of flimsy red plastic the color of cartoon blood, and I feel a little cheap when I use one to pronounce Mrs. Jones, as if I have shown up at a dinner party in a ripped tube top. But I make sure to treat Mrs. Jones's body with the same respect that I would afford a living, breathing patient. I always imagine her soul sitting in the corner of the hospital room in one of our beige visitor chairs, invisible to the eye but listening with her large, warty ears.

Until I pronounce her, Mrs. Jones is not officially dead. Even though she's stopped breathing and her heart is silent, legally she's still alive. Sometimes I have other tasks to do, and it takes me a while to get to Mrs. Jones's room. My thinking is that Mrs. Jones, whether her soul is sitting in the corner or not, doesn't really care whether I pronounce her dead at 4:07 or 4:53. I like to believe that time doesn't matter much to dead people.

It does matter to the living, though. If Mrs. Jones's husband or children are sitting at the bedside, that will make me hurry. The dead are dead, but the bereaved want closure. Invariably the family will ask me for the time of death, as if the information makes it more real for them.

It's traditionally a doctor's duty to pronounce patients. In the hospital where I work, only a few nurses have been given the pronouncing wand — mainly the nurse supervisors, like me, who oversee the hospital's day-to-day functions and happen to be available twenty-four hours a day, seven days a week. We can pronounce only under specific conditions, however. First, the patient's doctor has to order it. This can be done after the fact — and often is, especially if the patient dies in the middle of the night. Even during the day it's kinder to the family not to make them wait for the doctor, who is often reluctant to desert his living patients in order to rush to a dead person's bedside. Second, I cannot pronounce a patient who is a coroner's case; this includes victims of violence — even if the wounds are self-inflicted — and anyone who was admitted less than twenty-four hours prior to death. And third, I cannot pronounce a patient who was on a ventilator at the time of death, although I can and often do pronounce patients who've died just a few moments after we've withdrawn the ventilator.

But if there's no tube running into the patient's lungs, and the coroner has no need to confirm the cause of death, and no doctor wants to do the pronouncing (and, really, why would they — they're busy enough with the living), then I am called to pronounce the patient dead.

Pronouncing patients is only a small part of my work. Like the doctors, I spend most of my time with people who are still breathing and whose hearts keep something at least approximating regular time. Part of my job is also to figure out how to squeeze more patients into our already crowded hospital. Hospital rooms are becoming scarcer nowadays, and this can add a scavenger aspect to the news that a patient has died. When Mrs. Jones dies, she makes room for Mrs. Smith, who's been waiting five hours for an empty bed to become available. I can't help but feel a little grateful that

Mrs. Jones has finally passed. It was inevitable, and now Mrs. Smith will get the benefit of Mrs. Jones's already cooling bed.

All basements are creepy places, even those without a morgue. The hospital where I work stores its bodies in the basement, where pipes painted the same pinkish beige color as the low ceiling run the length of the halls. There are many twists and turns, and the hallways all seem to lead to nowhere or to end in locked doors.

Built in the 1930s, the windowless morgue has tiles the exact putrid green color of those seen in all TV and movie morgues. The rest of the hospital has been updated with laminated wood flooring and neutral color schemes, but the morgue remains untouched by a decorator's hand. At the center of the space is the autopsy table, with its sloping steel presence and its great drain. Above it is a faucet with an enormous sprayer head attached to a flexible steel hose, like the ones used to wash dishes in a commercial kitchen. I try not to think about what happens on that table, but, of course, the more I shun the thought, the more my mind conjures it.

I once worked as a staff nurse in the neonatal intensive-care unit. Whenever a baby died, I wrapped it in a blanket, and then around the blanket I wound a sky-blue disposable pad. I took the football-sized package—baby, blanket, and pad—down to the morgue and opened the door of the refrigerator there and placed the package on the glass shelf as gently as I could. Then I closed the door, pushing it until I heard the white seal grip, the way I might close the fridge door at home after putting away a chicken. There wasn't a way for me to close that refrigerator door with the reverence and honor the occasion deserved. This is a part of nursing that we learn early: how to do the unthinkable without falling to our knees and wailing.

The refrigerated drawers that house the larger bodies are on another wall, one above the other. The steel handle on one drawer is a little loose, and the other balks when the tray holding the deceased is moved along its rails. The dead don't mind a rickety ride.

We regularly need to move bodies from gurney to drawer and from drawer to gurney. The drawers are low and the gurneys are waist-high, so we use a mechanical lift to protect the backs of the living who handle the dead. Usually the morgue workers operate the lift, but I occasionally help out when it's the middle of the night and only one employee is working in the morgue. I'm not sure I provide all that much assistance—I'm about as coordinated as a toddler on stilts—but if I were them, I wouldn't want to manipulate a dead body in its white plastic shroud all by myself.

The lift is constructed of sturdy steel hoops that hang from the ceiling and yellow straps with strong clips at the ends, like those in rock-climbing harnesses. After clipping the straps securely around the feet, buttocks, and shoulders of the white-shrouded body, we activate the automatic lift, and the deceased begins to rise from the gurney. The parts of the body not supported by the straps sag in the white bag. Sometimes the balance is a little off, and we quickly lower the body back down. If the balance is perfect, the body moves straight and level until we bring it gently onto the tray, which we then slide into the drawer. When everything is aligned just so, it is like seeing a white plastic bag perform ballet.

The nursing supervisors keep track of the dead in a large binder we call the "Dead Book," although it bears the more dignified title "Deceased" on its spine. Paperwork is filed and moved in a complex system that tracks the whereabouts of the corpses, including bodies awaiting the family's choice of funeral home. Some supervisors describe a body that is legally ready to leave our morgue as being "on the launching pad," but I prefer the less dramatic "awaiting pickup."

The hospital recently bought a shiny new set of five refrigerated body drawers to replace the two old ones. One supervisor calls it our "five-holer." But still the morgue, like the rest of our hospital, often doesn't have enough room for its occupants. Families sometimes are too bereft or too poor to make timely arrangements. If we have more than five bodies, the overflow goes to a private storage facility, and we pay daily rent until the families are able to provide for disposition.

At one hospital where I worked, if there were too many corpses waiting to be picked up by mortuaries, we had to rotate them in and out of the drawers on a schedule. No one body was kept outside a drawer for more than a short time, and we kept a dry-erase board on the wall to track the in and out times of the corpses, the same way one might note when personnel have left or returned to an office.

I want to list here all the people I've pronounced: the former news anchor, the lady with the beard, the chronically ill twenty-year-old, the double amputee. But the list goes on and on and would become boring after a while.

There have been so many people that I've started to forget them. Each one is special at that moment when I am in the room with him or her. As I flash my light into each pair of eyes and feel each pulseless neck, I think, *Who were you?* But a few months later hundreds more names have paraded through the Dead Book, and the previous ones are forgotten.

The first time I pronounced someone dead, I felt like a nervous virgin on her wedding night. I remember the patient's family had disagreements about what we call "end-of-life issues," which really amount to how long we should stall the inevitable. I remember that the patient's granddaughter hugged me after I pronounced her grandmother dead. And I remember the patient's face, frozen in a waxy pose that could never have been mistaken for the face of a person still alive.

I'd seen dead people before in my career as a nurse, and I'd thought that pronouncing someone would be only an extension of this. I hadn't expected that I would want to linger with the body. I hadn't expected that I would want to comfort the deceased. I hadn't expected that I'd want to cry. And those impulses have never gone away.

The person to whom this pulseless neck and silent heart and these dilated pupils belonged is gone. Yet ten minutes ago, one minute ago, Mrs. Jones was still here, still breathing, still "Aunt Betty" to her nephew, still "darling" to Mr. Jones. That one minute changes everything. What happens in that liminal moment? How is it that we cease to be, while our body remains, quiet and still?

And every time it is just the dead person and I alone in the room, tears fill my eyes, and I feel as if my heart will burst through my skin. I didn't know these people, and yet, as my hands pass over their chests, their necks, their eyes, I grieve for them. Those moments remind me that everything and everyone I love in this world will one day die: my parents, my children, our dog, the tree in our front yard. One day someone else's hands will feel my neck and find no pulse; someone else's eyes will look into my pupils and see no contraction; someone else's ears will listen to my chest and hear no heartbeat. And then — I hope with reverence and grief befitting that mystery — they will pronounce me dead.

BRIAN DOYLE

Irreconcilable Dissonance

FROM *Oregon Humanities*

I HAVE BEEN MARRIED ONCE, to the woman to whom I am still married, so far, and one thing I have noticed about being married is that it makes you a lot more attentive to divorce, which used to seem like something that happened to other people, but doesn't anymore, because of course every marriage is pregnant with divorce, and also now I know a lot of people who are divorced, or are about to be, or are somewhere in between those poles, for which shadowy status there should be words like "mivorced" or "darried" or "sleeperated" or "schleperated," but there aren't, so far.

People seem to get divorced for all sorts of reasons, and I find myself taking notes, probably defensively, but also out of sheer amazement at the chaotic wilderness of human nature. For example, I read recently about one man who got divorced so he could watch all sixty episodes of *The Wire* in chronological order. Another man got divorced after thirty years so he could, he said, fart in peace. Another man got divorced in part because he told his wife he had an affair, but he *didn't* have an affair, he just couldn't think of any other good excuse to get divorced, and he didn't *want* to have an affair, or be with anyone else other than his wife, because he liked his wife, and rather enjoyed her company as a rule, he said, but he just didn't want to be married to her *every* day anymore, he preferred to be married to her every second or third day, but she did not find that a workable arrangement, and so they parted company, confused.

Another man I read about didn't want to get divorced, he said, but when his wife kept insisting that they get divorced because she had fallen in love with another guy, he, the husband, finally agreed to get divorced, and soon after he found himself dating the other guy's first wife; as the first guy said, who could invent such a story? I read about a woman who divorced her husband because he picked his nose. I read about a woman who got divorced because her husband never remembered to pay their property taxes and finally, she said, it was just too much. Is it so very much to ask, she asked, that the person who shares responsibility for your life remembers to pay your joint taxes? Does this have to be a crisis every year? She seemed sort of embarrassed to say what she said, but she said it.

It seems to me that the reasons people divorce are hardly ever for the dramatic reasons that we assume are the reasons people get divorced, like snorting cocaine for breakfast or discovering that the minister named Bernard whom you married ten years ago is actually a former convict named Ezzard with a wife in Wisconsin, according to the young detective who sat down in your office at the accounting firm one morning and sounded embarrassed about some things he had come to tell you that you should know.

I read about a couple who got divorced because of "irresolute differences," a phrase that addled me for weeks. Another couple filed for divorce on the grounds of irreconcilable dissonance, which seemed like one of those few times in life when the exact right words are applied to the exact right reason for those words. I read about another woman who divorced her husband because one time they were walking down the street, the husband on the curb side in accordance with the ancient courteous male custom of being on that side so as to receive the splatter of mud or worse from the street and keep such splatter from the pristine acreage of his beloved, and as they approached a fire hydrant he lifted his leg, puppylike, as a joke, and she marched right to their lawyer's office and instituted divorce proceedings. That particular woman refused to speak to reporters about the reasons for divorce, but you wonder what the iceberg was under *that* surface, you know?

The first divorce I saw up close, like the first car crash you see up close, is imprinted on the inside of my eyelids, and I still think about it, not because it happened, but because years after it happened it seems so fated to have happened. How could it be that two people who really liked each other, and who took a brave crazy leap on not just living together, which lots of mammals do, but swearing fealty and respect in front of a huge crowd, and filing taxes as a joint entity, and spawning a child, and cosigning mortgages and car loans, how could they end up signing settlement papers on the dining room table and then wandering out into the muddy garden to cry? How could that be?

The saddest word I've heard wrapped around divorce like a tattered blanket is "tired," as in "We were both just tired," because being tired seems so utterly normal to me, so much the rug always bunching in that one spot no matter what you do, the slightly worn dish rack, the belt with extra holes punched with an ice pick that you borrowed from your cousin for exactly this purpose, the flashlight in the pantry that has never had batteries and never will, that the thought of "tired" being both your daily bread and also grounds for divorce gives me the willies. The shagginess of things, the way they never quite work out as planned and break down every other Tuesday, necessitating wine and foul language and duct tape and the wrong-size screw quietly hammered into place with the bottom of the garden gnome, seems to me the very essence of marriage; so if what makes a marriage work (the constant shifting of expectations and eternal parade of small surprises) is also what causes marriages to dissolve, where is it safe to stand?

Nowhere, of course. Every marriage is pregnant with divorce, every day, every hour, every minute. The second you finish reading this essay, your spouse could close the refrigerator, after miraculously finding a way to wedge the juice carton behind the milk jug, and call it quits, and the odd truth of the matter is that because she might end your marriage in a moment, and you might end hers, you're still married. The instant there is no chance of death is the moment of death.

JOHN GAMEL

The Elegant Eyeball

FROM *Alaska Quarterly Review*

THEY AREN'T WHAT most people think they are. Human eyes, touted as ethereal objects by poets and novelists throughout history, are nothing more than white spheres, somewhat larger than your average marble, covered by a leatherlike tissue known as sclera and filled with nature's facsimile of Jell-O. Your beloved's eyes may pierce your heart, but in all likelihood they closely resemble the eyes of every other person on the planet. At least I hope they do, for otherwise he or she suffers from severe myopia (nearsightedness), hyperopia (farsightedness), or worse.

Such uniformity is essential: for an eye to focus properly, its length and optical system must match to within a fraction of a millimeter. When a man and woman toss their genes together to make a baby, nature sets the focal point (determined by the optical power of the cornea and crystalline lens) at a standard distance, then adjusts the length of the eyeball to that same distance—twenty-four millimeters, or about one inch, with a few millimeters of variation thrown in for good measure. Thus unlike livers and kidneys and hearts and brains—those ordinary, nonspherical organs—eyes tend to an impressive sameness all over the world. My spleen may be half again bigger than yours, intestines can vary by five feet in length from person to person, but, with rare and usually disastrous exceptions, eyes are like so many peas in a pod.

Trust me. I've handled hundreds of eyeballs, removed from their owners for a variety of unpleasant reasons. One of my jobs—that of the ophthalmic pathologist—is to slice these globes into wafer-thin strips, stain the strips with vivid colors, then examine the results under a microscope. Given these credentials, I can assure you that your lover's eyes differ from those of your most despised enemy in only the most superficial ways—in the color and texture of the iris and in the size of its pupil. When we wax eloquent about "beautiful eyes," we are usually moved more by the trimmings—the lids, the lashes, the prominence of the globe in its orbit—than by anything contained within the eye itself. The Japanese sometimes refer to Westerners as "big eyes," an illusion produced by the lid position and orbital structure of Occidentals, while in truth Asians exhibit a collective tendency toward myopia that gives them on average slightly larger eyeballs.

A crisis came upon me during my fourth year of medical school. This was the crucial moment, the ultimate decision: To what specialty would I devote my life? Should I tend to phlegmy children who wriggle and scream and scratch my flesh when I thrust an otoscope into their ear? Should I slice open bellies, wander among livers and spleens and gallbladders, grope my way through greasy omental fat pads to explore coil after coil of diseased intestines? Or should I tend to the human heart, throbbing in its nest between the foamy pink lungs?

I flirted with cardiology, then settled on neurology. Nothing rivals the complexity of the human brain, I reasoned, and no goal is more noble than curing its various ailments. The ultimate philosophical dialectic: using the skilled synapses of my own brain, I would diagnose and cure the diseased brains of others. Fortunately, before it was too late, a six-week elective in neurology revealed the terrible truth: almost every neurology patient suffers from a stroke or a seizure or an incurable brain tumor, and they never— NEVER—get better. Worse yet, the rare patient with a curable lesion is snatched up by the neurosurgeons, arguably the most arrogant species on earth. By the end of the elective I felt like a zombie myself.

How about ophthalmology? Clean, precise, offering its own dialectic: with my intact eye I would diagnose and cure the diseased eyes of others. It didn't take long, only one good look into the ocular depths through a dilated pupil, and my quest was finished. There before me lay a stunning image—a lacework of arteries and veins delicate as a spider's web, spread on a burnt umber palate swirled and streaked with shades of ocher. Most spectacular of all was the retina, a transparent wafer that gleamed like polished glass under the light of my ophthalmoscope. In the center the optic nerve shone like a risen sun. I was in love.

Since every normal eye displays a clear cornea and a white scleral coat, any notion of special beauty attributed to the globe itself must derive from the iris, the dynamic membrane that contains the pupil and rests in front of the crystalline lens. The iris comes in many colors, but if one trusts the obsession of poets and novelists, the most beautiful irises are always blue: light blue, velvety blue, sloe-eyed, peacock, midnight, cobalt, ice blue. Green gets an occasional nod—"she had jewel-bright emerald eyes, so lustrous and fetching they tore through my heart"—but most of the time blue runs the show: powder blue and baby blue, cerulean and aqua. Azure. Turquoise. The rankest discrimination. And a bit ironic, since blue irises contain no intrinsic pigment, showing only the raw color of the tissue itself. The pigment-secreting cells of Caucasians often remain inactive during the first few years of life, breaking the heart of many a parent when their blue-eyed special baby darkens over the years into brown-eyed mediocrity.

The texture of the iris is all but invisible to the unaided eye, but the ophthalmologist's slit-lamp microscope discloses a panorama of crypts and valleys, diaphanous spokes, flecks and spots and strands that dance about with each twitch of the pupil. Dark irises tend toward a tight weave, while light irises fluff up like a shag rug. And then there's the all-important pupil—squeezed into a dot by morphine and bright light; enlarged by fear, darkness, sexual arousal, and death. Yes, the coroner's final measure, the mark of a departed soul—enormous black pupils that give nary a twitch to even the brightest light. Despite this morbid association, many cultures consider large pupils a sign of beauty. "Belladonna," Spanish for "beautiful lady," is also the name of a poisonous, pupil-dilating extract from the plant *Atropa belladonna*, more commonly known as deadly nightshade.

A note on cosmetics: under an ophthalmologist's slit-lamp microscope, false lashes look like mutilated telephone poles, while mascara shows up as greasy black chunks that squiggle across the corneal tear film with every blink. For the efficiency-minded woman there is permanent eyeliner—a dark line tattooed along the lid margin. It works beautifully, provided styles don't change, and provided the tattooist, working millimeters from the cornea, doesn't inject ink into the eyeball.

About myopia—if you have it, be happy. As shown by numerous scientific studies, nearsighted men and women boast a higher average intelligence than their nonmyopic cohorts. The precise mechanism of this association remains unknown, but it is tempting to postulate an effect of myopia on early childhood development. Most nearsighted kids wander around undiagnosed for years, and during this formative period—unable to see the baseballs, Frisbees, and rocks thrown at them by their playmates—they spend a lot of time indoors. The nonathletic myopes who take up reading to while away the hours get high scores on their SATs, while those who take up eating tweak our claustrophobia by overflowing the adjacent seat on airplanes. Myopia also exerts a compelling influence on career choice: the great majority of my fellow ophthalmologists wear either myopic contact lenses or thick myopic spectacles. Pathology breeds preoccupation.

However beautiful the human eye, it serves a more important purpose than romantic allure. Forty percent of the brain is devoted to vision, which provides us with more information than our other four senses combined. Our optic nerves transmit millions of impulses to the brain every second, impulses that specify the location, color, and intensity of light for all the points in our visual space. Better yet, thanks to a mysterious algorithm that fuses the slightly disparate images from each of our eyes, our visual cortex, via a neurological miracle known as depth perception, shows us the world in three dimensions. An impressive feat, since a video camera, arguably the benchmark of modern technology, can muster only two dimensions.

Certain ocular tissues stand on the pinnacle of evolution. How does nature, so crude in claw and fang, create a surface that brings light to a pinpoint focus? This surface must be perfectly curved, perfectly transparent, perfectly smooth. It must be—water! Which is to say, the cornea owes its optical perfection to a tear film whose dissolved salts, lipids, and proteins maintain a flawless wetted surface. A man who has no tears stands on the brink of blindness.

Worse yet, that man will writhe in agony: a dry cornea, thanks to the most exquisite pain threshold in the human body, responds to each blink with a tormenting jolt. Dry- eye victims compare the sensation to that caused by rubbing the eyeball with shards of glass.

Another challenge surmounted by evolution: for light to reach the retina unimpeded, the cornea and lens must remain transparent, and yet, like all living tissues, they must be nourished. More than 99.9 percent of human cells obtain their nourishment from capillary blood flow, but capillaries passing through the cornea and lens would veil our vision in a net of opaque strands. To remain crystal clear, the outer portion of the cornea must survive on oxygen absorbed from the surrounding air, while the lens and the inner cornea depend on the flow of aqueous, a transparent, oxygen-poor fluid that circulates through the inner chambers of the eye. This fluid derives from cells sheltered behind the lens and exits through trabeculated channels located near the base of the iris. Blockage of these channels causes nauseating glaucomatous pain, while a deficiency of aqueous flow collapses the eye into a spitball. Thus pain-free normal vision, the presumed birthright of every human on earth, demands an arrangement of tissues so wondrous and complex its subtleties should take our breath away.

Of all the ugly things in this world, I would argue that diseases top the list: cancer, syphilis, leprosy, gangrene, fungating ulcers. Even the pictures lying flat and odorless on the pages of a textbook bring a surge of nausea. And let us not forget elephantiasis, an infestation by microscopic worms that wriggle into the lymphatic system, causing an accumulation of lymph so massive it forces the victim to stumble about on legs the size of tree trunks, carrying his scrotum before him in a wheelbarrow.

But surely the eye, the most delicate human organ, is afflicted by only the subtlest diseases. Or so one might think. I soon discovered the fallacy of this logic. Indeed, some of the most grotesque diseases known to medicine are those that disfigure the eye. Ophthalmology did not prove the sanitary refuge I had hoped for. On the second day of my student elective in the Stanford Eye Clinic, I examined Justine Jewell, a slender diabetic in her late teens. She was accompanied by a tall mother who carried twice her daughter's bulk. Justine complained, "My eyes are full of floaters." Good,

I thought. Floaters. No problem. Everything looked fine from the outside—white sclera, clear corneas, pale blue irises. Then I shined my ophthalmoscope through her pupils to examine the interior. "Excuse me," I said, and stepped out of the room.

By that time in my career, I had seen the interior of ten or twelve eyes, each a breathtaking panorama of amber and brown, yellow and pink, shading through a delicate lacework of arteries and veins. But Justine's eyes were filled with tangles of angry red spiders. Dark clots rose into the vitreous gel, trailing streamers of blood in all directions. I rushed into the hall to grab Doug Jacobson, the retinal specialist in the clinic that morning. It took only an instant. Doug focused the beam of his ophthalmoscope on Justine's right eye, then her left, removed the ophthalmoscope from his head, and hung it on the wall.

"You have diabetic retinopathy," he said. "And I'm sorry to say it's very advanced."

The mother burst into tears. "Oh, doctor," she sobbed, "my grandmother, my cousin Ernest, this woman across the street—so many people I know went blind from diabetes! Can't you do something?" Justine said nothing. Her eyes were dry, wide open, the blue irises stretched into pale rims around the blackness of her dilated pupils. Later, in private, Jacobson gave me her diagnosis in the vernacular—jungle-osis. Jungle-osis meant dense black clots, arching streamers of blood, a traction retinal detachment bound with scars so dense they defy the reparative efforts of even the most skillful surgeon. It meant blindness, both eyes, and soon—weeks, perhaps a month or two. Justine, not yet twenty years of age, was doomed to stumble through the remaining decades of her life with a white cane or a guide dog. Worse yet, she might develop absolute glaucoma, an intractable rise in pressure so painful and nauseating the victims often beg to have the eyes removed.

But—perhaps not. Justine's only hope was a treatment so recently developed we had no proof that it worked, a treatment whose promise was based on the crudest evidence. For decades, ophthalmologists had noted a strange phenomenon: when one eye of a diabetic showed widespread retinal scars from an old injury or infection, that eye often retained vision long after diabetic hemorrhages had blinded the unscarred eye. Apparently, by a mechanism no one understood at the time, these scars protected the surviving retinal tissue from the ravages of diabetes. And so, by a logic that might impress a blacksmith or a witch doctor, the new treatment called for obliterating much of the nonessential peripheral retina in an effort to save the central portion that gives us our sharpest vision. Since we had no other option, Jacobson advised Justine—a young girl poised on the brink of blindness, dry-eyed and speechless with fear—to let us perform an experiment on her.

Just months before Justine's arrival, our clinic had acquired the Coherent Radiation Model 800, one of the first lasers used to treat the human eye. Its console, six feet long and three feet high, looked like a coffin on legs. A glass tube buried deep within the bowels of its circuitry gave off a high-pitched whine. When activated by a foot switch, the tube emitted an eerie, bluish green beam of light. Shone against a wall, the beam formed a circle of shimmering motes that scurried about like atoms in a nuclear furnace. A fabulous instrument, more precise than any razor, but now its tightly focused beam was to serve a crude purpose—destroying retinal tissue. By the hundreds, by the thousands, the laser emitted tiny flashes, each flash the space-age equivalent of a magnifying lens burning a hole in a leaf. When the treatment was complete, lifeless white scars obliterated more than half of the patient's peripheral retina. Care was taken to avoid the central portion, assuring that, if the treatment proved successful, the patient might continue to read and drive.

Justine suffered. To dull the pain from those hundreds of burns, we injected Xylocaine deep behind the eye. The contact lens used to deliver the laser beam sometimes caused a painful corneal abrasion. For three or four days after every treatment, fluid leaking from the peripheral burns seeped into the central retina, blurring and distorting her vision. Her mother was always there, clutching an enormous purse against her chest, squeezing her eyes shut every time her daughter moaned under our long needle. But after six treatments the vitreous hemorrhages began to clear. The tangle of spiders melted away. Four months after Justine's first visit, Jacobson announced, "That's it. All the hemorrhage is gone."

Justine's mother burst into tears, dropped her purse on the floor, and threw her arms around Jacobson. His face blushed fiery red as he struggled against her grip, muttering, "No, no . . . it's too soon to tell . . . ," but he was a small man, an inch or two shorter and many pounds lighter than the joyful mother.

Four years later, during the last months of my residency, Justine's vision was still 20/20 in both eyes. There was no trace of hemorrhage, nor of the spidery vessels that signal recurrent proliferative retinopathy. Over the next three decades, recoveries similar to Justine's would number in the hundreds of thousands as laser treatment became the gold standard for diabetic retinopathy. A study published in 1976 showed a fourfold reduction in visual loss among treated patients, but modifications to the original method eventually reduced total blindness among diabetics to a tiny fraction of the original incidence. By the late 1990s, charitable institutions had delivered improved versions of the Coherent Model 800 laser to developing nations across the globe. Unfortunately, there remains a dark side to this story: many diabetics slip through the system, seeking care only when rampant scars have obliterated all hope of treatment, while some patients suffer an attack of retinopathy so fulminant and destructive, even the most timely therapy cannot sustain the acuity needed to drive or read.

Despite these limitations, laser surgery for proliferative retinopathy has proved a medical triumph of the first order. Here is something crude in principle, simple to perform, and easily learned, but it works. In the miracle that defeated jungle-osis, my role—treating thousands of patients with the laser, plus teaching the procedure to almost a hundred residents—has been the greatest privilege of my career.

Despite laser surgery and a host of other high-tech developments, the blind are still with us. If we live long enough, our eyes will always fail us. Most ten-year-olds can count the legs on an ant, while only the rare nonagenarian can see the ant itself. Sooner or later our eyes, along with our knees and our hearts and our hair, will surrender to the ravages of Mother Nature and Father Time. Before this vile duo sets upon their victim, the sclera is snowy white, the ocular media—composed of the cornea and lens and vitreous gel—remain crystal clear. Under a bright light, the retina shimmers like beaten silver. Indeed, the sparkle we see in children's eyes is no illusion. But by our twenties, the shank of young adulthood, the luster has begun to fade, foreshadowing the greenish cataract and rheumy yellow sclera of senescence.

When Father Time lets fly his first cruel arrow, the target is often our crystalline lens, a lentil-shaped tissue that hangs behind the iris, suspended by a thousand translucent filaments. Tension on these filaments allows youngsters to focus their eyes from near to far with the ease and precision of a Nikon camera. But in order to sustain its marvelous clarity, the lens must survive without capillaries, nourished only by a clear, oxygen-poor aqueous fluid. Such metabolic tenuousness leaves the lens vulnerable to every biological assault. Like the canary in the mine, it is often the first tissue to fall victim when subtle toxins or the ravages of aging attack our body. Over the years, our lenses first lose the elasticity that allows them to alter their focus from distance to near, heaping upon us the curse of bifocals or reading glasses. Then, over the following decades, inexorable as an unloved season, cataracts appear, diffracting light into halos, casting an odd tint on familiar objects, eventually drawing a dark veil over our world.

If granddaddy lives long enough, he won't be able to read, but if he's lucky—if cataracts are the only cause of his impairment—twenty minutes at the hands of a skilled surgeon will do the trick: voilà, the opaque lump is gone, sucked out through a vibrating needle and replaced by an acrylic lens the size of a corn flake. The next morning granddaddy will pore over his morning newspaper as happily as he did in his twenties.

"It's macular degeneration, isn't it, doctor?"

"Yes, I'm afraid so."

To see clearly, we need more than a clear cornea and a clear lens. Much more: a tissue that transforms light into nervous impulses (the retina), plus a cable to transmit these impulses to the brain (the optic nerve) and a sentient organ to receive and process them (the visual cortex). Of the tissues in this chain, arguably the most complex and vulnerable is the retina, a delicate, multilayered, altogether wondrous membrane. Alas, against the retina, as against the lens, Mother Nature and Father Time marshal their terrible forces. Among those patients who live beyond their sixth decade, an ever-increasing proportion show degeneration of the macula, the central portion of the retina and the site of its most active, densely packed neurons. First the macula begins to lose its silvery sheen, then it fades slowly into a ragged, lusterless wasteland known as dry macular degeneration—a progress akin to the inexorable wrinkles and liver spots that transform a baby's face into the face of a crone. Year by year, line by line on the acuity chart, the victims lose their vision. Worse yet, year by year the dread disease expands its roster of victims until, among the few that reach the century mark, virtually none are spared its cruel devastation.

"Doctor, when I got up this morning there was a black spot in my right eye. It blocks out everything I look at."

This was Sister Maria, an eighty-four-year-old nun. I have heard similar words from a sixty-nine-year-old railroad engineer and an eighty-six-year-old former prizefighter with a crooked nose. A colleague of mine, a seventy-three-year-old professor of pathology at the University of Louisville School of Medicine, spoke more succinctly. One afternoon he got up from his microscope, walked across the street, and barged into my clinic. "Goddammit, Gamel," he said, "what the hell's going on with my eye?"

These were the unlucky ones. Most patients with macular degeneration suffer the "dry" form, which steals vision slowly, year by year, but a small percentage suffer an abrupt hemorrhage or leakage beneath the retina that marks the onset of "wet" macular degeneration. From that point on, every object they look at disappears into a black hole. Fate makes only one concession: though the blind spot tends to enlarge over time, and though it quickly destroys the ability to read or drive, it rarely obliterates all sight, allowing the great majority of sufferers to navigate a familiar environment.

"Doctor . . . please . . . tell me . . . is there a treatment?"

Dry-eyed or weeping, motionless or wringing their hands, clear-voiced or choked with fear, sooner or later every patient with macular degeneration will ask the same question. Theory offers two potential cures: transplanting the eye or replacing the retina and its supporting structures. For the moment, both procedures remain well beyond the reach of science. The complexity of the retina rivals that of the brain itself. To transplant either organ, the surgeon must reconnect millions of axons—microscopic neural tubes so fragile the subtlest trauma destroys them forever. I suspect this achievement will elude the best surgeons for generations to come.

Thus at the moment we can boast only paltry progress against macular degeneration. For patients with the dry form, the only proven remedy is a regimen of vitamins and antioxidants that de-

lays—but does not stop—the insidious loss of vision. On a more
positive note, recent advances in molecular biology have given us a
panoply of new treatments for wet macular degeneration. Though
vastly more effective than the therapies available during my early
career, these miracle molecules remain an imperfect cure: they
must be injected repeatedly into the eye, they improve vision in
only a small proportion of patients, and of these only a lucky few
sustain the improvement for the remainder of their lives. Despite
the triumphs of modern medicine, Father Time and Mother Nature will eventually have their way with us. Decay is written into our
genes. It is our destiny.

Of all my patients with macular degeneration, Hans Bergerman
proved the most astute observer. No surprise, given his curriculum
vitae: professor emeritus, former chairman of Stanford's Department of Anthropology, editor of five books, author of two hundred
academic publications. His bushy brows and bald, sun-darkened
head gave him a gnomish look. Born in Brazil of German parents,
he spoke with a crisp accent and sat stiff as a soldier in the exam
chair. He never took his dark eyes off me for a moment.

"Let's see how this matches yours," he said, handing me a
sketched outline of the dark blur he had noted in his right eye. I
had just finished my exam and was drawing my own picture of the
lesion that lurked beneath the macula of that eye. Both drawings
resembled a childish doodle of a wolf's head, but in my doodle the
snout and ears were marked with a red pencil to show streaks of
subretinal blood. The wolf's bulbous jowl was formed by a tangle of
vessels that threatened to hemorrhage at any moment, destroying
forever Bergerman's central vision. The diagnosis was crystal clear:
wet macular degeneration. Several years before, the same disease
had destroyed the central vision in the patient's left eye.

Bergerman was lucky. Wet macular degeneration usually strikes
precisely in the central portion of the retina, where laser therapy,
the only option available back in the 1970s, would cause instant
blindness. His lesion lay a fraction of a millimeter removed from
the center. A shiver of anxiety ran down my spine. I had to treat the
poor man by cauterizing the tangle of vessels with a laser beam.
The zone that divided success from disaster was devilishly narrow,
no greater than the width of a few human hairs. Doug Jacobson,

the faculty attending who watched my every move through the viewing tube on the slit-lamp microscope, could not have guessed the quantity of sweat that soaked my armpits as I fired dozens of blue-green flashes into Bergerman's eye.

Three months later, Bergerman said, "Thank you, doctor." His vision was 20/30. The tangle of vessels had shrunk to a dry, flat scar. He thanked me again two years later, the day he awoke to find a huge black spot in the center of his vision. My treatment had failed. I knew it would fail—all laser treatments eventually failed, unless the patient died first—but the sight of that dark clot mounded beneath his retina broke my heart.

"Thank you very much," he said. "Your laser allowed me to read for an extra two years." On his way out of the exam room, he stopped to shake my hand and squeeze my shoulder. He gave me a rueful smile. "Why so sad, doctor? You look like you just lost your best friend. Who do you think you are—a magician, a god who turns old men into young men?"

Boris Osterhaus was a gray-haired farmer from Cecelia, Kentucky. His potbelly stretched the bib of his denim overalls tight as a drum. Minutes after arriving in my office, he pulled a pouch of Red Man chewing tobacco from the pocket of his denim shirt, then—remembering that this was neither the time nor the place to tuck a wad into his mouth—grimaced and stuffed the pouch back in the pocket. An optometrist in Cecelia had referred him to an ophthalmologist in Elizabethtown, the ophthalmologist had referred him to me, and now, after a hundred miles over backcountry roads, Boris learned from my lips that he would never read or drive again. A dry, pockmarked wilderness had destroyed the macula in both of his eyes. When I finished my dismal spiel—a diplomatic version of "Mother Nature is a bitch, Father Time is a son of a bitch, and there's not a damn thing we can do about it"—Boris leapt out of his chair to grip me in a knuckle- cracking handshake.

"Thank you, doctor, thank you so much. I just can't tell you how good it is to finally hear the truth straight up and down. Now I can get that confounded woman"—he gestured toward the stern-faced daughter who had brought him—"to stop dragging me all over the county. She keeps saying nowadays you doctors can fix anything. What a load of rubbish! I've lived eighty-three hard-bit years, and ain't nobody in my family been able to read much after they was seventy-five or eighty. That's just the way it is. I knowed it all along, but she wouldn't listen."

Patients are more than the sum of their failing parts. The wisest among them know that life cannot be cured, but even they need someone to inform them, and—when healing fails—to accompany them on the lonely road to disability and death. I did not learn this truth in a book or a laboratory or a lecture hall. My patients taught it to me. They came in desperation, returned year after year to share their struggles, and, as the years passed, they died. One way or the other I always lost the battle, but they gave me many precious moments. The eye begins as a perfect thing, a miraculous organ, but its luster, mortal and doomed as life itself, fades with each passing year. I watched it all through my slit-lamp microscope. I watched my patients grow old, and slowly, decade by decade, they taught me how to do it.

WALTER ISAACSON

How Einstein Divided America's Jews

FROM *The Atlantic*

ALBERT EINSTEIN'S FIRST tour of America was an extravaganza unique in the history of science, and indeed would have been remarkable for any realm: a grand two-month processional in the spring of 1921 that evoked the sort of mass frenzy and press adulation that would thrill a touring rock star. Einstein had recently burst into global stardom when observations performed during a total eclipse dramatically confirmed his theory of relativity by showing that the sun's gravitational field bent a light beam to the degree that he had predicted. The *New York Times* trumpeted that triumph with a multideck headline:

> Lights All Askew in the Heavens / Men of Science More or Less Agog Over Results of Eclipse Observations / EINSTEIN THEORY TRIUMPHS / Stars Not Where They Seemed or Were Calculated to Be, but Nobody Need Worry

So when he arrived in New York in April, he was greeted by adoring throngs as the world's first scientific celebrity, one who also happened to be a gentle icon of humanist values and a living patron saint for Jews.

Newly published papers from that year, however, show a less joyful aspect to Einstein's famous visit. He found himself caught in a battle between ardent European Zionists led by Chaim Weizmann, who was with Einstein on the trip, and the more polished and cautious potentates of American Jewry, including Louis D. Brandeis,

Felix Frankfurter, and the denizens of established Wall Street banking firms. Among other things, the disputes about Zionism apparently caused Einstein not to be invited to lecture at Harvard and prompted many prominent Manhattan Jews to decline an invitation from him to discuss his pet project, the establishment of a university in Jerusalem.

The full extent of this controversy, which has been only touched upon in previous books (including a biography I wrote in 2007), is revealed in a volume of Einstein's correspondence and papers for 1921 that was recently published by the Princeton University Press. None of the letters are newly discovered (all are available in public archives), but most have not been published before. The six-hundred-page volume, the twelfth compiled so far by the editors of the Einstein Papers Project, pulls all of the letters and related documents together in a way that allows us now to see, even more clearly than Einstein did at the time, the political and emotional struggle he stumbled into.

Einstein was raised in a secular German-Jewish household, and (except for a brief fling with religious fervor as a child) he disdained religious faith and rituals. He did, however, proudly consider himself Jewish by heritage, and he felt a strong kinship with what he called his fellow tribesmen or clansmen. His outlook in 1921 can be seen in the brusque answer he sent early that year to the rabbis of Berlin, who had urged him to become a dues-paying member of the Jewish religious community there. "In your letter," he responded, "I notice that the word Jew is ambiguous in that it refers (1) to nationality and origin, (2) to the faith. I am a Jew in the first sense, not in the second."

German anti-Semitism was then on the rise. Many German Jews did everything they could, including converting to Christianity, in order to assimilate, and they urged Einstein to do the same. But Einstein took the opposite approach. He began to identify even more strongly with his Jewish heritage, and he embraced the Zionist goal of promoting a Jewish homeland in Palestine.

He had been recruited by the pioneering Zionist leader Kurt Blumenfeld, who paid a call on Einstein in Berlin in early 1919. "With extreme naiveté he asked questions," Blumenfeld recalled. Among Einstein's queries: With their intellectual gifts, why should Jews create a homeland that was primarily agricultural? Why did it have to be its own nation-state? Wasn't nationalism the problem rather than the solution? Eventually, Einstein came around. "I am, as a human being, an opponent of nationalism," he told Blumenfeld. "But as a Jew, I am from today a supporter of the Zionist effort." He also became, more specifically, an advocate for the creation of a Jewish university in Jerusalem, which became Hebrew University.

Einstein had initially thought that his first visit to the United States, which he jokingly called "Dollaria," might be a way to make some money in a stable currency. He and his first wife had gone through a bitter divorce, and they were still fighting over finances. Hamburg banker Max Warburg and his New York–based brother Paul tried to help Einstein line up lucrative lectures. They asked both Princeton and the University of Wisconsin for a fee of $15,000. In February 1921, Max Warburg informed him, "The amount you wish is not possible." Einstein was not terribly upset. "They found my demands too high," he told his friend and fellow physicist Paul Ehrenfest. "I am glad not to have to go there; it really isn't a pretty way to make money." Instead, he made other plans: he would go to Brussels to present a paper at the Solvay Conference, the preeminent European gathering of physicists.

It was then that Blumenfeld came by Einstein's apartment again, this time with an invitation—or perhaps an instruction—in the form of a telegram from the president of the World Zionist Organization, Chaim Weizmann. A brilliant biochemist who had emigrated from Russia to England, Weizmann asked Einstein to accompany him on a trip to America to raise funds to help settle Palestine and, in particular, create Hebrew University in Jerusalem. When Blumenfeld read the telegram to him, Einstein balked. He was not an orator, he said, and the idea of using his celebrity to draw crowds to the cause was "an unworthy one." Blumenfeld did not argue. Instead, he simply read Weizmann's telegram aloud again. "He is the president of our organization," Blumenfeld said, "and if you take your conversion to Zionism seriously, then I have the right to ask you, in Dr. Weizmann's name, to go with him to the United States."

"What you say is right and convincing," Einstein replied, to the "boundless astonishment" of Blumenfeld. "I realize that I myself am now part of the situation and that I must accept the invitation."

Weizmann was thrilled and somewhat surprised. "I wholeheartedly appreciate your readiness at such a decisive hour for the Jewish people," he later cabled Einstein from London.

Einstein's decision reflected a major transformation in his life. Until the completion of his general theory of relativity, he had dedicated himself almost totally to science. But the anti-Semitism that was oozing up around him in Berlin led him to reassert his identity as a Jew and to feel more committed to defending the culture and community of his people. "I am not keen on going to America, but am just doing it on behalf of the Zionists," he wrote to his French publisher. "I must serve as famed bigwig and decoy-bird . . . I am doing whatever I can for my tribal brethren, who are being treated so vilely everywhere."

And so Einstein and his new wife, Elsa, set sail in late March 1921 for their first visit to America. On the way over, Einstein tried to explain relativity to Weizmann. Asked upon their arrival whether he understood the theory, Weizmann gave a puckish reply: "Einstein explained his theory to me every day, and by the time we arrived I was fully convinced that he really understands it."

When the ship pulled up to the Battery in lower Manhattan on the afternoon of April 2, Einstein was standing on the deck, wearing a black felt hat that concealed some but not all of his now graying profusion of uncombed hair. One hand held a shiny briar pipe; the other clutched a worn violin case. "He looked like an artist," the *New York Times* reported. "But underneath his shaggy locks was a scientific mind whose deductions have staggered the ablest intellects of Europe."

Thousands of spectators, along with the fife-and-drum corps of the Jewish Legion, were waiting in Battery Park when the mayor and other dignitaries brought Einstein ashore on a police tugboat. The crowd, waving blue-and-white flags, sang "The Star-Spangled Banner" and then the Zionist anthem, "Hatikvah." The Einsteins and the Weizmanns intended to head directly for the Hotel Commodore, in Midtown. Instead, their motorcade wound through the Jewish neighborhoods of the Lower East Side late into the evening. "Every car had its horn, and every horn was put in action," Weizmann recalled. "We reached the Commodore at about 11:30, tired, hungry, thirsty, and completely dazed."

*

One group was missing at most of the subsequent welcoming ceremonies and celebrations: the leaders of the Zionist Organization of America. Supreme Court Justice Louis D. Brandeis, who was its honorary president, did not even send pro forma official greetings or congratulations. Brandeis had traveled with Weizmann to Palestine in 1919, and the following year had gone to London to be with him at a Zionist convention. But shortly afterward they began to feud. Their fight partly stemmed from a few differences over policy; Brandeis wanted the Zionist organizations to focus on sending money to Jewish settlers in Palestine and not on agitating politically. It was also partly an old-fashioned power struggle; Brandeis wanted to install efficient managers and take power from Weizmann and his more ardent eastern European followers. But above all, it was a clash of personalities. Weizmann was born in Russia, emigrated to England, and shared Einstein's disdain for Jews who tried too hard to assimilate. Brandeis was born in Louisville, Kentucky, graduated from Harvard Law School, prospered as a prominent Boston lawyer, and was appointed by President Wilson to be the first Jewish justice on the Supreme Court. His crowd tended to look down on unrefined and unassimilated Jews from Russia and eastern Europe. In a letter to his brother in 1921, Brandeis revealed the cultural and personal underpinnings of his rift with Weizmann: "The Zionist [clash] was inevitable. It was one resulting from differences in standards. The Easterners—like many Russian Jews in this country—don't know what honesty is & we simply won't entrust our money to them. Weizmann does know what honesty is—but weakly yields to his numerous Russian associates. Hence the split."

Brandeis was initially happy that Einstein was coming to America, even though he was accompanying Weizmann. "The Great Einstein is coming to America soon with Dr. Weizmann, our Zionist Chief," he wrote to his mother-in-law. "Palestine may need something more than a new conception of the Universe or of several additional dimensions; but it is well to remind the Gentile world, when the wave of anti-Semitism is rising, that in the world of thought the conspicuous contributions are being made by Jews."

But two of Brandeis's closest associates expressed misgivings. His protégé Felix Frankfurter, then a professor at Harvard Law School, and Judge Julian Mack, the person Brandeis had tapped to be president of the Zionist Organization of America, argued that it would be better if Einstein's visit were cast primarily as a trip to lecture on physics, rather than one to raise money for Palestine.

Frankfurter and Mack sent Weizmann telegrams urging him to make sure that Einstein scheduled some physics lectures during his trip. But they quickly changed their minds when they were informed that Einstein had tried to extract large fees from various universities for such lectures, even though he was speaking about Zionism for free. That was even worse. So they sent another telegram, this one warning of the danger that Einstein would be seen as trying to "commercialize" his science. Such crassness would hurt his image and that of Jews, Frankfurter and Mack feared. Some of the physics lectures should be done for free. As Mack cabled to Weizmann: "EINSTEIN SITUATION EXTREMELY DIFFICULT EXPEDIENT YOU EXPLAIN US FULLY HIS EXACT NEGOTIA- TIONS . . . ALSO AWAITING YOU PROMISED CABLE WHETHER HE ACCEPT YOUR SUGGESTION COUPLE UNI- VERSITY LECTURES FREE." In one telegram, they went so far as to urge that Einstein's trip be canceled. Another telegram made clear that there would be no lecture at the university where Frank- furter was an influential professor. "HARVARD ABSOLUTELY DE- CLINES EINSTEIN," the telegram read. It did add that he would be welcome to come for an informal visit without a lecture or a lecture fee. When Einstein found out about the telegrams, he was furious. Mack defended himself and Frankfurter—and by exten- sion Brandeis—in a letter to Einstein insisting that their only mo- tive was "to protect you against unjust attacks and to protect the organization against the result of such unjust attacks."

Brandeis and his cohorts at the Zionist Organization of America made matters worse, during Einstein's visit, when they reacted to a deadly clash between Arab and Jewish rioters in Jaffa by reinforc- ing their desire that adequate "safeguards" be in place before money was raised for Hebrew University. Einstein confided that this attitude made him suspect that the Brandeis crowd was "com- mitting sabotage" of his mission. When Brandeis's friend and sup- porter Rabbi Judah Magnes proposed hosting a gathering in Man- hattan for intellectuals to talk about the university, Einstein replied that he would come only if Magnes made the event a fundraiser. "I did not have in mind a fund-raising meeting," Magnes replied in a cold and curt letter. "Under the circumstances, it is probably better to forego the meeting."

The resistance to Einstein's mission came not only from the Brandeis camp of cautious and restrained American Zionists, but also from successful New York Reform Jews of German heritage, many of whom were opposed to Zionism. When Einstein invited fifty or so of New York's most prominent Jews to a private meeting in his hotel, many of them declined. Paul Warburg, who had served as his agent soliciting lecture fees, wrote: "My presence would be of no use; on the contrary, I fear that, if at all, its effect would be rather to cool things down. As I already told you on another occasion, I personally have the greatest doubts relating to the Zionist plans and anticipate their consequences with genuine consternation."

Other rejections came from Arthur Hays Sulzberger of the *New York Times;* the politically connected financier Bernard Baruch; the lawyer Irving Lehman; the first Jewish cabinet secretary, Oscar Straus; the philanthropist Daniel Guggenheim; and the former congressman Jefferson Levy.

On the other hand, Einstein and Weizmann were wildly embraced by less assimilated and more enthusiastic Jews, the ones who tended to live in Brooklyn or on the Lower East Side rather than on Park Avenue. More than twenty thousand showed up at one event, causing "a near riot," the *Times* reported, when they "stormed the police lines." After three weeks of lectures and receptions in New York, Einstein paid a visit to Washington. For reasons fathomable only to those who live in that city, the Senate decided to debate the theory of relativity. On the House side of the Capitol, Representative J. J. Kindred of New York proposed placing an explanation of Einstein's theories in the *Congressional Record*. David Walsh of Massachusetts rose to object. Did Kindred understand the theory? "I have been earnestly busy with this theory for three weeks," Kindred replied, "and am beginning to see some light." But what relevance, he was asked, did it have to the business of Congress? "It may bear upon the legislation of the future as to general relations with the cosmos."

Such discourse made it inevitable that when Einstein went with a group to the White House, President Warren G. Harding would be faced with the question of whether *he* understood relativity. As the group posed for the cameras, he smiled and confessed that he did not. The *Washington Post* carried a cartoon showing him puzzling over a paper titled "Theory of Relativity" while Einstein puzzled over one on the "Theory of Normalcy," which was the name Harding had given to his governing philosophy. The *New York Times* ran a front-page headline: "Einstein Idea Puzzles Harding, He Admits."

During the Washington visit, the noted journalist and power broker Walter Lippmann tried to set up a peace meeting between Weizmann and Brandeis. Negotiations between the camps of the two Zionist leaders broke down over a variety of issues, and the summit never occurred. Einstein, however, was happy to pay a call on Brandeis, even though Weizmann urged him not to. They hit it off well. Einstein told the friend who arranged the visit that he came away with an "utterly different" opinion of Brandeis than the one pushed on him by Weizmann. Brandeis was also pleased. "Prof. & Mrs. Einstein are simple lovely folk," he wrote his wife the next day. "It proved impossible to avoid some discussion of the 'break,' though they are not in [it]. They specialize on the University." The one day of personal harmony, however, ended up doing nothing to heal the rift between the Weizmann-Einstein camp and the Brandeis-Frankfurter one, which continued to worsen during the visit.

Einstein subsequently went to Princeton, where he delivered a weeklong series of scientific lectures and received an honorary degree "for voyaging through strange seas of thought." He did not get the $15,000 fee he had originally requested, but he did receive a more modest one, plus a deal that Princeton would publish his lectures as a book and give him a 15 percent royalty. Einstein's lectures were very technical. They included more than 125 complex equations that he scribbled on the blackboard while speaking in German. As one student admitted to a reporter, "I sat in the balcony, but he talked right over my head anyway."

Einstein seemed to like Princeton. "Young and fresh," he called it. "A pipe as yet unsmoked." From a man who was invariably fondling new briar pipes, this was a compliment. It would not be a surprise, a dozen years hence, that he would decide to move there permanently.

Harvard, where Einstein went next, did not endear itself quite as well. Einstein graciously took a tour of the campus, dropping in on labs and commenting on students' work, even though he had been explicitly not invited to give a formal lecture there. For the rest of his U.S. trip, he and Frankfurter engaged in an exchange of letters in which the Harvard professor tried to deflect the blame for the snub. People have "accused me of having wanted to prevent your appearance at Harvard," Frankfurter wrote in a short note. "The accusation is absolutely untrue." Einstein, however, knew of the telegrams that Frankfurter and Mack had sent objecting to Einstein's request for lecture fees. "It now does seem plausible to me that you acted the way you did with honest, good intentions," Einstein replied, not quite accepting Frankfurter's denial. He added a humorous jab at Jews such as Frankfurter who were eager to avoid ruffling the refined sensibilities of non-Jews. "It would not even have been serious if all universities had withheld invitations," he wrote, "although I certainly know that it is a Jewish weakness always anxiously to want to keep the Gentiles [*Gojims*] in a good mood."

One of the final stops on the grand Einstein-Weizmann tour was Cleveland, where several thousands thronged the train depot to meet the visiting delegation. The parade included two hundred honking and flag-draped cars. Einstein and Weizmann rode in an open car, preceded by a National Guard marching band and a cadre of Jewish war veterans in uniform. Admirers along the way grabbed onto Einstein's car and jumped on the running board, while police tried to pull them away.

The Zionist Organization of America was about to meet in Cleveland for its annual convention, and the "downtown" Jews loyal to Weizmann were preparing for a showdown with the "uptown" Jews loyal to Brandeis. The convention turned out to be raucous indeed, with bitter speeches that included denunciations of the Brandeis camp for, among other sins, not showing enthusiasm for Einstein's trip. Weizmann's supporters, fortified by his presence, were able to block a vote of confidence endorsing the leadership of Brandeis and his point man, Julian Mack. Mack immediately resigned as president, Brandeis resigned as honorary president, and others in the Brandeis camp—including Felix Frankfurter and Stephen S. Wise—resigned from the executive committee. The deep rift in American Zionism would persist, and would undermine the movement, for almost a decade.

Einstein was not at the convention. He had already boarded

a ship back to Europe, feeling somewhat baffled and amused by what he had seen in America. "It is more easily aroused to enthusiasm than other countries I have unsettled with my presence," he wrote to his best friend, Michele Besso. "I had to let myself be shown around like a prize ox . . . It's a miracle that I endured it. But now it's finished and what remains is the fine feeling of having done something truly good and of having worked for the Jewish cause despite all the protests by Jews and non-Jews—most of our fellow tribesmen are smarter than they are courageous."

The opposition he encountered served only to deepen his support for the Zionist cause. "Zionism really offers a new Jewish ideal that can give the Jewish people joy in its own existence again," he wrote Paul Ehrenfest right after the trip. In this regard, he was part of a trend that was reshaping Jewish identity, by choice and by imposition, in Europe. "Until a generation ago, Jews in Germany did not consider themselves as members of the Jewish people," he told a reporter on the day he was leaving America. "They merely considered themselves as members of a religious community." But anti-Semitism changed that, and there was a silver lining to that cloud, he declared. "The undignified mania of trying to adapt and conform and assimilate, which happens among many of my social standing, has always been very repulsive to me."

The fundraising part of Einstein's tour was only a modest success. Even though poorer Jews and recent immigrants had poured out to see him and donated with enthusiasm, few of the eminent and old-line Jews with great personal fortunes became part of the frenzy. Only $750,000 was collected for Hebrew University, far less than the $4 million that Einstein and Weizmann had hoped for. But that was a good enough start. "The university seems to be financially secured," Einstein wrote Ehrenfest.

Four years later, the university did indeed open, on top of Mount Scopus, overlooking Jerusalem. In an ironic twist, some of the New York financiers who initially spurned Einstein ended up supporting it, and they insisted on installing as chancellor Rabbi Judah Magnes, the person who had clashed with Einstein in 1921 and canceled a reception when Einstein insisted on turning it into a fundraiser. Einstein was so upset by the appointment of Magnes that he resigned from the board in protest. Nevertheless, he would eventually leave his papers and much of his estate to the university.

There was one other ironic footnote. In 1946, after he had emigrated to America, Einstein again became associated with fundraising for a Jewish university. The organization was initially called the Albert Einstein Foundation for Higher Learning, and it acquired the campus of a dying university near Boston. But once again, Einstein clashed with some of the donors and their choices for administrators. When they asked whether they could name the university after him, Einstein refused. So the founders decided instead to honor their second choice, who had died five years earlier. They named the new university Brandeis.

STEVEN L. ISENBERG

Lunching on Olympus

FROM *The American Scholar*

THE BRITISH WRITERS W. H. Auden, E. M. Forster, Philip Larkin, and William Empson paid respectful attention to one another: Larkin wrote "English Auden was a superb and magnetic wide-angled poet, but the poetry was in the blaming and the warning." Empson thought Auden a "wonderful poet" and put Larkin among the "very good poets." Auden wrote a sonnet for Forster, and Empson wrote a poem called "Just a Smack at Auden." Forster's novels were touchstones for Auden, who cabled "Morgan" Forster on his eightieth birthday these good wishes: "May you long continue what you already are stop old famous loved yet not yet a sacred cow." Empson thought Forster's *Aspects of the Novel*—lectures he had heard as a student at Cambridge—"a model."

For me the four have another thing in common, the unlikely and unexpected occasions of my having met each of them for lunch. Those visits are always with me, and while I kept no diary and so remember fewer of their words than I wish, the memories I do have are testimony to their humanity and kindness.

W. H. Auden: "Oh, don't bother much about that."

It all began with Auden in New York in 1962. I had recently graduated from Berkeley and started to work at McGraw-Hill as a reader of manuscripts that senior editors wanted cleared out. Unauthorized and unanticipated by my boss, I looked Auden up in the phone book and called him at home. I said I was in McGraw-Hill's trade editorial department and had recently been a student of and reader for Mark Schorer, the head of the English department at Berkeley. I wondered if we could meet to discuss whether he might write a biography. I'd come up with this because Auden was not our author, and I had been told that exclusivity clauses in publishing contracts sometimes omit a genre in which the author had never written.

Auden said he didn't write biographies, but was curious about whom I had in mind as a potential subject. E. M. Forster, I said, or Thomas Mann, or—the third is fuzzy in my memory, but it was either Carl Jung or Hermann Hesse. "Forster is alive," he said. "Well, perhaps, that one might wait," I replied, and somehow I got from there to setting a date for lunch. I chose the Oak Room at the Plaza Hotel because I had looked in there once and it seemed old world, serious, and comfortable.

A few days later my boss, Ed Kuhn, the head of the trade editorial department, summoned me to his office. "I have just had a call," he said, "from Bennett Cerf [I knew who he was from the television panel show *What's My Line?*], the head of Random House, asking who the hell you were. I couldn't imagine why he had heard of you and why he sounded so damn put out. Cerf asked, 'What does he do for you? He is poaching on one of our authors.' I asked Cerf who that was. 'W. H. Auden. He is trying to get him to write a biography.' I told Cerf you were just a kid out of college, and I had no idea about this, and Cerf said, 'Well, Auden is having lunch with him.'"

For McGraw-Hill to publish W. H. Auden was virtually unthinkable. We had brought out Schorer's biography of Sinclair Lewis, but our biggest-selling authors were Eugene Burdick with *Fail Safe* and Robert Ruark with *Uhuru*. So it was on a few counts that Kuhn was astonished. I could tell Cerf and Kuhn had enjoyed a laugh at my expense. Nevertheless, the whole matter pricked Kuhn's pride. Why shouldn't his house be a place for the likes of Auden?

Kuhn asked what biographies I had suggested. I told him. He was even more stunned after I got out one name. "How much Auden have you read?" he asked. "Not much," I admitted. He told me to take afternoons off for the next several days to read Auden so the lunch would have less danger of being embarrassing. I asked him if he would like to come with us. "No," he said, "that wasn't what Auden had in mind"—and if he went, Cerf would be on the phone again, and this time it wouldn't be so amusing.

The day before the lunch, though, Kuhn appeared in my office and suggested I include John Starr, a senior editor who had taken a shine to me. Starr was a friend and editor of Richard Condon, the author of *The Manchurian Candidate,* and that was as much as I knew about his literary taste. He was a seasoned hand at picking up a check on the lunch circuit and had been especially kind to me, so I was happy to ask him. It wouldn't hurt to bring along someone with the bona fides of adulthood and the publishing business.

We waited for Auden in the leathery den of the Oak Room. Neither of us had ever seen him in person. He came in carrying a pile of newspapers, which seemed to include lots of cut-out crossword puzzle pages from the *Times* of London. He wore a tweedy sports coat and pants, his shirt and tie were dominated by academic brown and allied shades. His face was like a plowed field.

We never spoke of biographies at all. Or of his writing anything for us. Auden and Starr began talking about good food and wine. The substance of it was beyond me, but they were at ease and familiar with each other's distinctions and discriminations. They didn't show off; they were just appreciative critics. They then spoke of World War II. Starr had served as an army officer in Europe, while Auden had famously emigrated from England to New York in 1939. In 1940 he wrote "In Memory of W. B. Yeats," set amidst the backdrop of war:

> In the nightmare of the dark
> All the dogs of Europe bark,
> And the living nations wait,
> Each sequestered in its hate

Again I was separated from the talk by age and experience, having been born in 1940, but they made me feel included. I had a front-row seat; I had made the lunch happen, and they were both happy to be together talking.

Then Auden asked me about Berkeley. I had just done my senior paper on Yeats and said something about his mysticism. "Oh," he said, "don't bother much about that. Just a contrivance, a device, a stage, more than anything else." I gathered from the familiar tone that he knew Yeats, about whom "In Memory" says:

You were silly like us: your gift survived it all;
The parish of rich women, physical decay,
Yourself; mad Ireland hurt you into poetry.

As the lunch drew to its close, we asked Auden what he liked best about New York, and he said Jewish jokes. He asked if we knew any. I said I was from Los Angeles and couldn't really do a good accent, but my aunt from Brooklyn and my father told some good jokes. He laughed at the couple I told him, and then he told one of his favorites. A man from the Upper West Side goes to his psychiatrist. The doctor listens and tells him he is depressed and hostile. The doctor suggests a hobby or a pet, something to bring him out of it. The man says he lives in a small apartment; it would be difficult. The doctor says even a small pet would do. After several weeks, the doctor noted improvement, and asked if the man had bought a pet. "Yes," the man said. "What kind?" "Bees," he replied. "Bees?" the doctor said, puzzled. "I thought you said you had a small apartment. Where do you keep them?" "In a cigar box," said the patient. "But how do they breathe?" the doctor asked.

"How do they breathe?" said the patient. "Fuck 'em."

E. M. Forster: "I will tell you when it's time to go."

In 1965, while I was a student at Oxford, NBC was trying to make a television show about the Genizah Scrolls from Cairo (an archaeological find second only to the Dead Sea Scrolls). But NBC wasn't having any luck in getting access to the Genizah archives in the Cambridge University library. Fortunately for me, someone at a dinner party in New York said he knew a student at Oxford who might help. So, I got the job of producing the show.

In the course of visiting Cambridge, I arranged an introduction to the professor of Near Eastern languages and literature, and through him to the curator of the scrolls. Once the curator had gotten used to both the astounding news that television existed and the bemusing fact that I was American, he granted me some kind of honorary Oxbridge status and so the scrolls—actually scraps of parchment journals—were seen on television for the first time.

Because the show's sponsor was the Jewish Theological Seminary, the professor asked me if I was religious. I said I'd had a bar mitzvah and been confirmed, but after that I had gone to services rarely—so, no, I wasn't religious. He probed a bit further, laughed, and said, "You are a pagan. Would you like to meet another one?" I had no idea whom he had in mind, but I said yes. He knew I was reading English at Oxford and perhaps that explained his next words: "Write me when you have read all of E. M. Forster, and I will ask him to see you."

Some months later I did, and I received a short note from Forster proposing a day and time when I might visit him and saying he hoped I had other business, as it seemed a long trip to make only to see him. One gray, chilly March day in 1966, I planned to take the train down to London and then up to Cambridge. As I was leaving the college, I ran into my tutor, Christopher Ricks. "Remember you are meeting an old man," he said, "so you should leave after about twenty minutes."

At ten the next morning, I walked into King's College, one of the grandest Oxbridge colleges, whose cathedral-sized chapel is one of the most famous buildings in Europe. The porter gave me the staircase and room number and directions. I walked up the wooden stairs (five flights; a lot, I thought, for an old man; Forster was then eighty-six) and knocked on the door.

It opened to reveal a small, slightly stooped, demure man, smartly but modestly dressed, who welcomed me in and offered me a chair. It felt straightaway as if I were a visitor rather than a student having come for a tutorial. He asked my plans for the day, as once again he said it was an awfully long way to come just to see him. I said I had no other plans and that compared to my travel from California, this trip was short. The visit with him more than justified it.

He seemed to want me to ask questions, but first he talked about living in college and how generous King's had been to him and how much enjoyment he reaped from it and how convenient it was. He asked after my college at Oxford, Worcester—where were my rooms and did I enjoy it?

He asked what I had been reading lately. I said Dickens and George Eliot and that I was going to do the special paper on the novel in my exams. This to the man who wrote *Aspects of the Novel*. I asked Forster if we could talk about Lawrence, and he responded,

"David or T. E.?" He told me that in his bedroom he had several letters from D. H. Lawrence. I told him my mother had picked Lawrence as my middle name, after Lawrence of Arabia, and he laughed happily at that. But I found that I didn't have much more to ask him. It was one of those moments, as in all these meetings, when my self-doubt was playing as hard inside me as my excitement.

I was hoping he would get out the D. H. Lawrence letters, but suddenly it occurred to me that it was getting to be around the twenty-minute marker. I said he had been kind to see me and I ought to be going and leave him to his work and reading.

"Someone told you that you are going to see an old man and you ought to leave after a short time," he said, and my expression told him that that was just what had happened.

"Anyone who says that should also remember when you go to see someone old, it may be the last time. Please stay, if you can, and I will tell you when it's time to go."

That exchange stays with me because of its simple kindness. I remember the moment better than anything else that was said, other than his asking me "Did you ever know Gide?"

"I know who he was," I replied.

"No," Forster said, "did you ever have lunch with him?"

I almost laughed out loud at the absurdity, but I just said no, and no more was said of André Gide.

Forster asked me to open the mail piled on a nearby table and to go through it, setting aside anything personal or seemingly important for him to look at. And then, as it was nearing eleven, he suggested that we go to the Senior Combination Room for coffee. He put on his overcoat, as I did mine, and slowly but surely he descended the staircase. We walked through the college—it was out of term, so not many students were around—and went into the SCR lounge. It was populated only by a few extraordinary-looking old men, bent under the weight of age and the burdens of study. No one spoke, and everyone sat so as to have no need to converse.

We were served our coffee and biscuits, and after a short time Forster got up and led me outside. It was cold and clear. He suggested a walk along the River Cam. "Would that suit you?" he asked. "Of course," I said. As we began to walk, he laced his arm through mine. Can you imagine how I felt—a boy from my circumstances, so American, so unfinished—walking along the backs of the Cambridge colleges with the man who wrote *A Passage to India* and *Howards End* on my arm as a silent companion?

At some point Forster began to remark on things he loved about particular colleges—their gardens and parts of the river. I followed his lead, and we wound up walking down the main street of the town; soon we were in front of Heffer's, the university's bookstore. Only then did I realize I hadn't brought a book for him to sign. I asked him if I could run in and buy one. He said yes, and that he would wait outside.

I ran in, totally unfamiliar with the store and suddenly worried about leaving Forster in the street alone. I don't know what I thought would happen, but I imagined headlines reporting an accident: "Forster Accompanied and Then Abandoned by a Visiting American Student." I couldn't find the novels section, but I caught sight of a hardbound edition of Lionel Trilling's book on Forster and bought it in a desperate rush.

We then walked back to King's and up to his room. "Now it is time for me to go," I said, and I told him how grateful I was for his kindness. He asked where I would go, and I said back to Oxford. He said, "Let me sign your book," and without explanation I showed him the Trilling. He smiled and drew a line through the title—his name—and signed his name.

Philip Larkin: "I never like to be more than five miles from home."

Fifteen years later, when my family paid a summer visit to Christopher Ricks in England, Ricks had the idea that I ought to try to see Philip Larkin and offered to write Larkin and ask if he would see me. The year before in New York I had set up a lecture that Ricks had given about the poet. I asked Ricks if he would come with me. Absolutely not, he said. He wanted to ask for me—that would make him happy.

I do not have a copy of Ricks's letter to Larkin, but I do have a copy of Larkin's answer:

28 June 1982

Dear Christopher,

Thanks for your letter — this is the fourth week of having the painters in, which is why I haven't replied.

It's true I generally decline, with such gentleness as I can muster, self-proposed visits by chaps like yours, but I suppose I can break my own rules. On condition that

i. You name your man, & he isn't someone I detest;

ii. It's understood that this isn't a precedent but a single exception;

iii. This is a private meeting and not an interview — very important this —

iv. He realizes I am seriously deaf & hard to talk to;

v. The meeting doesn't last more than an hour or two; then I should be willing to oblige you.

Venue doubtful: I shall be in London in July. *Here* less trouble, but makes [rule] v. harder to observe. However, I leave this rather doubtful ball in your court.

Your life sounds exciting. If it isn't the Faculty, it's the College! Must be wearing.

Kind regards,
Yours, Philip

A day was set, and with every Larkin rule in mind, I drove to Hull, where Larkin was university librarian. On campus, I was directed to the library and asked for the librarian's office. Larkin's secretary promptly announced my arrival, and I was summoned into a large office. From behind his desk, a taller, balder, more affable Larkin than I had imagined came to shake my hand.

"Good morning, Professor Isenberg."

"Good morning. Thank you for letting me come to see you. But first, I am not a professor."

"Well, I see you are young, but surely you must be at least an associate professor."

"No, I'm not an academic."

Larkin's smile widened with open delight. "Good. But somehow I got the impression of Ricks giving a lecture you helped arrange."

"I will tell you about the setting — I think you would like it."

"Please do. But what is your job now?"

"I have just begun working in newspapers."

His face showed less of a smile.

"What do you do?"

"I'm assistant to the publisher of *Newsday,* a large newspaper in Long Island, New York, where I'm learning the business and hope one day to run one."

"Good," he said, his face brightening again. "You're neither a reporter nor an academic. Come," he said. "I propose we go for a pub lunch in the country. I will be happy to drive."

We walked out to his car, which was some sort of mini–station wagon. Larkin had large thick glasses, and I was apprehensive about his driving skills, but he wouldn't hear of me driving. "That would make me an awful host, and anyway I would have to keep giving you directions, and as a publisher, you are a direction giver."

His tone and manner were anything but that of the Larkin of despair and loneliness; he was fast, funny, and friendly. I laughed often and was struck by the precise and fresh turns of phrase in his conversation.

At the pub, we had beer. I am a slight drinker; Larkin went at a seasoned Englishman's lunchtime pace. I told him about the evening of the Ricks lecture and he was pleased.

He was, by his own admission, wary of Americans; they wanted either to ask academic questions about his poems or to try to get him to visit America. He said he was the sort of Englishman who did not want to go anywhere else. He told me of going to Germany to get an award. When he went to the hotel's front desk in the morning to ask for a newspaper, he discovered that "although they tell you the people in those places speak English, they don't."

At some point, I asked him about contemporary poets. He was jokey and dismissive, refusing to be caught up in "Ted Hughes worship," as he put it, "or anything like that."

He told me he had a friend who visited New York and was mugged outside the New York Public Library on 42nd Street. I told him that when he came, I would get my younger brother, who was a strong guy, a criminologist, and knew a lot of policemen, to see that he was protected. He laughed. "You see? You are working on trying to get me there."

He seemed in no rush to begin lunch, and I started to fear the rule about an hour or two. I didn't want to drink too much without eating, but I had another beer with him.

When we did sit down, I remember two things I said. First, I misquoted a word in a snatch of a John Betjeman poem, and he corrected me, gently. (At the end of our visit, he gave me an edition of

Betjeman's poems and signed it: "For Stephen (or even Steven), commemorating a delightful day, Kindest regards, Philip.") Second, I said that the way he wrote about death and growing old, staring them in the face, summoning unshopworn, unexhausted everyday words, all newly woven and unflinching, ironically, gave me a certain comfort against my own fears. He listened quietly.

He then raised the matter of going to see well-known people and asked had I done it before. I told him of going to see Forster.

He told me that when he was young he had gone to see Forster too. Forster had entertained a circle—literally—of young men. Every ten minutes or so, he made them change chairs so someone new sat on his right. Larkin said he had taken the manuscript of his first novel, *Jill*, and tried to press it on Forster to read, but he wouldn't take it. Larkin laughed at himself. It was an embarrassing and amusing memory—not painful, though I got the clear impression he would have been happier if Forster had taken and read his manuscript. I think he told me this story to put me at greater ease —we both knew it takes nerve to arrange one of these meetings, and there is a certain nervousness once you are there.

He had another tale of meeting the famous. When he was librarian of Belfast University, the Queen visited, and he was introduced to her. He told her an Irish joke, which he said was sort of a triple faux pas—telling the Queen a joke, an Irish one, and doing it in Northern Ireland.

At some point the chemistry felt right, and so I did take up the question of a visit to America. What stops you? I asked. He said, "I don't like to be in hotels, and I really don't know anyone." I said, "Here's a proposition. You know Ricks—he always stays at my home. Get him to vouch for us. Why don't you stay with us at our apartment? It overlooks Central Park. There's my wife and our son, who's nine. You don't have to talk to us. You can come and go as you please, invite anyone over you like."

He said, "The idea sounds appealing," and I thought that if I could get him on a plane that day, he would do it. Then he said, "I never like to be more than five miles from home."

Well, here's another idea, I said. Why don't you fly to New York? We'll get a helicopter to take you to Manhattan, take you to see whatever you want, and then take you back to the airport, and you can fly home.

"Oh," he said, "I like that very much. But you can't do that."

"Oh yes I can," I said. I told him of a friend who was the head of the Port Authority. "They run the airports, and my newspaper will find a way to get it done."

He roared. "That's the best offer I have ever had." Years later, I read that Larkin said he would like to go to China—if he could come back the same day.

It is faces we remember, and his was big, enlarged by his baldness and the glasses and the animated intensity of his speech. For all his poems, which often showed a glum, lonely, and struggling self, the man I met was strong, confident, terrifically alive, welcoming, relaxed, engaged, engaging. He had another beer, finished his lunch, and insisted we have something sweet. I tried to pay; he wouldn't allow it.

As he drove back, I was thinking how much he had drunk and how narrow the country roads were. I must have given off some whiff of apprehension, because he turned to me and said, "I hope we don't have an accident or the headline in your paper will be 'Our Beloved Assistant Publisher Dies with Unknown English Poet.'"

William Empson: "My boy, it is just like a symphony."

A year later, Ricks asked me if I would like to join him on a visit to William Empson in London. I was staying with a friend in Hampstead Heath, quite near Empson's home, so Ricks and I met late on a Saturday morning, planning to take Empson out to lunch, somewhere close by and informal.

The eccentricity of Empson's genius was almost as well known as his important critical works: *Seven Types of Ambiguity, Some Versions of Pastoral,* and *Milton's God.* Robert Lowell, then the American poet of highest standing, had once written to Empson that he was "the most intelligent poet writing in our language and perhaps the best. I put you with Hardy and Graves and Auden and Philip Larkin." A prized possession of mine is a recording of Empson reading his poems in a tone of voice that I believe no other human being can match, even if that person also combined Wykehamist, Cantabrigian, and Chinese accents.

Ricks is said by Empson's biographer, John Haffenden, to be

Empson's "greatest fan and friend," and Empson himself once said gruffly to Ricks's mother, "Your son saved me." This invitation was a great privilege for me.

We were met at the door by Empson himself, unkempt white hair and beard prominent. His shirt and pants were a faded gray and looked to have been worn unwashed for several days. The sitting room itself was strewn with newspapers and was visibly dusty; it looked as unkempt as Empson. Almost at once I could tell I was going to have a very hard time understanding him. I had to listen for key words. He said his wife was away, so we would have to put up with him.

In honor of "our American guest," he would make bloody marys. He was a skinny man whose clothes hung on him, and as he walked about he continually hooked his thumbs in the front of his pants and stretched them forward. Ricks and I had to avoid each other's eyes.

Empson picked out of the kitchen sink three large glasses that may have been washed within the week. On the counter was a large open can of tomato juice with a rusted top. He poured juice into each glass and, after that, generous amounts of something that could have been either gin or vodka—I couldn't see. Then he sprinkled on something that might have been Worcestershire sauce and from a bin dredged up browned celery stalks. And then he stood back to admire his work and repeatedly stretched and fanned his pants.

He bade us to keep our seats and served his magic drink, which I knew I was meant to praise as thoroughly authentic, if not hygienic. The real challenge was to drink some of this warm slop—no ice cube ever was evident—without spluttering. We toasted Empson and set to work. It had to be done in slow sips; every chance for him to offer a second one had to be eliminated.

Ricks and Empson had a few things to talk about, and they laughed together. I was concentrating on getting enough of the drink down to be neither insulting nor sick. By now, Ricks and I were having a harder time with the drinks and pants-stretching—it was just so outrageously funny, but we contained ourselves. I tell my classes that I believe America has weird and idiosyncratic people, but only England has naturally, fully formed eccentrics. Empson is the paradigm. (Recently Ricks remarked of Auden, Forster,

Empson, and Larkin that because they were centric in so many ways, their eccentricities were all the more interesting.)

I told him about meeting Auden and being astonished by his wrinkled face. "It was all those sailors," said Empson, who had written of Auden and Dylan Thomas that they were the only contemporaries "you could call poets of genius."

After a time, Empson said he wanted to make us lunch, and we would eat in the garden as it was such a fine day. Glancing again at the kitchen, I almost pleaded that he let us take him out to the closest place he enjoyed. Ricks added his solicitation. Empson wouldn't hear of it.

He went into the kitchen. I asked if I could help. He said I could set the table outside. I began a search for silverware, plates, and glasses. We were to switch to beer, warm of course. He provided no direction, so I had to look in cabinets and drawers. It gave me the chance to rinse and towel everything as unobtrusively as possible. He said we needed soup bowls and spoons and knives for cheese. I found three rolls, butter, and cheese. The rolls had seen a better day, but I hoped they could be buttered into edibility.

Ricks was ordered to stay seated, and then the soup-making began. First, Empson produced a large, dirty pot, which I had no chance to rinse. He ran water into it and set it to boil. From strange corners he found an onion, leeks, parsley, and some of the browned celery. He threw in some other things, but by then I couldn't look. At least it was all floating in hot water.

After a time Empson told me to bring the bowls to him, and he ladled out full portions for each of us, stopping between scoops to make pants adjustments. We sat outside in the lovely air and quiet garden, which did not have much beyond grass and some shrubbery. We were at a wooden table, with Empson at its head. He was obviously proud of his culinary work. There was no choice but to get it all down.

I tasted it and was shocked to find it was good. I didn't know what it was, but I was so relieved that I would be able to eat it at all that I blurted out my compliments.

"My boy," Empson said, "it is just like a symphony. You get the right instruments together—here, the ingredients—and the conductor then blends it all together." We laughed at his delight.

He told us that when he had taught for a semester in America, at a small college, he was assigned to teach Shakespeare to a class full of engineers (perhaps because he had taken the first part of his Cambridge degree in maths). Without slighting them, he said they knew nothing, not even what the Avon was. But what he liked best about them was that they were so well disciplined by their engineering training that they looked up every word they didn't know—so they met the first test of close reading.

I left with his voice even clearer in my head than on my old Caedmon recording of him reading his poems, my favorite being a Gertrude Stein pastiche, "Poem About a Ball in the Nineteenth Century":

> Feather, feather, if it was a feather, feathers for fair, or to be fair,
> aroused. Round to be airy, feather, if it was airy, very, aviary, fairy,
> peacock to be well surrounded. Well-aired, amoving, to
>   peacock, cared
> for, share dancing inner to be among aware.

There then: visits to four men who lived and died by, with, and for the English language. What most remains for me, beyond their words and genius, is their generosity. Today Christopher Ricks is the Oxford Professor of Poetry, just as Auden was over a half century ago, finishing his five-year appointment in 1961, the year before our luncheon.

As I have grown older, read more, and now teach, becoming what J. D. Salinger called a "lifetime English major," how many times I've wished for another meeting with each of them, because I have so much more to ask. And to hear again how each was so indelibly himself, to say some thanks to them for their part in making my teaching years full, to show them how much these meetings meant to me.

JANE KRAMER

Me, Myself, and I

FROM *The New Yorker*

EVERY FRENCH SCHOOLCHILD learns the date: February 28, 1571, the day a well-regarded and uncommonly educated nobleman named Michel de Montaigne retired from "the slavery of the court and of public duties," moved a chair, a table, and a thousand books into the tower of his family castle, near Bordeaux, shut the door, and began to write. It was his thirty-eighth birthday, and, by way of commemoration, he had the first two sentences he wrote that morning painted on the wall of a study opening onto his new library—announcing, if mainly to himself, that having been "long weary" of those public duties (and, presumably, of his wife, at home in the castle, a few steps across the courtyard), Michel de Montaigne had taken up residence in "the bosom of the learned Virgins, where in calm and freedom from all cares he will spend what little remains of his life, already more than half expired." His plan, he said, was to use the second half looking at himself, or, as he put it, drawing his portrait with a pen. He had his books for company, his Muses for inspiration, his past for seasoning, and, to support it all, the income from a large estate, not to mention a fortune built on the salt-herring and wine trades, which, in the last century, had turned his family into landed gentry. (His full name, as most enophiles can tell you, was Michel Eyquem de Montaigne.)

Montaigne's pursuit of the character he called Myself— "bashful, insolent; chaste, lustful; prating, silent; laborious, delicate; ingenious, heavy, melancholic, pleasant; lying, true; knowing, ignorant; liberal, covetous, and prodigal"—lasted for twenty years and produced more than a thousand pages of observation and revision that he called *"essais,"* taking that ordinary word and turning it into a literary occupation. When he died, at fifty-nine, he was still revising and, apparently, not at all surprised, since Myself was a protean creature, impossible to anticipate but also, being always at hand, impossible to ignore. I like to think of the essays as a kind of thriller, with Myself, the elusive prey, and Montaigne, the sleuth, locked in a battle of equals who were too close for dissimulation and too smart for satisfaction. And it may be that Montaigne did, too, because he often warned his readers that nothing he wrote about himself was likely to apply for much longer than it took the ink he used, writing it, to dry. "I am myself the matter of my book," he said, when the first two books of essays appeared, in 1580. "You would be unreasonable to spend your leisure on so frivolous and vain a subject."

He was wrong. By the time he finished a third book, eight years later, everyone in France with a philosophic bent and a decent classical education had read the first two—lured, perhaps, by the writer's promise that "my defects will here be read to the life, and also my natural form, as far as respect for the public has allowed" —and, given that some 90 percent of the French were illiterate, that probably means that everyone who could read the essays did. By sixteenth-century standards, Montaigne had produced a bestseller, although he maintained the pretense that he wrote only for himself or, at most, "for a few men and a few years." ("The public favor has given me a little more confidence than I expected" is how he described the effect on him.) News of the essays traveled fast. The first known English translation, by an exuberantly prolific language tutor named John Florio, went on sale in London at the turn of the seventeenth century, in time for Shakespeare to buy a copy. It was followed, in 1685, by the poet Charles Cotton's lovely version—the one that most Englishmen and Americans read until 1957, when Donald Frame, a Columbia professor who went on to become Montaigne's preeminent American biographer, produced his own translation. Thirty years later, the Oxford professor M. A. Screech did the same for Britain. I have used all three, along with, in French, my old, dog-eared Flammarion copy of the essays and the seriously intimidating new Pléiade edition, which came out in Paris in 2007, doubled in size by nearly a thousand pages of endnotes and annotations incorporating four hundred years of Montaigne research. (I admit to tweaking a few of the English quotes, in the spirit of competition and interpretation.)

However you read them, Montaigne's books were utterly, if inexplicably, original. They were not confessional, like Augustine's, nor were they autobiographical. You could call them the autobiography of a mind, but they made no claim to composing the narrative of a life, only of the shifting preoccupations of their protagonist in an ongoing conversation with the Greek and Roman writers on his library shelves—and, of course, with himself. His belief that the self, far from settling the question "Who am I?," kept leaping ahead of its last convictions was in fact so radical that for centuries people looking for precedents had to resort to a few fragments of Heraclitus on the nature of time and change—or, eventually, to give up and simply describe Montaigne as "the first modern man." It didn't matter if he was quoting Seneca in an essay called "To Philosophize Is to Learn How to Die" or, a few pages later, in an essay about imagination, musing on the vagaries of penises: "We are right to note the licence and disobedience of this member which thrusts itself forward so inopportunely when we do not want it to, and which so inopportunely lets us down when we most need it; it imperiously contests for authority with our will: it stubbornly and proudly refuses all our incitements, both of the mind and hand." He followed himself wherever his attention settled, and his regard was always the same—intent, amused, compassionate, contrarian, and irresistibly eclectic. (He could jump from Plato's discourse on the divinatory power of dreams to dinner at the castle—"a confusion of meats and a clutter of dishes displease me as much as any other confusion"—and do justice to them both.) One of his favorite philosophers, starting out, was the skeptic Sextus Empiricus, who had famously cautioned his followers to "suspend judgment" on everything but the experience of their own senses. Voltaire called Montaigne one of history's wise men, but when it came to the big philosophical questions that absorbed him—the nature of justice, say, or morality—he seemed to be saying, like Sextus, that there may be no truths, only moments of clarity, passing for answers.

The best way to read Montaigne is to keep watching him, the way he watched himself, because the retired, reclusive, and pointedly cranky Michel de Montaigne is in many ways a fiction—a mind so absorbingly stated that by now it can easily pass for the totality of Montaigne's "second" life. In fact, he went to the best parties in the neighborhood. He attended all the important weddings—and never mind that, by his admission, he'd practically been dragged to his own; the bride was a suitable Bordeaux girl named Françoise de la Chassaigne and the alliance more or less arranged. (His view of marriage, he wrote in the essay "On Some Verses of Virgil," was that he was "not so fit for it" but had acquiesced for "posterity," and he held to the common wisdom that the secret of a peaceful, companionable marriage was to keep one's wife permanently unaroused, the better to fix her thoughts on the details of hospitality and "sound housekeeping.") He had everybody's ear. He corresponded with beautiful, educated women who read his drafts. He dined at the castle with wellborn men who had learned to value his advice and, more to the point, his tact during his years of "public duties," both as a local emissary to the court of Charles IX, in Paris, and as a magistrate at the law court known at the time as the Parlement de Bordeaux.

He claimed to have forsworn his youth, which was apparently so unruly that eight years of it are missing from the public record; "I burned myself at [lust] in my youth, and suffered all the furies that the poets say come upon all those who let themselves go after women without restraint and without judgment" was how he described those years, when he was in his fifties. But he never forswore women or, for that matter, the thrill of watching a good battle, or any of the other indulgences of his class. ("For the intimate companionship of my table I choose the agreeable not the wise; in my bed, beauty comes before virtue," he once said.) He left his tower in 1580 for a year of traveling. He left it again in 1581 to become the mayor of Bordeaux—at the time the country's third-largest city and its richest port. Two years later, he agreed to a second term. And, while an avowed Catholic royalist (whether by conviction or, as a few of the essays suggest, because of a suspicion that taking a leap of faith on the big loyalties of his time was the best way to clear his mind for more enticing subjects), he was also a close friend and confidant of the Protestant Henri de Navarre, and was Navarre's emissary to the Catholic court of Charles's brother and successor, Henri III. His lifetime encompassed the spread of

Calvinism through France, and the eight Catholic-Protestant wars provoked by conversions like Navarre's within the royal family. And if Montaigne did not take sides in those wars, it may be that he thought of them as a family matter, which in a way they were. The Henris were both directly descended from Louis IX—the paterfamilias of three hundred years of French kings—and by 1584, with the death of Henri III's brother, Navarre was himself first in line to the French throne. "My house, being always open, easily approached and ever ready to welcome all men (since I have never let myself be persuaded to turn it into a tool for a war in which I play my part most willingly when it is farthest from my neighborhood), has earned quite a lot of popular affection," Montaigne wrote, about a year later, in the essay he called "On Vanity."

Authors are, of course, sneaky. (Montaigne put it nicely: "All is a-swarm with commentaries: of authors there is a dearth.") They lead you exactly where they want to go, and no farther. By the end of the essays, you know a great deal about Montaigne's mind and temperament, but, as for his promise that "my defects will here be read to the life," you are still waiting for the details of that life and most of the people in it. His evasions are legendary. He writes a great deal about the tyranny of laws but nothing about his fourteen years as a magistrate or his four years as a mayor, or even about his response, as mayor, to the plague that struck Bordeaux toward the end of his second term, leaving a third of the population dead. (He fled.) He writes a great deal about wives but rarely refers to his own and never by name, though he claims to have made himself "fall in love" to marry, a task perhaps made briefly pleasant by the fact that Françoise is said to have been an exceptionally beautiful and lively girl. Montaigne, at the time, was thirty-two and, he says, ready to be a dutiful and respectful husband. But he was not much interested in Françoise—nor, it may be, she in him, since some scholars have thrown her into the arms of his younger brother Arnaud, a good-natured and *sportif* army captain who died young, from a tennis ball to the ear. Montaigne himself rarely slept in his wife's bed, except for purposes of procreation; she gave him six daughters in thirteen years, and only one of them, Léonor, lived past infancy—a fact he dismissed with the unnerving remark (Montaigne experts are still arguing about why he made it and what it meant) that he had "lost two or three."

As for his mother, he alludes to her twice, but only in passing. Her name was Antoinette Louppes de Villeneuve. She came from a far-flung merchant clan, similar to the Montaignes in wealth and influence, but with the notable exception that, while the Montaignes were then solidly and safely Catholic, some of the Louppes were Protestant, and the family themselves were Sephardic *conversos* from Saragossa, where their name was Lopez de Villanueva. (Several had left Spain before the expulsions of 1492, and were thriving in Europe as properly minted Christians, or, as the new Pléiade edition chooses to put it, a Christian family *"anciennement convertie."*) Antoinette grew up in Toulouse. She arrived at the castle a reluctant bride of sixteen, to marry Pierre Eyquem, an eccentric but apparently exemplary chatelain (and a future mayor of Bordeaux himself), and once having settled her duty to her children by bearing them, she was attached mainly to herself. She claimed that Michel had exhausted her getting born—eleven months of pregnancy, by her calculations—and was furious to learn that, by her husband's last will, he was not only heir to but steward of the estate she had expected to manage in her lifetime. Their relations were, by anyone's standards, sour. The year after Pierre died, she threatened to sue Michel over the ownership of a family necklace; he discovered it in his wife's jewel box and gave it back, hoping to avoid the scandal of a court case—after which she spent a long, bitter, and contentious widowhood in the company of a granddaughter who seems to have been the only relative she liked.

But Montaigne was not much interested in family histories of any sort, and his own was apparently untouched by not only the anti-Semitism that attached to the children of "new Christian" immigrants like the Louppes but also the Catholic-Protestant wars at home. Some of Montaigne's siblings became Protestant, with no evident disruption to the family—even during the St. Bartholomew's Day massacres of 1572, when thirty thousand French Calvinists died. He doesn't mention those massacres in the essays, either. For him, the subject of Protestants and Jews (who had been barred from practicing their religion in France since the end of the fourteenth century) seems to have been, at most, food for his meditations on the absurdities of persecution and the fatal distractions of disharmony. He efficiently wrote off Martin Luther for leaving behind in Germany "as many—indeed more—discords and disagreements because of doubts about his opinions than he himself ever raised about Holy Scripture." He quoted Josephus and admired the Maccabees. But, when it came to seeing an old Jew herded naked through the streets of Rome, he remained a reporter—curious, compassionate, but not particularly disturbed. He did not expect much better from the world. Relatives, to his mind, were accidents of birth, consideration, and proximity. The genealogy that interested him was the genealogy of thought. He was far more interested in thinking about religion with the Sophists and Skeptics in his library than he was in the part that religion, even his own Catholicism, played in him.

For all that, he was a passionate traveler. His search for the spa that would cure his kidney stones—the disease had killed his father and would eventually help kill him—took him to Switzerland, Austria, and Germany. His love of the classics took him to Italy. In Rome, where his own copy of the essays had been seized by the Inquisition, he walked the streets of his dead mentors: "I like thinking about their faces, their bearing and their clothing," he said. "I mutter their great names between my teeth and make them resound in my ears." (Latin, by his father's decree, was not only his first language but the only one he was allowed to speak for his first six years.) He prowled the ghetto, visiting a synagogue, watching a circumcision, and happily cross-examining the rabbi. (By the end of his visit he had met the Pope and was made an honorary Roman citizen.) Today we would call him a gentleman ethnographer, more enchanted than alarmed by the bewildering variety of human practices. "Yes. I admit it," he wrote in "On Vanity." "Even in my wishes and dreams I can find nothing to which I can hold fast. The only things I find rewarding (if anything is) are variety and the enjoyment of diversity." He was interested in all things unfamiliar and exotic, from immolations in India to cannibalism in the New World. In the essay he called "On the Cannibals," he described "a very long talk" he had once had with a Tupi chief, brought to France from Brazil and, at the time, on display in Rouen for a royal visit. He admired the Indian's gentleness and his evident perplexity at the pomp and the poverty and the cruelty displayed so indifferently and indiscriminately to *him*. "I think there is more barbarity in eating a man alive than in eating him dead," he wrote, "more barbarity in tearing apart by rack and torture a body still sentient, in roasting him little by little and having him bruised and bitten by pigs and dogs (as we have not only read about but seen in recent memory, not among enemies in antiquity but among our fellow citizens and neighbors—and what is worse, in the name of duty and religion) than in roasting him and eating him after his death." No one has said it better.

"Anyone can see that I have set out on a road along which I shall travel without toil and without ceasing as long as the world has ink and paper," Montaigne wrote at the beginning of "On Vanity," his late and perhaps greatest essay. "I cannot give an account of my life by my actions: fortune has placed them too low for that, so I do so by my thoughts." He compares himself to a nobleman he once knew who would keep his chamber pots for a week to display, seriatim, to his friends—"He thought about them, talked about them: for him any other topic stank"—saying, "Here (a little more decorously) you have the droppings of an old mind, sometimes hard, sometimes squittery, but always ill-digested." He starts to extrapolate—"Scribbling seems to be one of the symptoms of an age of excess. When did we ever write so much as since the beginning of our Civil Wars? And whenever did the Romans do so as just before their collapse?"—and catches himself in time to add that "each individual one of us contributes to the corrupting of our time: some contribute treachery, others (since they are powerful) injustice, irreligion, tyranny, cupidity, cruelty: the weaker ones bring stupidity, vanity, and idleness, and I am one of them." He accuses himself, a little pridefully, of pride—in writing at all, with his country at war, and in the small, stubborn habits with which he flaunts his disregard, saying that "if one of my shoes is askew then I let my shirt and my cloak lie askew as well: I am too proud to amend my ways by halves . . . The words I utter when wretched are words of defiance."

Montaigne called "On Vanity" one of those essays which, being quite long and not at all confined by the titles he gave them, "require a decision to read them and time set aside." It is a meditation on dying and, at the same time, on writing—or, you could say, on writing oneself to life in the face of death, on getting "lost" in words and in "the gait of poetry, all jumps and tumblings" and in the kind of space where "my pen and my mind both go a-roaming." ("My mind does not always move straight ahead but backwards too," he says. "I distrust my present thoughts hardly less than my past ones and my second or third thoughts hardly less than my first.") And it draws pretty much the whole cast of characters from his library into the conversation—the kings and philosophers and poets and historians and statesmen and assorted saints and scoundrels whom he introduced on the first pages of Book I, with the words "Man is indeed an object miraculously vain, various and wavering. It is difficult to found a judgment on him which is steady and uniform." Since then, they have appeared and reappeared through the essays like characters in a novel, demolishing one another's arguments. Now, in a way, he both honors and discards them, along with their cluttering truths, their most congenial wisdom, and the deceptive comfort they sometimes bring.

Thus his ruminations on vanity move quickly from disreputable shoes (and the way that the "forlorn state of France" mirrors his "forlorn age") to Petronius, Horace, and Lucretius, each discoursing, in Latin, on the metaphysics of droughts, storms, crop failures —the deaths of nature. But he isn't interested. He interrupts them to complain about the burden of managing his own land, and the difficulty of economizing, in lean years, for someone "used as I am to travel not merely with an adequate retinue but an honorable one." He says that, unlike Crates, who "jumped into the freedom of poverty . . . I loathe poverty on a par with pain." He prefers the freedom that money gives him to go away. "I feel death all the time, jabbing at my throat and loins. But I am made otherwise: death is the same for me anywhere. If I were allowed to choose I would, I think, prefer to die in the saddle rather than in my bed, away from home and far from my own folk. There is more heartbreak than comfort in taking leave of those we love . . . I would willingly therefore neglect to bid that great and everlasting farewell." He considers the case of Socrates, who, preferring death to banishment, took the hemlock—and then nails him with praise as one of those "heaven-blessed" men whose qualities are "so soaring and inordinate that . . . I am quite unable to conceive them."

At the same time, he worries, or pretends to, about his inattention at home. He agrees with Diogenes, who said that the wine he liked best was always the wine somebody else had made, but then, typically, berates himself. He describes the good husbandry of his father: "I wish that, in lieu of some other part of his inheritance, my father had bequeathed me that passionate love for the running of his estates. If only I can acquire the taste for it as he did, then political philosophy can, if it will, condemn me for the lowliness and barrenness of my occupation." (Pierre, he said, was "the best father that ever was"; he had studied law to please him, and once spent more than a year translating Raymond Sebond's enormous treatise *Theologia Naturalis* from Latin to French so that his father, who rued the lack of Latin in his own education, could read it.) A few lines later, he remembers that he is a father himself—and he turns to the problem of finding "a son-in-law who would fill my beak, comfort my final years and lull them to sleep, into whose hands I could resign the control and use of my goods . . . provided that he brought to it a truly grateful and loving affection." But he doesn't mention Léonor, or, for that matter, his dead children. When he thinks about loss now, at fifty-three, it is his father he mourns and, more than anyone, his "soul's" friend Étienne de la Boétie, a Bordeaux poet who was arguably the love of his life and whose early death, he once said, drove him to marriage in the hope of solace and then into his tower for escape. They are the absent interlocutors of "On Vanity": the people he talks to about death, talking to himself; the only ones he describes with what could be called a deep sense of relationship.

How to describe the dazzling ramble of "On Vanity"? For nearly all of its sixty pages, it has no arguments, personal or philosophical, to expound, no revelations on the nature of man to offer, no path to salvation to propose. What we get instead is the gift he has given himself: "scope and freedom" of interpretation; language that is "blunt" and "raw"; and, most of all, the experience of Montaigne thinking. (Ralph Waldo Emerson, in a classic essay on Montaigne, wrote that the "marrow of the man reaches to his sentences . . . Cut these words, and they would bleed.") He can move in a few paragraphs from the admonitions in 1 Corinthians 3:20 — "Those exquisite subtleties are only good for sermons: they are themes which seek to drive us into the next world like donkeys. But life is material motion in the body, an activity, by its very essence, imperfect and unruly: I work to serve it on its own terms"—to a riff on the corruption of judges, the hypocrisy of moralists and diet doctors, and the secret sex lives of Greek philosophers, as described by an exceptionally expensive fourth-century-B.C. courtesan named Lais, who said, "I know nothing of their books . . . but those fellows come knocking at my door as often as anyone."

You could call this intellectual free association, but it is far too sterile a term for the mind of Michel de Montaigne running after itself, arguing against argument, reading his thoughts and his aging body at least as carefully as he reads his books. (His copy of Lucretius's *De Rerum Natura,* at the Cambridge University Library, is filled with enough Latin and French margin notes to make a book themselves.) But he thinks of himself as a browser, and in a way he is, because, by his account, a couple of interesting thoughts or stories in one book will always remind him of something smarter, or more interesting—or, better still, contradictory—in another book, and he opens that. By the time he begins "On Vanity," most of his favorite quotes have been carved into the beams and woodwork of the tower—for inspiration, fast access, and, perhaps, distraction. (He would have loved Google.) Those words are the preferred company of his old age, however spurious their counsel. He wants to "die, grinding [his] teeth, among strangers," and what more accommodating strangers than dead ones, speaking across millennia from his rafters—the kind of strangers who, like paid companions to the old and frail, "will leave you alone as much as you like, showing you an unconcerned face and letting you think and moan in your own way." Death, he says, "is not one of our social engagements: it is a scene with one character."

But the truth is that writing about death—surrounded by the books that he says "console me and counsel me to regulate my life and my death"—has put him off dying. The world intrudes on his gloom, battles for his attention, and almost always wins. He longs to revisit Rome. His wife must have been against this, because he says, "Truly, if any wife can lay down for her husband how many paces make 'far' and how many paces make 'near,' my counsel is to make him stop half-way . . . and let those wives dare to call Philosophy to their aid." Like the clueless Professor Higgins, he wishes that women were more like men. "In a truly loving relationship—which I have experienced—rather than drawing the one I love to me I give myself to him," he says, remembering La Boétie. "Not merely do I prefer to do him good than to have him do good to me, I would even prefer that he did good to himself rather than to me: it is when he does good to himself that he does most good to me. If his absence is either pleasant or useful to him, then it delights me far more than his presence." The question, of course, is what the absence called death means.

The penultimate pages of "On Vanity" are an homage to Rome (and perhaps to himself, since he quotes in full the papal bull that made him a Roman citizen). But he ends the essay in the oracular heart of Greece, with the Delphic admonition to "know thyself," and in a few pages turns the idea of vanity on its head, defending his pursuit of himself, however fractured, transitory, or imperfect, as the only knowledge he, or anyone, can hope to gain. It is the one argument for a "truth" he makes in a hundred and seven essays: "Nature has very conveniently cast the action of our sight outwards. We are swept on downstream, but to struggle back towards our self against the current is a painful movement; thus does the sea, when driven against itself, swirl back in confusion. Everyone says: 'Look at the motions of the heavens, look at society, at this man's quarrel, that man's pulse, this other man's will and testament'—in other words always look upwards or downwards or sideways, or before or behind you. Thus, the commandment given us in ancient times by the god at Delphi was contrary to all expectations: 'Look back into your self; get to know your self; hold on to your self' . . . Can you not see that this world of ours keeps its gaze bent ever inwards and its eyes ever open to contemplate itself? It is always vanity in your case, within and without, but a vanity which is less, the less it extends. Except you alone, O Man, said that god, each creature first studies its own self, and, according to its needs, has limits to his labors and desires. Not one is as empty and needy as you, who embrace the universe: you are the seeker with no knowledge, the judge with no jurisdiction and, when all is done, the jester of the farce."

When Montaigne moved his books to the third floor of his tower, he moved a bed to the floor below. He would cross to the castle for dinner, after which he would say good night and leave. It is tempting to imagine him at his desk then, pen in hand, books scattered around him, and candle flickering, but in fact he never wrote or read after the sun set—a habit he recommended to his readers, saying that with books "the soul disports itself, but the body, whose care I have not forgotten, remains inactive, and grows weary and sad." He was seven years into the essays when he suffered his first serious attack of kidney stones, writing that illness and sleep, like madness, "make things appear to us otherwise than they appear to healthy people, wise men, and waking people." He lived in fear of the next attack, and, even more, of what he called "emptiness." He was the man who (*pace* Roosevelt and Thoreau) first said, "The thing I fear most is fear . . . It exceeds all other disorders in intensity."

Toward the end of his life, he claimed to have accepted emptiness. He had once called his essays "monstrous bodies, pieced together of diverse members, without definite shape, having no order, sequence, or proportion other than accidental," and blamed the fact that "my ability does not go far enough for me to dare to undertake a rich, polished picture, formed according to art." But there is every indication that, growing older, he missed the statesman's life. When Navarre succeeded to the throne, in 1589, becoming Henri IV of France—and, after four more years of religious war, making a shrewd conversion to Catholicism with the words "Paris is well worth a Mass"—Montaigne wrote to volunteer his services again. Henri replied, delighted, and in January of 1590, when his letter arrived, Montaigne wrote back, saying that he had always wished for the succession, "even when I had to confess it to my curate," and then offering the advice that "where conquests, because of their greatness and difficulty, could not be thoroughly completed by arms and by force, they have been completed by clemency and magnanimity, excellent lures to attract men, especially toward the just and legitimate side." The passage is vintage Montaigne: a prescription for wise rule lurking in a few fine, flattering phrases about the fruits of victory; a strategic detour into the real world to say that "if rigor and punishment occur, they must be put off until after the possession of mastery"; and, finally, an appropriate classical example—in this case, Scipio the Elder. In July, Henri summoned Montaigne to Paris, but by September, when he had hoped to go, Montaigne was too sick to travel.

ARTHUR KRYSTAL

When Writers Speak

FROM *The New York Times Book Review*

THAT'S VLADIMIR NABOKOV on my computer screen, looking
both dapper and disheveled. He's wearing a suit and a multibut-
toned vest that scrunches the top of his tie, making it poke out of
his shirt like an old-fashioned cravat. Large, lumpish, delicate, and
black-spectacled, he's perched on a couch alongside the sleeker,
sad-faced Lionel Trilling. Both men are fielding questions from a
suave interlocutor with a B-movie mustache. The interview was
taped sometime in the late 1950s in what appears to be a faculty
club or perhaps a television studio decked out to resemble one.
The men are discussing *Lolita*. "I do not . . . I don't wish to touch
hearts," Nabokov says in his unidentifiable accent. "I don't even
want to affect minds very much. What I really want to produce is
that little sob in the spine of the artist-reader."

Not bad, I think, as I sit staring at the dark granular box on
my YouTube screen. In fact, a damned good line to come up with
off the cuff. But wait! What's that Nabokov's doing with his hands?
He's turning over index cards. He's glancing at notes. He's reading. Fluent in three languages, he relies on prefabricated responses
to talk about his work. Am I disappointed? I am at first, but then I
think: Writers don't have to be brilliant conversationalists; it's not
their job to be smart except, of course, when they write. Hazlitt,
that most self-conscious of writers, remarked that he did not see
why an author "is bound to talk, any more than he is bound to
dance, or ride, or fence better than other people. Reading, study,
silence, thought are a bad introduction to loquacity."

Sounds right to me. Like most writers, I seem to be smarter in print than in person. In fact, I am smarter when I'm writing. I don't claim this merely because there is usually no one around to observe the false starts and groan-inducing sentences that make a mockery of my presumed intelligence, but because when the work is going well, I'm expressing opinions that I've never uttered in conversation and that otherwise might never occur to me. Nor am I the first to have this thought, which, naturally, occurred to me while composing. According to Edgar Allan Poe, writing in *Graham's Magazine,* "Some Frenchman—possibly Montaigne—says: 'People talk about thinking, but for my part I never think except when I sit down to write.'" I can't find these words in my copy of Montaigne, but I agree with the thought, whoever might have formed it. And it's not because writing helps me to organize my ideas or reveals how I feel about something, but because it actually creates thought, or at least supplies a petri dish for its genesis.

The Harvard psychologist Steven Pinker, however, isn't so sure. In an e-mail exchange, Pinker sensibly points out that thinking precedes writing and that the reason we sound smarter when writing is because we deliberately set out to be clear and precise, a luxury not usually afforded us in conversation. True, and especially true if one writes for magazines where nitpicking editors with expensive shoes are waiting to kick us around for every small mistake. When people who write for a living sit down to earn their pay, they make demands on themselves that require a higher degree of skill than that summoned by conversation. Pinker likens this to mathematicians thinking differently when proving theorems than when counting change, or to quarterbacks throwing a pass during a game as opposed to tossing a ball around in their back yards. He does concede, however, that since writing allows time for reveries and ruminations, it probably engages larger swaths of the brain.

I agree. I'm willing to bet that more gray matter starts quivering when I sit down to write than when I stand up to speak. In fact, if you were to do an MRI of my brain right now, you would see regions of it lighting up that barely flicker when I talk. How do I know this? Because I'm writing! In fact, I'm so smart right now that I know my cerebral cortex is employing a host of neurons that are cleverly and charmingly transforming my thoughts and feelings into words. But if I were talking to you about all this, a different set of neurons would be triggered, different connections and associations would be made, and different words and phrases would be generated. In short, I'd be boring the pants off you.

OK, I'm just guessing, but I do think that whoever wrote that he never thinks except when he sits down to write was using hyperbole to make a valid point. There's something about writing, when we regard ourselves as writers, that affects how we think and, inevitably, how we express ourselves. There may be no empirical basis for this, but if, as some scientists claim, different parts of the brain are switched on by our using a pen instead of a computer—and the cognitive differences are greater than what might be expected by the application of different motor skills—then why shouldn't there be significant differences in brain activity when writing and speaking?

Along these lines, it seems composers sometimes pick up different instruments when trying to solve musical problems. It's not that a violin offers up secrets the piano withholds, but that the mind starts thinking differently when we play different instruments. Or maybe it's just that the flow of thought alters when we write, which, in turn, releases sentences hidden along the banks of consciousness. There seems to be a rhythm to writing that catches notes that ordinarily stay out of earshot. At some point between formulating a thought and writing it down falls a nanosecond when the thought becomes a sentence that would, in all likelihood, have a different shape if we were to speak it. This rhythm, not so much heard as felt, occurs only when one is composing; it can't be simulated in speech, since speaking takes place in real time and depends in part on the person or persons we're speaking to. Wonderful writers might therefore turn out to be only so-so conversationalists, and people capable of telling great stories waddle like ducks out of water when they attempt to write.

So the next time you hear a writer on the radio or catch him on the tube or watch him on the monitor or find yourself sitting next to him at dinner, remember he isn't the author of the books you admire; he's just someone visiting the world outside his study or office or wherever the hell he writes. Don't expect him to know the customs of the country, and try to forgive his trespasses when they occur. Speaking of dinner, when the German naturalist Alexander von Humboldt told a friend, a Parisian doctor, that he wanted to meet a certifiable lunatic, he was invited to the doctor's home for supper. A few days later, Humboldt found himself placed at the dinner table between two men. One was polite, somewhat reserved, and didn't go in for small talk. The other, dressed in ill-matched clothes, chattered away on every subject under the sun, gesticulating wildly, while making horrible faces. When the meal was over, Humboldt turned to his host. "I like your lunatic," he whispered, indicating the talkative man. The host frowned. "But it's the other one who's the lunatic. The man you're pointing to is Monsieur Honoré de Balzac."

A Rake's Progress

FROM *The Weekly Standard*

Let me live in a house by the side of the road,
Where the race of men go by;
The men who are good and the men who are bad,
As good and as bad as I.
— *from Sam Walter Foss's "House by the Side of the Road," the first poem Marion Barry recited in church as a boy*

IN MOST CONCEPTIONS OF Washington, D.C., the city operates on Eastern Standard Time. But those who pass through Marion Barry's orbit know there's another zone that has nothing to do with the mean solar time of the 75th meridian west of the Greenwich Observatory. It's called "Barry Time." The former four-term mayor of D.C. will show up for speeches, meetings, and civic events whenever he damn well pleases.

This translates into many minutes, even hours, of waiting for Barry to appear. So after being slated to hang out with Barry for several days, I am surprised to receive a call from his spokesperson, Natalie Williams, two days before we're supposed to meet.

"Mr. Barry wants to start early," Natalie informs. "He wants you to come to church with him tomorrow."

"Great," I say. "What time does church start?"

"Eleven A.M.," she says.

"OK. And what time should I meet him before church?" I ask.

"Eleven-thirty," she responds with complete seriousness.

Barry, now in his second postmayoral term as a councilman representing the city's poorest ward, is these days something less than a political powerhouse, but my interest had recently been rekindled in the man universally known as one of the two or three finest crack-smoking politicians our nation has ever produced. A 1990 FBI sting yielded grainy video of Barry holding a crack pipe to his lips which was broadcast around the world (launching a booming "Bitch set me up" T-shirt industry), and his name became a late-night comic's rim shot, especially as he won one more mayoral term in 1994 after serving six months in jail.

Now, after a relatively dormant postmayoral period of local politicking, serial brushes with the law, health and taxman problems, with the occasional drug relapse, Barry seemed to be enjoying a renaissance for both good and bad reasons. The good, for him, has come in the form of a balanced, years-in-the-making documentary called *The Nine Lives of Marion Barry*, now in regular rotation on HBO. It traces Barry's arc from an idealistic, dashiki-wearing civil rights activist, through his rise and fall as mayor, to his current redemptive plateau-period, a life that has made him the singular figure in the history of D.C.'s municipal politics.

The bad came this past Fourth of July weekend, when Barry was arrested for "stalking" his former girlfriend, Donna Watts-Brighthaupt, after an argument they'd had on the way to Rehoboth Beach. She changed her mind about the trip and returned to D.C., flagging down an officer when Barry was allegedly pursuing her in his car. The stalking charge looked like an honest lover's tiff, amounted to nothing, and was quickly dropped.

In typical Barry fashion, however, there were baroque touches that gave the story national oxygen. For instance, the Barry team called a late-night press conference to denounce Watts's psychiatric fitness, and she showed up in the middle of it, loudly denouncing their denunciation. Scribes at the Washington *City Paper*, who still enjoy riding Barry like the village Zipcar, detailed the knotty love triangle between Barry, Donna, and her ex-husband—whom Barry had had banished from the city council building—and ran transcripts from leaked voicemail tapes of a lovesick Barry trying to woo Donna back. They did the same with a taped fight in which Donna proclaimed that Barry had booted her out of a Denver hotel room "'cause I wouldn't suck your dick," a quote that provided likely the most memorable cover line in *City Paper* history.

Still, this was just the entertainment portion of the program.

The real trouble was Watts-Brighthaupt's employment arrangement with Barry, who had (legally) garnered nearly $1 million in earmarks for various nonprofits in his ward—which journalistic Nosy Neds discovered had all sorts of irregularities, such as outfits overseen by Barry's city council staffers, contracts thrown to women he'd dated (not just Watts-Brighthaupt), people being paid for do-nothing jobs, alleged forgeries, etc.

Nobody's yet alleged Barry personally profited. For all the perceptions of Barry over the years as a dirty politician, he's been a remarkably clean one on the financial front. Having periodically teetered on the edge of personal insolvency, even as two of his deputy mayors went upriver for embezzlement and corruption in the 1980s, Barry has never been caught with his hand in the cookie jar, and not for lack of investigators trying.

Barry has audaciously proclaimed he's done nothing wrong—if you can't throw work to qualified girlfriends with city council–approved taxpayer money, just who can you throw work to? Barry insists he wouldn't give a job to his mother if she wasn't qualified. Still, as Barry points out, "Old Man Daley gave his son the insurance contract, and was criticized for it. He said, 'If a father can't help his son, what the hell is he here for?'"

The whole messy business has resulted in the city council's authorizing an ethics investigation of Barry by superlawyer Robert Bennett (something of an expert on ethically challenged politicians, having represented Bill Clinton). It has also reportedly piqued the more serious investigative interest of the feds, who've never lacked for zeal in building cases against Barry, having spent tens of millions doing so going all the way back to the FBI's 1967 file on "Marion S. Barry, Jr., Negro Militant."

When I ask a Barry staffer if her boss is spooked by the new attention, she says, "No. He never gets spooked. We get spooked." By the lights of longtime Barry aficionados, this latest doesn't rank very high on his scandal Richter scale. A ward boss throwing sketchy patronage jobs to friends? It could make a Barry connoisseur very sleepy. Plus, some Barry watchers think he might be losing a step. There wasn't even any cocaine involved.

Yet the scandal wasn't my reason for visiting hizzoner. Barry-bashing has been a near-ubiquitous sport, and approaching him in order to find holes in his stories is about as sporting as taking candy from a quadriplegic preemie. Rather, I was curious to take his measure as a human being, which many forget he still is, despite the caricatures and self-parodies. For seventy-three years, over forty of them in public life, Barry has kept rearing up like a plastic varmint in a Whac-a-Mole game. No matter how many times he's batted about the head with a mallet, he relentlessly reappears.

Like countless Maryland commuters, I drive past the turnoff to Marion Barry's house every time I go to the District without ever giving his Congress Heights neighborhood in Southeast Washington a thought. The Suitland Parkway that runs past it doubles as the most common artery from the city to Andrews Air Force Base — *Air Force One* frequently casts shadows on your car as you drive it. The denizens of Ward 8 commonly refer to their locale as "east of the river"—by which they mean the Anacostia River, an 8.4-mile-long, meandering toxic soup that is about as clear as Swiss Miss and where up to 68 percent of the brown bullhead catfish have been found to have liver tumors. Flowing into the much more celebrated Potomac, it's the kind of river most people tend to forget, just as they do the ward that nestles it.

For decades, Ward 8 has been the crime and poverty and every-other-dubious-statistic headquarters of D.C. It is the land that the real estate bubble forgot. Amidst the check-cashing places and screw-top liquor stores, it contains such tourist meccas as the reeking Blue Plains Wastewater Treatment Plant and St. Elizabeths psychiatric hospital, where Ezra Pound sweated out his insanity plea for treason and John Hinckley Jr. can compose rock operas for Jodie Foster in peace. While only minutes from Capitol Hill, and from the more prosperous black suburbs in Maryland's Prince George's County, Ward 8 might as well be in Burkina Faso to the commuting class. The only reason to pull off there is if you needed to buy a quick fifth of Hennessy for the ride home, or possibly something less legal.

It is here, after cruising past street signs bearing the names Martin Luther King and Malcolm X, that I find Barry's house, a rented red-brick duplex. (He lives alone, as Cora Masters Barry, his fourth wife, left him in 2002, without going through the formality of getting a divorce.) The window shades are yellowed and drawn. There is bird splat on the bricks. A Metro bus-stop pole is posted right in front of it, meaning Barry sometimes has a chance to involuntarily meet constituents, as some end up waiting for their ride on his barren concrete porch.

I knock on the door—the doorbell's missing—even though I'm a good half hour early. I don't want to make Barry late for being late to church. "Come in!" he yells. And as I do, I find him sitting on the couch, wearing track pants and a loose workout shirt, eating a greasy, four-course IHOP takeout breakfast on a TV tray in front of his big-screen. He looks both gaunter and more appealing than during the glory years, when the drugging and boozing often swelled him up like a sweating, smirking sausage. His skin is smooth—he believes in the healing balm of moisturizer—and the lines on his face make him look more avuncular and settled.

The furniture is no-frills—the dining room table is pushed against the wall, and some chairs still have the plastic on them. There is no vanity wall of past glories. Décor is minimalist, besides the Afrocentric statuary and Barack Obama's beatific mug on a commemorative "From Slavery to the White House" blanket draped over his couch. The coffee table is littered with books of the self-improvement variety: the Bible, M. Scott Peck's *The Road Less Traveled,* Gary Chapman's *The Five Love Languages: How to Express Heartfelt Commitment to Your Mate.*

Most jarring is the end table littered with prescriptions—thirteen bottles in all—and syringes. It looks like Elvis's medicine cabinet, circa 1977. At first I think maybe I have the wrong day and have walked into a Vista Hotel scene redux (the location of his 1990 crack bust). But I'm looking instead at all the meds he takes after a February kidney transplant. The syringes, he explains, are for "taking my sugar," which he has to do as a longtime diabetic. Barry has other health issues, too. He has hypertension. His cancerous prostate is a distant memory, the surgery for which caused some incontinence issues. He keeps a urinal next to his bed for middle-of-the-night emergencies. It's not the most ideal arrangement for a legendary Romeo, but, as he points out, "The alternative is worse."

Barry speaks in a mumbly whisper ("I'll talk louder," he repeatedly promises when I keep checking my tape recorder for pickup), but seems in fine spirits. He's used to dodging bullets. With varying success, as he reminds me of the time in 1977 when Muslim terrorists took hostages in the District Building when Barry was a council member. It was shortly before his first mayoral run, and he caught a bullet in the chest. "Do you have a scar?" I ask. "Let's see," he says, lifting up his shirt, so that within ten minutes of arriving, I'm eyeball to areola with Barry's left nipple. It's a move that's very Barry. Most times, he reveals nothing at all. Then he reveals too much.

After about thirty seconds of examination, we can't decide if what we're looking at is a fading gunshot wound or a skin blemish. But for Barry's seminakedness, he's still adept at showing less than everything. The point I shouldn't miss, one of the reasons he wants to bring me to church, is that "I go through this time and time again, when if it weren't for God, I wouldn't be here." He catalogs various dramatic happenings in his life: making it out of Mississippi as the son of sharecroppers, near misses during his SNCC-organizer days in the civil rights movement, the Vista Hotel.

I wasn't even going to bring the latter up until our second date, as it's generally bad manners to mention your host's crack bust straightaway. But since he mentions it, I pursue a bit, asking him how he felt when he realized he'd been stung. "I didn't realize what happened," he says. "It happened so fast. And so my instinct was, as I said, 'This bitch set me up.'"

"She kinda did," I offer, an objectively indisputable point.

"Not kinda—she did!" he reiterates of Rasheeda Moore, the former model and Barry paramour. While Barry admits to using cocaine "recreationally" beforehand (several witnesses at his trial said he "recreated" habitually), he says he had not smoked crack before (also at odds with the testimony of witnesses), claiming he even needed to go to the bathroom to practice holding the pipe, so as not to look like an amateur in front of Moore. In the video, Barry is seen asking her multiple times how to do it and brushing off her initial invites. But, he adds, "Rasheeda could talk an Eskimo into buying a refrigerator."

One of the more underappreciated, pathos-laden aspects of the video is how the main impetus for Barry's being present "was sex," as he freely admits, and he repeatedly grovels to Rasheeda on the video. I mention that I recall him grabbing her breast. "Tried to," he readily agrees. "The manly instincts took over . . . I guess what was probably in my mind—first time I thought about it—was if I took a hit, maybe she would change her mind about sex."

"So your motives were pure," I note.

His cell phone rings, as it incessantly does, and he answers it. "I'm gettin' ready to go to church, let me call you back." He hangs up, saying, "I'm glad you're interested in all that. Very few people ask me."

Of his own culpability in the matter, Barry's a little less forthright. He says he's thankful to God, as it "could've turned out another way." I point out that the incident and resulting trial turned out pretty badly: serial humiliation, his third wife leaving him, and eventually six months in jail (not, actually, from the Vista incident, but from another misdemeanor possession that was part of the fourteen-count indictment). "People assume there was crack cocaine in there. The jurors didn't believe it," he says.

Some pro-Barry jurors did speculate that the pipe was filled with baking soda. But he at least assumed there was crack in it, I assert. "How do you know?" he asks, now defensive. Well, that's what most people assume is in a crack pipe, I proffer, hence the name "crack pipe."

"I don't know," he says, completely straight-faced. "I didn't think about it . . . Who knows what the FBI put in there? I know this: they tried to kill me. That's for sure."

We are joined for church by a slew of younger women, many roughly half his age, in their Sunday finery. Barry gives off the whiff of a black Hugh Hefner: old enough to seem a fatherly elder that younger women like to mother-hen, lusty enough that you're never sure which of his female relations goes beyond platonic. There's Natalie Williams, his spokesperson, and her friend in from Los Angeles, who is a dead ringer for the actress Robin Givens. There's Chenille Spencer, Barry's sometime companion and personal assistant, and her nine-year-old son, Fats, who is Barry's godson. (Barry has five godsons, as he says it's important for the kids around his ward, often raised by single mothers, to have "positive male role models.")

Barry is often circumspect about who he has seen romantically. Though when I point out to him that he's entitled to see whoever he wants, he agrees: "That's right. I'm free, black, and twenty-one." There is Kim Dickens, though, who Barry admits he "takes out" sometimes and who was kind enough to donate a kidney to Barry after his renal failure. She basically saved his life but makes no great to-do about it. I ask Kim if she misses her kidney. "I do have separation anxiety," she says. "But I visit him enough. So the kidneys see each other."

There is also a CW network cameraman along for the morning, collecting B-roll for a two-part series on Barry. The star goes upstairs to get suited up, right down to his silver wraparound cufflinks. "A professor told me if you want to be a millionaire, look like a millionaire," explains Barry. We finally gather ourselves to go to church, about forty-five minutes after the opening bell. Kim waves off our lateness. "Marion likes to get there to hear the Word," she says. "They'll still be praising the Lord, honey."

Before we go, Barry huddles everyone in the center of his cramped living room and instructs us to grab hands for prayer. I join in, but we decide I should fall out, as the praying white reporter kind of confuses the cameraman's visual. Barry lifts his voice to the heavens, which is still mumbly, so my tape doesn't pick up the particulars. But I am struck by two things while listening to him:

The man prays with the familiarity of someone who regularly talks to God.

Who prays in front of a cameraman and *before* they go to church?

We arrive in a blue Cadillac with a missing hubcap (a loaner, since his 2000 BMW is in the shop). The ushers at the Temple of Praise in Southeast show Barry a deference due a visiting dignitary, though it has been his home church for some years. The congregants are in the full throes of Holy Ghost power when we arrive. The percussion from both the band and all the stomping comes up through the floor, rattling the soles of your shoes. Rookies would do well to wear a mouthguard, as they might catch a stray elbow, as I did, from rapturous church ladies performing the Pentecostal shake. At one point during a song, I watch a beefy elder onstage square his shoulders, tuck his head, and dash down the steps like a fullback hitting a hole, then into a breakaway open-field sprint around the sanctuary. Natalie asks if I'm OK. "Sure," I tell her, "this is just like my church."

My vantage point is excellent, since even though we arrived an hour late, the front pew is cleared out for Barry and his entourage. He has a standing reservation whenever he wants it. Bishop Glen

Staples, a silky prosperity-gospeler, welcomes "Our dear mayor-for-life. We are thankful that he is here." Staples alludes to Barry's recent troubles, saying, "I love him because he's taught me how to get back up."

Staples finds the old rhetorical rhythms, as congregants whoop on the rests. "You got to learn how to get up. [*Whoop.*] Because everybody in this life, if you are alive and breathing, that is the one thing you can be sure of, making mistakes. [*Whoop.*] When you fall down 'cause of mistakes, get back up, dust yo'self off, and start over again. [*Whoop.*]" Staples instructs us to grab one person and tell them, "I know you're going to make it!" The audience obliges, and whoops some more, as Barry is called to the stage over pumping, orgasmic organ.

"Praise the Lord!" Barry says. "Hallelujah!" He is echoed by the audience. "Whenever you see me, I'm going to praise the Lord, because with all that I've been through. [*Whoop.*] You understand." The thought doesn't need to be finished. They understand.

Barry says the media have tried to demonize him. "But y'all know how much I care. [*Whoop.*] There are a lot of people who don't like what I do. [*Whoop.*] Lookin' out for black people. [*Whoop.*] Lookin' out for black people. [*Whoop.*] Standin' up for black people. [*Whoop.*] They don't like it, and so I'm constantly attacked. But because of God's mercy and grace and power. [*Whoop. Whoop. Whoop.*]"

Again, he doesn't need to finish. The crowd is all about extending however much forgiveness he needs, even if he doesn't feel he needs any, and it was never asked for. "So I want to thank this congregation and the bishop for your prayers," Barry continues. "Thank you Temple of Praise. You love me, and I love you!"

Bishop Staples retakes the pulpit and whips the crowd into a frenzy with a hell-for-leather singsongy sermon that is half T. D. Jakes, half Otis Redding. Only amateurs wait for the altar call. Most just come up front during the sermon, wailing and whooping and feeling the electric surge of Holy Ghost power hitting in jolts like the Staples-punctuating organ.

Staples laces the sermon with plenty of Barry references. But the main subject is Paul and his thorn-of-the-flesh, which God wouldn't remove. Instead, Staples says, God told Paul, "'I'm gonna leave it right there, to keep you humble.' . . . You better believe that everybody in here got a thorn in yo' flesh . . . But God said the prescription that I'm gonna give you for your malady of being a human being is called grace."

Barry is by now transported himself. He gets up and joins the mosh pit of ululators, swinging his arms like a child readying himself for the standing broad jump at a school track meet. When asked afterward what part of the sermon spoke to him most, he says, "All of it," then starts throwing some Bible himself. "It says, 'Greater is he that is in us, than he that is in the world,'" Barry says, adding his own interpretation: "Greater than devils, and evildoers, and haters . . . Barry critics."

It's a tad ironic that, while all but emperor-for-life in Ward 8, Barry didn't make his bones as mayor by standing up for "the last, the least, and the lost," as he has spent the post-Vista half of his career rebranding himself in these parts. While his signature summer-jobs program for youth ensured that you can swing a cat in a local black neighborhood and hit five adults for whom Barry provided their first gig, his primary accomplishment was riding '80s-era real-estate-boom market forces.

Barry threw the city open to development the likes of which D.C. hadn't seen before. He was so proactive that old staffers tell how, early in his mayoral tenure, he used to have weekly brainstorming brown-bag lunches with architects and developers and would fast-track formerly glacial construction-approval processes with Post-it notes saying "Good idea, do it!" When he assumed office in 1979, whole quadrants of the city were ghost towns, and there were streets untouched since they were torched in the '68 riots.

During Barry's first term, seventy new buildings were either started or completed, and millions of new square feet of downtown office space were added. Even Republicans, after rolling through their mental Rolodexes of Chris Rock crack-smoking jokes or using Barry as a handy excuse to deny D.C. statehood, sometimes recall the '80s-era Barry with fondness. Even if there were accusations of untoward cronyism, he was a mayor you could do business with. "The one thing Barry fundamentally understood is that nobody—not the city, not the private sector—profits off a weed-strewn lot. In that way, he was a supply-sider," says one.

In other ways, though, he was a raging redistributionist. "Some call it socialistic, some call it democratic," Barry tells me. "I don't go by labels, they don't mean s—— to me." Figuring if the Poles and Italians could feather nests in Chicago and the Irish could dominate Boston, Barry ruthlessly insisted that all of his departments meet minority set-aside contracting quotas, up to 30 percent. At the same time, his knack for creating patronage jobs would've left Huey Long gaping in awe. At one point in the late '80s, the city didn't even know how many employees it had on its own payroll (an independent commission estimated there was one city worker for every thirteen residents). By the end of Barry's third term, shortly before the Vista bust, the size of the municipal payroll had swelled to 52,000—that's 14,000 more taxpayer-funded jobs than Los Angeles, a city five times the size of D.C.

Barry, always intent on buffing the scratches out of his legacy, tells me that he didn't foster a black middle class just in D.C., but also in neighboring Prince George's County. He's more right than he'd like to be. For much of the newly created black wealth fled the city, as they had a much better chance of enjoying their spoils without getting shot in the suburbs.

Barry's early electoral success was also partly attributable to lily-white, affluent do-goodniks, enamored of the exotic former black radical taking on the establishment. He was championed by the *Washington Post*, which endorsed him in three out of his four runs for mayor, though the *Post*'s editors later publicly wished they could rescind the last one. But his consistent racial polarization and claims of martyrdom when running into various ethical and personal lapses eventually cost him that goodwill.

In the late '80s, most of the poor black wards became drug-ravaged killing fields, and it was their voters that saved Barry's hide in subsequent elections. (Barry's talents as a political Machiavelli are grossly underrated—he's lost only one election ever, for an at-large council seat right after his trial. "I had to get that out of my system," he jokes. "Even then, I got fifty thousand votes.") Some of these circumstances were far beyond Barry's control. But then, some of them weren't. As Harry Jaffe and Tom Sherwood detailed in their 1994 book *Dream City*, D.C. became an inefficient, pothole-ridden sinkhole, and even Barry himself admits that he'd lost all energy by the third term (1987–91). "I was getting tireder and tireder," he tells me, "because the job was so damn hard."

Most of the talent that had graced his first administration had left through attrition and indictment. The schools ranked as some of the worst in the nation. The hobbled police force was literally outgunned by homegrown drug dealers and their imported Jamaican rivals. Barry was distracted, disconnected, and partying like he was getting paid by the gram of whatever he ingested. As *Dream City* suggested, some of his more suspicious hospital visits for things like "hiatal hernia" were likely cocaine-related.

Things grew so bleak that the liberal *Washington Monthly* even ran a piece in 1989 that jeopardized Detroit's civic pride, with a detailed house-of-horrors portrait entitled "The Worst City Government in America—Washington D.C."

But here at the Temple of Praise, people don't break out the scales and stack Barry's good deeds versus his bad ones. His popularity here transcends such minutiae. Supporting him, in spite of his struggles—even because of them—is almost a symbolic sacrament. Plus, he does something few other politicians in the District, even the city's later black mayors, do: he shows up.

Over the course of my time with him, he shows up to senior centers, where he gives twenty bucks to the oldest doll in attendance, which often takes some sorting out, what with senility. He shows up to the planning of the Labor Day picnic that he throws out of his own budget, overseeing details down to the hot dogs and what go-go bands are hired. The fact that he regularly gets raked over the coals by newspapers—which Barry tells me Ward 8ers largely don't read—for tax evasion and traffic arrests and addiction issues and many of the pathologies that plague their community in such numbers might help him rather than hurt him.

One morning, Barry hauls me to a "Ward 8 Leadership Council" breakfast at the gleaming, new IHOP—considered a Ward 8 development triumph, which Barry helped champion. I find out that there isn't technically a "Ward 8 Leadership Council." Barry has merely assembled seventeen people in a back room—everyone from activists to ministers to community leaders to a Giant store manager (the first grocery chain to do business in the ward in a decade). There's even a white real estate developer named Jeff Epperson, who has a Texan accent, used to work for the National Republican Senatorial Committee, and speaks from experience that "politicians and perfect behavior should never be mentioned in the same sentence."

They tell me of Barry's tireless devotion to the ward, of how "he remembers people that don't have no title, no nothing," of how after forty years of public life he will "stand at the gate" for Ward 8 "and knows every crook and cranny in city hall, he knows exactly where the money is at, where the dead bodies are," and can therefore put people with resources.

They tell me how the ward is finally moving in the right direction (Epperson's company is investing there), even if Bishop C. Matthew Hudson of Matthews Memorial Baptist says he's preaching two funerals that week — one for a gunned-down eighteen-year-old, the other for a seventy-six-year-old man beaten by a group of teenagers on Malcolm X Boulevard. (One afternoon, when tracking home with Barry, we get out of the car to see a dozen squad cars at the Congress Heights Metro station as a young man in a wife-beater is being cuffed and put into one of them, while the woman he just assaulted, and who dropped her baby in the melee, lies crying on the ground. "In Ward 8," Barry tells me, "if it ain't one thing, it's another. But it's always something.")

The IHOP convocation is a Barry-engineered Potemkin exhibit, to be sure. But the intensity of their possessiveness is no put-up job, and is similar to what I encounter all over the ward. When I interview Barry standing on Alabama Avenue, a random car pulls up and a woman yells out the window, "Are they pickin' on you again?" The IHOP amen corner pisses blood over the way their man has been pilloried for behavior that's conveniently forgotten when it comes to the likes of Bill Clinton or Ted Kennedy.

As James Coates, senior minister of Bethlehem Baptist Church, says, "He understands our path — 'stony the road we trod.' So when someone attacks Mr. Barry, they attack all of us." I push back, and ask the ministers and others what it would take for Barry to lose their support. Would they still support him if he killed somebody? "Yes, I would," says Coates without blinking, then breaks into laughter. The ministers then give biblical murder precedents — Moses killed, David killed Bathsheba's husband, etc. "I'm coming to your church next week," says Epperson.

When I visit Barry's constituency office one day in the ward, conveniently located a few floors above the local welfare office, the intensity of this devotion is put quite explicitly to me by a woman who mans Barry's phones and who's been volunteering for him for years. She wears a matching African-print gown and head wrap, and she is called Mother Boone. She says she came to D.C. decades ago, when her husband was laid up overseas in a hospital after getting injured in the war — she doesn't remember which war.

"It started with a K," she says, her spotty memory failing her.

"Korea?" I ask.

"Maybe," she says.

After arriving from St. Louis, she lived in her car with her baby. "The front seat was my living room, the back was my bedroom." Who gave her shoes and milk for her baby? "Mr. Barry!" Boone says. Who found her a place to live? "Mr. Barry!" When she was shot in the stomach after getting carjacked, she got a special room at the hospital with extra flowers and nightgowns and the works. "Guess who was there with me," Mother Boone intones, practically grabbing my lapels. "Gawwwd, and Jesus, and MR. BARRY!"

A few minutes later, I ask Barry if she in fact got shot when she was carjacked. He shrugs and says, "I don't know." Mother Boone "goes in and out," a staffer explains. In some parts of the city, Barry can't buy credit for things he's legitimately done. In Ward 8, he gets credit even for the things he hasn't.

After church, Barry is famished. If you participate in a Temple of Praise service, your cardio requirement is fulfilled for the day. Barry insists on taking me and the Barry Angels to the pricey Old Ebbitt Grill downtown, since the only sit-down restaurants in Ward 8 are the IHOP and a former topless bar, the Players Lounge, where Barry likes to order the liver and onions and occasionally takes the stage to sing his theme song, T-Bone Walker's "Stormy Monday."

Before we go, however, we have to deposit "what little money I have" in his account so his debit card can cover it. The Caddy rolls up to a Safeway grocery store in neighboring Ward 7, which contains a SunTrust bank counter that sits behind bulletproof glass. Barry and I go in, and he spies the long line. "Oh my God, I gotta cut that," he says. So he heads to the front of the line and negotiates with a woman, telling her he's with a reporter, and he's in a hurry (after cutting, he'll later work every person in the line, as he's a perpetual campaigner).

While I wait behind him, a woman with a neck tattoo and bandanna-covered head approaches, assuming I'm a Barry staffer. Her name is Vicki Mitchell, and she's on the phone with her son, Lejeevan Toudle, who's currently in lockup for armed robbery. Telling her son that Mayor Barry just walked in, she tells me, "My son said to tell you D.C. jail ain't got no air. You wanna speak to him?"

I grab the phone, and Lejeevan proceeds to tell me how it's 110 degrees in his cell. Not only that, "the canteen is messed up, they don't give us what we ordered." Spying my notebook, his mother adds, "Put that on the list." I ask Lejeevan if he wants to speak with the mayor, who's technically a city councilman. He does. I hand the phone to Barry. "Yeah, what's happenin'?" Barry says, hearing his complaints. "All right," says Barry. "I can deal with that tomorrow, can't deal with that today." Barry gives me Lejeevan's phone number to write down, but is a digit short. No matter. He never asks me for it anyway.

Back in the car outside the Safeway, a booty-shaking lass walks by, giving Barry the eye. Kim, the kidney donor, offers play-by-play from the back seat: "We call it grinnin' and skinnin'."

"Y'all leave her alone, now," says Barry, adding, "I'm glad I'm in the car."

"We glad you are too," says Kim, "or you'd be out there another fifteen minutes."

"God gave me the gift of being gregarious," Barry explains. "I'm a touchy-feely kind of person." I offer that that's gotten him in a spot of trouble in the past. "A little bit," says Kim caustically. "Everybody has some trouble sometimes," Barry assents. Another Safeway patron extends well wishes through the car window. "I don't care what nobody says. You my man!" he says. "I can't come in here," Barry says to me. "If I were to shop, I wouldn't be out of here till three hours later."

Arriving at Old Ebbitt, we are seated in a side room in the front of the restaurant ("the slave quarters," one of the girls calls it). Barry orders his favorite, the trout parmesan, and shows a sign of aging, as he occasionally does, when asking the waiter where his spinach and mashed potatoes are—they're under his fish.

I order a postchurch bourbon, and Barry joins me by ordering a white zinfandel, having sworn off the cognac—along with the cocaine, he insists—that used to cause him so many problems. If he bothers ordering any, he stops at one glass of wine during the many meals we have together. Still, I'm pretty sure that's not in the program of the AA meetings he's attended for years. Isn't even one glass of wine bad for his sobriety?

"No, it's bad for my kidney," he says, telling me everybody deals with addiction differently. "I do it my way," he says. "Oh no," says his spokeswoman, Natalie, sitting beside him.

I hadn't visited Barry to put him on the rack. But his responses to addiction issues, along with a host of his other troubles, practically dictate that any self-respecting reporter play prosecuting attorney. Barry is gentlemanly, never malicious, but he's also eternally argumentative. Anything you preface with "I read in the *City Paper* or *Washington Post*" will immediately elicit an objection. So that if, for instance, you told him you'd read that he loved his mother, he'd have to insist he didn't.

It's understandable, perhaps, that a man who is constantly under attack tends toward the defensive. But Barry frequently loses track of his own narrative, contradicts his former public utterances, and shows a less-than-straightforward hold on the truth. Over the entirety of our time together, we incessantly play cat-and-mouse. At various times, he insists he never really had an alcohol or serious drug problem—that his post-Vista trip to Hazelden was a "tactical move" for the upcoming trial. Then later he'll admit that alcohol is his only real addiction.

When I ask Barry how a seventy-three-year-old man can still find so much trouble, he says, "I don't get into trouble. People *get* me in trouble." But he does have a knack for getting into more trouble even when he's seemingly in more trouble than he could already be in. For instance, when already in prison, he was transferred to another facility after witnesses reported seeing him receive oral gratification from a female admirer in the visitation room. (He denies it to this day.) And after failing to pay his taxes for roughly seven years, repeatedly getting hauled before judges for his negligence, and having his pay garnisheed for roughly $3,050 per month (he says it was due to "procrastination"), Barry was put on probation by a judge and subsequently failed a drug test in 2006. Barry insists it was an unfortunate relapse. As with most of his problems, "a woman was involved," he admits.

Yet he swears that despite persistent rumors and even public declarations by his friends calling for him to take his sobriety more seriously, he did not use drugs from the time of his 1990 arrest until the 2006 relapse. When I bring up a 2002 incident, when police found a $5 rock in his car and claimed Barry had white powder on his face (they didn't charge him, saying they were trace amounts), Barry insists it was a frame-up. "It's really not consistent," he says. "If I'm smoking crack, I don't have powder on my face." He decided not to run for city council afterward, and his fourth wife left him two weeks later, but he insists none of this was related.

I mention to Barry that his real addiction seems to be women. And in fact, in the early '90s, he confessed to sex addiction. "I never said that," he insists. Yes he did, I inform him. I had just read the clip the night before. He said it on an episode of *Sally Jessy Raphael.* "No, that's bulls——," he says. "We made a tactical mistake. We were trying to get our story out about what happened at the Vista, and she put me on with a sexually addicted person. We corrected that." I recheck the *Washington Post* clip later. Headline: "Marion Barry, Airing His Vices; On Sally Jessy Raphael, the Ex-Mayor Tells of Sex Addiction."

So naturally defensive is Barry that at one point, when driving around Ward 8, I ask him what pisses him off most about what he sees. "Some things don't piss me off, some things make me angry."

That's the same thing, I tell him. Natalie laughs and shakes her head, as though I'm seeing what she's up against.

"Nah, nah, there's a difference," he says.

"You argue about everything!" I tell him.

"I have to!"

Barry feels like he's been in a fight his entire life. He was born to Mississippi sharecroppers, and his mother, who used to carry him around in a cotton sack in the fields, split for Memphis with Barry and his sisters when he was eight, leaving his father behind. Barry never saw him again. "I used to be ashamed of that," says Barry. "So in my bio, I used to say he died. 'Cause I was ashamed that I didn't have a natural father."

Growing up, he says, "I was very insecure. Didn't like my name. It was a lady's name. Didn't like my looks. Didn't like anything about myself." Kids would tease him about his name, and "I'd pop 'em in the mouth, damn right I would. Then I got to the point where I said what the hell. That's what God gave me. That's how I was born. This is how I look. To hell with them. Though I wasn't cussin' back then."

Sure, Barry has taken a beating over the years. "But I'm not supposed to be here," he tells me. When he was in high school, he'd never even heard of college, didn't know what it was. "In fact," he says, "my sixth-grade teacher told me, 'Marion Barry, you not gonna be anything. You're not gonna be anywhere.' I went home and cried to my mother. She said, 'Now don't listen to that stuff. You can do anything you want to do.' Here's a woman with a fourth-grade education talkin' about what I could do."

"I felt depressed for a couple days, then I said I'm not gonna buy that in my own mind." He became an achiever. He consistently made the honor roll. He was an Eagle Scout. He recited poems in church. He went to college, and stopped one year short of getting his doctorate in chemistry, quitting to join the civil rights movement. "In chemistry, there's order," he says wistfully. "In politics, there's disorder. The rules change just about every other day."

I mention to Barry that for all his biblical invocations, the Bible teaches us to be humble, a trait he doesn't often display. "But there's a time to be humble, and a time not to be humble."

"When's the time not to be?" I ask.

"In front of your enemies," he says. "Because if they're trying to break your spirit, even if your spirit is broken, you can't let them know it . . . God gave me a strong spirit. People expect me to come in with my head down and out. Not me. I'm not doing it. I hold my head up. High."

Barry's spirit is sung home to me by longtime Barry watcher and critic Mark Plotkin, a political analyst for WTOP radio. In 1986, Plotkin unsuccessfully ran for city council, and in the midst of his campaign he went to see Barry, who shared some advice. "I don't remember anything else he said," says Plotkin. "But the one thing that sticks in my mind twenty-three years later, which sums him up, is he told me, 'My whole life, people have told me what I can't do. And I'm not going to abide by that.'"

"I think that's what motivates him more than anything," says Plotkin. He remembers talking to Barry right before sentencing in the income tax case. "I said, 'How do you feel about this?' He said, 'Well, you never know how these things turn out.' He was majorly calm. I'd be a sweating wreck. He was literally flirting with the clerk who announced the verdict. Talk about chutzpah."

After lunch at the Old Ebbitt, the check comes. I offer to split it, but Barry waves me off and throws down his debit card. The waitress disappears, then returns apologetically, informing Barry that his card's been rejected. I throw my credit card instead, and Barry's spokesperson Natalie panics, saying she should pay so I won't write about it. I tell her I will anyway, so she might as well let it ride.

A symposium commences at the table on the journalistic pros and cons of what just happened. The only person who doesn't care in the least? Marion Barry. "It just shows I'm human," he says. "Millions of Americans go through this every day. Think they got the bank thing straight, don't have it straight. Come on . . . We make mistakes. We have frailties." It turns out Barry has a big wad of bills in his pocket, which we notice when he tips the valet outside. "You could've paid for lunch," observes Natalie. "I had it," says Barry. "But whenever the *Weekly Standard* offers to pay, I'm takin' it."

"Welcome to the family," Natalie says with a grimace.

A few days later, Barry wants to return the favor, taking me and Natalie to lunch at Acadiana, a New Orleans–style eatery where he'll have the fried catfish and watermelon salad. First, though, he has to go to a downtown SunTrust and see what's what with his card and his retirement check, which seems to be missing from direct deposit.

"Who do I see about a problem with my card?" he says, once in the bank. As Barry cools his heels, customers, both white and black, come up to make small talk and take cell-phone pictures. The branch manager, Yolette Olufemi, sits down with Barry and checks the damage. She looks a little sheepish about what she's discovered and gingerly informs him that Thrifty Car Rental has billed his card for $1,353.10, which has caused him to be overdrawn and to be assessed an additional penalty.

Barry mutters that the police impounded his car during the stalking-charge episode, and, though they didn't press charges, "the police had my car. For a week. Illegally." He must've forgotten to pay for the rental car he needed in the meantime. He tells her apologetically that he should have his paycheck soon, and can cover the shortfall. She sees me taking notes, and seems somewhat embarrassed for him, telling Barry she waited on him six years ago, and thanked him then, because he was responsible for her first summer job when she was a high school student. "Those lifetime experiences helped to put me where I am today. So I always say, 'Kudos Mr. Barry,'" she adds with somewhat strained cheer, offering to reduce his overdraft penalty.

Marion Barry was, is, and will always be a ladies' man. We talk about women plenty. When I chat up one of his supporters, commenting on the fake gemstones glued to her eyelashes, Barry leans over my shoulder and says, "Don't hit on those women. That's my job."

One of the women he won't talk about much is Donna Watts-Brighthaupt, the central character in his current troubles. But when I ask him what the biggest regret of his life is, he has only one woman on his mind: "Effi."

He's referring to the late Effi Barry, his third wife and mother of his son, Christopher. Effi was an elegant former model with an aristocratic bearing, best known for sitting by Barry every day during the six-week Vista trial, hooking a rug in supportive silence, while a parade of witnesses detailed sex 'n' drug specifics that would've caused any normal wife to have a stroke.

She stuck with Barry for a while longer, then left him before he went to prison. They remained close, however. And he says that in the years before she died, of myeloid leukemia in 2007, they even talked about getting remarried. The depth of his affection for her was evidenced from what he said at her funeral at the National Cathedral: "I was not late this time, Effi. I was on time."

One afternoon, in Barry's city council office, after a vigorous interrogation, he says, "Wanna go to lunch? I ain't got no money. Card's still messed up." Before we do, however, he walks over to a framed photo of himself with a laughing Effi at a chamber of commerce dinner. "Come look at this over here. Look how fine she looks. Yeah, my God." I ask if he misses her. "Absolutely," he says. "I do. I miss her. For about the last ten years or so, I didn't dream. After my transplant, I started dreaming again. I dream in color. The toxins are out of my body . . . Two or three nights ago, I dreamed about her."

I ask what he dreamed. "I don't want to get into that," Barry says, as he often does about subjects he brings up.

Later that day, she comes up again. Barry has insisted we visit Linda Greene, his "fine" former chief of staff and decades-long friend, at her beautiful restored Victorian at the foot of a national parkland hill in Anacostia, atop which sits Frederick Douglass's old house.

Inside Linda's living room, the television is on, showing the "beer summit" between Obama, Skip Gates, and the Cambridge cop who arrested him. Barry and I both agree the spectacle of Obama and Co. pretending they're just regular guys having a brew is preposterous. When I suggest it might be useful for him to have a beer summit with the police, he grunts: "They'd probably poison my beer."

Barry sinks back on his shoulders into Linda's luxurious couch, while eating pineapple and cheese slices from an hors d'oeuvres tray. She takes a seat on the arm of the couch beside him. They flirt, they reminisce, she fusses over his tie, telling him she doesn't like it much. They seem like an affectionate old married couple. I ask if they've ever been romantic. They both insist not, though Linda says her ex-husband still asks her if they ever got it on.

Linda was one of Effi's best friends and was with her at the end, so she and Barry start trading off, giving me the blow-by-blow of Effi's last days. Barry had seen Effi shortly before, in what ended up being her deathbed in Annapolis. "Even then," he recalls, "She said, 'Marion, I'm getting tired. I'm getting tired.' I said, 'You're not getting tired. It's gonna be all right. You're gonna make it through this. We've gone through worse than this.'"

Shortly thereafter, he left for Memphis to see his ailing mother. Linda called him while he was there and told him this was it. He knew he couldn't get back in time. "About ten minutes later," Barry says, "Linda called back again and said she's gone." His face pinches when he says this. His lip starts quivering. He shuts his eyes tight, and tears stream from them, which he quickly covers with his hand so nobody can see.

He eventually lightens the mood, looking at Linda. "Linda complains about me sometimes. But Effi willed me to you. So I'm stuck."

Both Barry and Linda talk freely about how much he cared for

Effi, which prompts me to ask how he could put her through what he did: the infidelity, the public humiliation. Linda covers for him: "He's not doing it out of disrespect, or less love for the person he's committed to at that time."

Barry takes this in, meditatively chewing on a pineapple slice. "I haven't thought about it much," he confesses. "First of all, I love people. Attractive women. They're all attractive to me if they're female." We laugh.

"No, really," he insists:

> But I guess part of what happens in life is you are what you see. Growing up without a natural father, I didn't see these one-on-one relationships. I'm just thinking about it for the first time, quite frankly. I mean I've thought about it, but not in this depth . . . I think there ought to be fidelity between a man and a woman . . . But you are what you see. And when I was growing up, I didn't see men who were one-woman men. So I guess it sort of got caught in my personality. I'm not rationalizing it. It is what it is.

We're ready to leave Linda's. We go out to the car, and on the floor of the back seat is a Häagen-Dazs cup filled with melted butter-pecan ice cream. Natalie had bought Barry a cone when she was driving us around D.C., as Barry showed me his mayoral-era development triumphs. But the cone started dripping all over his suit. I suggested throwing it out the window, but this is Barry's city. He adamantly refused. He might run afoul of the law every now and then, but he's not some kind of litterbug. So instead, he quickly ate it while letting the rest drip into the cup.

When he slides into the car at Linda's, he reaches down, drinks the melted ice cream, then hands the empty cup to Linda. "Oh, thanks," she says. "Now I'm the trash woman."

Several days later, I follow Barry to New York for the premiere of *The Nine Lives of Marion Barry.* He is in his glory, disembarking from a stretch limo with his Angels for a screening high atop the HBO building, which overlooks the yoganauts and ping-pong players of Bryant Park. He sings a few bars of the old gospel hymn "Victory Is Mine" when he takes the microphone after the screening (*I told Satan to get thee behind / Victory today is mine*). He accepts well wishes from statuesque blondes, who are aroused at the sight of a young, militant Barry in a leopard-print dashiki. "You're a beautiful man, I just want to put that out there," says one.

At a reception buffet line, I run into Jim Vance, a tall, well-dressed, barrel-chested African-American news anchor from D.C. —half of the longest-running anchor team in Washington—who has known and covered Barry since the late '60s. Vance, too, was addicted to cocaine for seven years back in the '80s.

Around Barry, Vance is all hugs and smiles. But I ask him to give me his straight-up assessment of Barry. He raises his eyes to the ceiling, thinks a bit, then says, "There were so many of us who had so much hope for Marion. I don't know too many people that were more blessed or that had more skills than Marion had, nor too many people who were a bigger disappointment, quite frankly."

Vance said his own addiction "snuck up on me":

> It was a pattern of behavior that was nobody's fault but my own. I think the same applied to Marion. A pattern of behavior began that Marion couldn't blame anybody, or anything, except Marion for. There comes a point for most of us who are addicts, that today, I'm either gonna live, or gonna die. And you begin the process of living, or continue the process of dying. I don't know that Marion's got to that point yet.

After the screening, Barry and the Angels and I load into the limo and head uptown for chicken 'n' waffles, fried catfish, and shrimp étouffée. It's supposed to be the last of our time together, but he insists on breakfast the next morning, to clear a few things up. Just as he'll do when he calls me a few days later, unbidden, at home.

The specifics of what he says turn out not to be that important. But it feels as though he is addressing some advice I'd given him when catching him at the screening. Earlier that afternoon, from my hotel, I'd watched him tussle with an MSNBC anchor while promoting the film, Barry insisting yet again that he'd done nothing wrong at the Vista. I suggested to him that if he didn't insult people's intelligence regarding the things they already know about him, he might get a fairer hearing regarding the things they don't know.

So, for instance, at breakfast the following morning, Barry offers, "When I told you about recreational use, I don't want you to think I'm trying to minimize it. It was a serious problem, yeah.

But the good news is, look at me now!" Of course, such rare moments of honest disclosure come between hours and hours of amnesia, revisionism, suspect self-justification, airbrushing, and legacy-buffing.

But that's OK. It felt, over the time I was with him, that there were several moments where Marion Barry was trying to tell me something. Maybe even the truth. If he can't quite always get there, it's still a commendable effort. After all, he hasn't had much practice.

PHILLIP LOPATE

Brooklyn the Unknowable

FROM *Harvard Review*

I SING OF BROOKLYN, the fruited plain, cradle of literary genius and standup comedy, awash in history, relics from Indian mounds, Dutch farms, Revolutionary War battles, breweries and baseball. In Brooklyn, miles of glorious townhouses and brownstones, among the most architecturally effective residential neighborhoods in urban America, coexist not far from dismal slums with some of the highest infant mortality rates in the country. Brooklyn is home to millions of immigrants, many of whom never learn to speak proper English, so surrounded are they by Brooklynese, a curious hardy dialect. Brooklyn is my hometown.

There must be some mercury in the water that promotes a need to recount, show off, or intimidate. Brooklyn breeds writers, performers, and gangsters as effortlessly as Detroit turns out convertibles, coupes, hatchbacks. Malamud and Mailer, Stanwyck and Streisand, Woody Allen and Mel Brooks, the Miller Boys (Henry and Arthur), Al Capone and the Amboy Dukes, Red Auerbach and Spike Lee, all came up in the encouraging yet fanatically competitive atmosphere of Brooklyn schoolyards. Even more numerous are the illustrious who, though born elsewhere, took to the hospitality of Kings County: Marianne Moore, Walker Evans, Hart Crane, Richard Wright, Truman Capote, Gypsy Rose Lee, Carson McCullers, Thomas Wolfe . . .

Brooklyn is vast and unassimilable. Like the Great Wall of China, it mocks our hankering for finitude. For all its braggadocio, the place is so diffident and secretive that even a homeboy like me is hard pressed to characterize it. When you've said that it is the most populous borough in New York City, that some 2,300,000 people live here on eighty-one square miles, you haven't begun to describe it. When you note that it's a patchwork of neighborhoods on the southwestern tip of Long Island, and zero in on Crown Heights, Fort Greene, Williamsburg, Bensonhurst, Bay Ridge, Dyker Heights, you're a little closer to the essence of Brooklyn, though not much. A friendly place (I knew more about the people on my block a few weeks after returning to Brooklyn than I had about the occupants in the next building after ten years on a Manhattan street), it can also exhibit a fortress mentality. How to explain the contradiction that Brooklynites can be so inviting to newcomers within the neighborhood enclave, yet so xenophobic and murderously guarded toward strangers from ten blocks away? Recall the sad episode of Yusuf Hawkins, a black youth killed for straying into the wrong white neighborhood while trying to buy a car. The novelist Pete Hamill recalled this Brooklyn territoriality in an interview:

> Where I grew up there were hamlets that were sometimes two blocks wide in which everybody knew everybody . . . But they didn't know people from the hamlet nine blocks away. Often they fought each other. All these fights that street gangs would have over turf, or girlfriends—they acted as if the people from 18th Street were totally different from the people from 9th Street.

If, as the pop song goes, there is a "New York state of mind," what might be the Brooklyn equivalent? I would characterize it as combative, wry, and resilient. From General Washington's strategic retreat over the East River to the present, it often consists in making a virtue of setbacks. Brooklyn Dodger fans were famous for their fortitude and their obstinate slogan: "Wait till next year." It is no accident that when the Dodgers finally won a World Series, they quit the borough almost immediately for the sunnier climes of Los Angeles. The Brooklyn mentality is not that of a winner, but a stoic. Brooklyn likes a beautiful loser.

Perhaps the defining loss was municipal identity. In 1898, when Brooklyn was the third-largest metropolis in the United States, it amalgamated with spindly Manhattan and three other boroughs, Queens, Staten Island, and the Bronx, to form modern New York City. In amalgamating with Brooklyn, Manhattan became the python that swallowed the elephant. I am not one of those who rue consolidation; I rejoice that Brooklyn feeds the greater whole. But there are those who still speak of Brooklyn as its own city. Perhaps they have in mind a symbolic rivalry along the lines of Minneapolis and St. Paul. I am a realist, I consider it a borough. But what a borough! I will go so far as to say that the spicy character of Brooklyn derives in large part from its "co-dependent relationship" with Manhattan. Having relinquished its municipal birthright, it haunts Manhattan Island like a doppelgänger. Manhattan is the tower, Brooklyn the garden; Manhattan is Faustian will, Brooklyn, domestic life. Manhattan preens, disseminates opinion; Brooklyn is Uncle Vanya schlepping in the background to support his flamboyant relative.

For over a century, millions of men and women commuted every day to make their living in Manhattan, my father and mother among them. They spent their vital essence as clerks in the garment center, riding the subway into Times Square every weekday morning, coming back at night with the *New York Post* (then a liberal tabloid) in my father's arms, relinquished to my brother and me for the sports pages. Before the *Post* it was the *Brooklyn Eagle,* a well-written local paper but lacking, as we say, an edge.

Brooklyn spirit remains a mixture of pride and provincialism. That its citizens have much to be proud of is an indisputable fact. But what's odd, for such a world-renowned place, is the rinky-dink sound of its boosterism, the narrow perspective of its free newspapers, which reprint the police dockets and church bingo schedules like a small-town gazette, the defensive character of its borough president's horn-tooting. Brooklyn's provincialism, be it said, is not, or not entirely, a failure to achieve cosmopolitan worldliness; it is also a painstaking, willed achievement. It's not easy to be situated next to the most *au courant* place on the planet and hold on to one's rough edges.

Though Tiresias's passage between genders has always struck me as exhausting, I seem to have conducted my life so as to crisscross the identity border between Manhattanite and Brooklynite. I grew up in Brooklyn, my family having resided just above the poverty line in the ghettoes of Williamsburg and Fort Greene/Bedford Stuyvesant, before clawing their way up the lower-middle-class ladder to

Flatbush. When I went off to college in Manhattan, I vowed never
to look back. Manhattan was the City, the Party, Heaven and Hell.
When out-of-state friends (who didn't know any better) settled in
Brooklyn, championing its civility and low-key grace, I took in the
fact that they had more space and prettier apartments, but I did
not envy them. For me, the borough carried a stigma. Brooklyn
was the primeval ooze out of which I had crawled in order to make
something of myself, and a move back would be a relapse, a defeat,
a regression to childhood and family entrapment.

The rest of my family, including my parents curiously enough,
followed me in time to Manhattan, except for my youngest sister,
who chose to live on Cheever Place, a cul-de-sac in the backwaters
of Cobble Hill. Each time I took the F train to visit, I pitied her for
still living in Brooklyn. The wheel turns: I now live seven blocks
from her old address. Just as I had expressed unconscious resistance to trekking to Brooklyn by never memorizing the directions
there, asking her anew each time, so now my Manhattan friends
toy the same way with me. It is as if they secretly hope to erode my
patience with directional amnesia, until, in the midst of repeating
these tedious instructions, I will break down and say, "Oh, all right,
let's meet in the City." (So Brooklynites call Manhattan, in spite of
the fact that we are just as much a part of New York, technically
speaking.)

On the face of it, the barrier between the two boroughs should
not be so great: after all, it is quicker to hop from Wall Street across
the river to Brooklyn Heights than to traverse the island all the
way to northernmost Manhattan. Yet I have known many people
who lived in Manhattan for years and never set foot in Brooklyn.
I remember once asking a highly cultivated elderly couple if they
might want to join me and my wife for a baroque opera at the
Brooklyn Academy of Music (or BAM) only to be told, "My husband and I don't go to Brooklyn." These were people who had
traveled all over the world and lived in Europe. Even the more in-
trepid downtown Manhattan types who, in the 1980s, started going to BAM for its avant-garde performances, would often travel in
packs, emerging from the subway with a look of suppressed terror,
clinging to their chums like roped mountaineers until they had
reached the safety of the Brooklyn Academy.

As it happens, the area around BAM *is* rather choppy and unprepossessing, usually under construction or partly boarded up, a classic transitional zone caught between commercial, residential, and traffic conduit. I do not blame Manhattanites for being afraid to venture left or right into unknown streets. But there is more to their hesitation than fear of muggers. There is also profound confusion at the vagueness of Brooklyn's urban design. They have moved from the clear, insular certitude of the Manhattan grid to the vaster landmass of Brooklyn, which is more like the continental United States in its potential for inspiring agoraphobia. Manhattan's grid is like a tall menu offering a hierarchical suite of neighborhoods: the merest change in signage, street lighting, or fenestration signals to the trained local a world of information about income and class. Brooklyn is no less class-bound, but its cues may be harder to read, especially for the Manhattanite, so used to precisely calibrated progressions of luxury and distress.

Then, too, the arrival in Brooklyn brings with it a drop in sophistication and tension (Manhattanites often equate the two) that registers immediately in the body. I have experienced it myself as a kind of decompression: a weight lifting from my shoulders. The low-rise streetscape, compared to Manhattan, is like going from a tense verticality to a semiprone position. This unstiffening is eventually recognized as one of the delights of living in Brooklyn, but for the casual day-tripper it can be alarming, like the woozy onset of a tranquilizer. The Manhattanite has learned to convert wariness into a muscle, which twitches unhappily when not stimulated; the Brooklynite has adapted to greater quantities of boredom and is consequently less afraid of it. Everything on the Brooklyn side of the bridge is more casual, you see fewer fashion statements, the passersby seem like ordinary people rather than out-of-work actors projecting a cameo-worthy intensity. Even the slackers in Brooklyn have less of an air of ideological anti-ambition than Manhattan dropouts. The furniture in a Brooklyn coffeehouse looks like throwaways from your aunt's living room. There is, in short, a touch of the amateur, the voluntaristic, the homemade about the place.

I remember when my wife became pregnant and we began looking for larger living space than our one-bedroom fifth-floor walkup in the West Village. I was determined not to leave Manhattan, but we looked uptown and down and grew fed up with the overpriced,

jerry-built crawl spaces pretending to be duplexes, or the peniten-
tial apartments darker than a jail cell. I had somehow forgotten to
save several million dollars to purchase a brownstone in the Village, so we began, reluctantly, to consider buying a house in Brooklyn. On our second day of looking in that borough, we fell in love
with a Carroll Gardens brownstone and made an offer, which was
accepted. That night, we had second thoughts, stealing peeks up
and down a near-deserted Court Street on a Saturday night. There
was an emptiness in my stomach—the gut of a Manhattanite at-
tuned to urban excitement. Were the quiet streets an omen of our
soon-to-be-dulled existence? Were we about to make a huge mistake? Fifteen years later, we have more than adjusted, while the surrounding neighborhood has accommodated us by growing livelier
and hipper. We love our house, we love our block, and we love the
borough of Brooklyn. Perhaps, like the pod people in *Invasion of
the Body Snatchers,* we have simply been taken over by some Gowanus legume that insidiously makes us accept a blander life.

All I know is that, when I go into Manhattan, which I do on the
average of three times a week, I enjoy the City but I do not miss living there. Not at all. Yet I realize I may never be whole: I have been
both Manhattanite and Brooklynite, I have identified with the imperial contempt of the former and the complacent inferiority complex of the latter, I have sampled the champagne and the Ovaltine
and will forever be split.

Not so much when world-weary as when feeling chipper, I sometimes saunter over from my house to the Union Street Bridge to
take in the restorative waters of the much-maligned Gowanus Canal. To do so, I first go past the modest brick three-story homes
of Union Street, with their stoops, stone angel fountains, patriotic
American flags, and an occasional Italian tricolor—this being a
long-standing Italian neighborhood, where immigrant stevedores
labored to raise a roof over their families' heads, with a renter
downstairs. These are not the fancy brownstones selling for several million, but awkward, cozy row houses, whose lack of cachet
increases as you approach the canal. No one of class ever wanted to
live near the Gowanus, legendary for its stink and for the mobsters'
bodies fished out of the canal.

The old Gowanus creek had been enlarged in the 1840s to service nearby factories and move construction materials for the burgeoning habitations of Brooklyn, and this dinky little canal, one hundred feet wide and less than a mile long, no deeper than fifteen feet in high water, became one of the most trafficked watercourses of nineteenth-century America. In the twentieth century, it devolved into a one-use channel—a conveyer of heating oil, whose toxic leakage into the creek bottom and the nearby shores complicated any future development for recreational or residential uses. The daunting cleanup costs have not prevented local community planners from fantasizing the lowly Gowanus's becoming a Little Venice, with outdoor cafés hugging the narrow banks. (Inshallah, it will never happen.) The tides being too sluggish to rid the channel of pollutants, a flushing tunnel has been installed, whose pumping action goes a long way toward alleviating the olfactory insult.

Standing on the span, looking outward toward the north, I see what is most astonishing for this city, a good deal of sky and clouds above low-scaled structures, and a vast sweeping view of Brooklyn that would have quickened the pulse of any Delft landscape painter. You can luxuriate in the profligate empty space ("waste" to a developer's eye) framed by the canal. On the canal's western bank, a small grassy meadow with wildflowers, bisected by oil pipes, slopes down to the greenish, petroleum-iridescent water. Along the eastern bank are lined the back ends of mostly abandoned factories, painted with graffiti and faded words like "Conklin Brass." The *thump-thump* of cars passing over the bridge competes with the contemplative mood.

Looking south toward Red Hook, there is a parking lot filled with Verizon telephone trucks, in the distance the elevated trestle of the F train, and the Kentile Floors sign, and a factory placard that reads "Alex Figliola Contracting: Water Mains and Sewers." All this prosaic attention to infrastructure and repair strewn haphazardly on either side of the canal amid weeds and ailanthus trees, this strange combination of industrial, residential, and bucolic, speaks to the poignantly somnolent essence of Brooklyn. The genius of Brooklyn has always been its homey atmosphere; it does not set out to awe, like skyscraper Manhattan, which is perhaps why one hears so much local alarm at the luxury apartment towers that are starting to sprout up in parts of the borough closest to Manhattan. Being a native Brooklynite, I never romanticized the place as immune from modernity, nor do I see why such an important piece of the metropolis should be protected from high-rise construction when the rest of the planet is not. But my feelings are mixed. For, if the sleeping giant that is Brooklyn were to wake and truly bestir itself and turn into a go-getter, I would deeply regret the loss of sky. Perhaps it is some deep-seated, native-son confidence that Brooklyn will never quite get it together that allows me to anticipate its bruited transformation with relative sanguinity.

Meanwhile, I stand on the Union Street Bridge, a fine place from which to contemplate the Brooklyn that was, that is, and that is to be.

Brooklyn occupies an oddly sentimental corner of the American consciousness. Recently I was in a breakfast place in Santa Fe called Bagelmania where the walls were covered with old, blown-up photographs of the Brooklyn Bridge and other quaint scenes from my native borough. I immediately became mistrustful. I thought also of the Brooklyn Diner on West 57th Street in Manhattan, yet another railroad-car-theme diner devoted to a bygone era. What is it about Brooklyn that makes it serve as such a ready hieroglyph of earthy reality to the outside world?

In the World War II era, when more battleships were built in the Brooklyn Navy Yard than in all of Japan, Brooklyn became the symbol of democratic, pluralistic tolerance and common decency—in short, the values for which we were fighting against the fascists. Every war movie had its GI played by William Bendix or someone of his ilk, who swore that Flatbush was "the greatest spot on oith." In the 1945 *Anchors Aweigh,* the chorine with a heart of gold is called simply "Brooklyn." When soldier Robert Walker meets single girl Judy Garland at Pennsylvania Station in *The Clock* (also 1945) and they fall in love, the two, having only a weekend to commit to each other before he returns to action, and needing a glimpse of domesticity to inspire them, go to Brooklyn where they encounter a gruff, kindly milkman (James Gleason) and his family. Another Gleason, Jackie, immortalized the frustrated hopes and dreams of working-class Brooklyn in *The Honeymooners.* Just as British playwrights used to typecast Cockneys as working class and proud, refusing to take any guff from superiors or even envy them (read: knowing their proper station in life), so American popular culture celebrated the Brooklynite as Everyman bittersweetly contented, in the end, to stay in that grubby lower-middle-class environment, with the El train rattling the windows, because somehow it was still "the greatest spot on oith." All these Ralph Kramden caricatures may be condescending at the core, but they also contain a grain of truth. There *is* something earthy and appealing about folk Brooklyn. Or was.

Nostalgia can be a hazardous distortion. *When Brooklyn Was the World* is the schmaltzy title of a book by Elliot Willensky. But Brooklyn was never the world, except perhaps for those children who never left their neighborhood, so that to long for that time is to wish to stay arrested in a kingdom of egg creams and stickball, or at the very least, provinciality. And of course, Dem Bums: the Brooklyn Dodgers with their loyal fans, Hilda Chester and the cowbells. I'm so sick of hearing about Jackie Robinson and Pee Wee Reese with their arms around each other—how it satisfies our need to believe in a simplified myth of racial harmony; and team owner Walter O'Malley cast as Judas, selling the team to Los Angeles with the connivance of archdemon Robert Moses. I was ten years old in 1953 and a more passionate Dodger fan did not exist. I *loved* Jackie Robinson, Pee Wee Reese, Carl Furillo, and Duke Snider. But let's be real: Dodger attendance figures were declining before Walter O'Malley moved the team to Los Angeles. The borough's breweries started closing in the 1950s, not the 1960s. So it's stretching things to say that the '50s were the heyday of Brooklyn and then blame everything bad on O'Malley.

As painful as the departure of the Dodgers may have been, the real decline in Brooklyn's fortunes came about from the shifting of the port to New Jersey and the closing of the navy yard, along with the city's loss of most of its manufacturing base. Ironically, the country was falling in love with white working-class ethnics at just that moment they were starting to leave the city, soon to be replaced by African Americans, Hispanics, and Asians, who would find it much harder to obtain unskilled, entry-level jobs. I dislike Brooklyn sentimentality, but if I am sentimental about anything it is the working-class world of my childhood, and the opportunity it gave to millions of people without college degrees to work with their hands and take home a paycheck. All the candy stores and dairy cafeterias and delicatessens and trolleys that Brooklyn nostalgists lament were actually cogs of that functioning working-class culture. When several hundred thousand manufacturing jobs left Brooklyn in the 1950s and 1960s, never to return, it broke the back of the neighborhoods. Decades of massive disinvestment by redlining banks accompanied the deindustrialization process.

Fortunately, the tide has turned in the past fifteen years, and money has flooded back to Brooklyn. In retrospect, it's hard to see how Brooklyn could have ever fallen out of favor for long, given its superb housing stock and proximity to Manhattan's overheated real estate market, which makes it seem a relative bargain. However, Brooklyn's new prosperity, with its bistros and boutiques, looks different: it's no longer as homey and amateurish (which may be for the best), but a more self-consciously trendy, consumerist culture, driven by trust funds and the twin processes of globalization and gentrification.

At the same time, almost invisibly, a whole different, labor-driven Brooklyn is taking shape, fueled by recent immigration from India, China, the Dominican Republic, Russia, Israel, and Guyana. Present-day Brooklyn is both a more dynamic and a more perilous place than the cozy myths allow. Parts of Brooklyn are bursting with hidden economies, and sentimentality about Brooklyn's past obscures this new, emerging reality with its opportunities and its dislocations.

"Only the Dead Know Brooklyn." How often have I thought of that aptly grim title of Thomas Wolfe's. What did Thomas Wolfe know, you may ask; he grew up in Asheville, North Carolina. True, but he put in his time here, he tried to grasp its true nature. In that short story, he gives his narrator a thick Brooklyn accent: "Dere's no guy livin' dat knows Brooklyn t'roo an' t'roo, because it'd take a guy a lifetime just to find his way aroun' duh f——town." Our narrator witnesses a debate after someone asks directions to "Eighteent' Avenoo an' Sixty-sevent' Street." Some say it's in Bensonhurst, others, Flatbush. It turns out the direction-seeker is an oddball trying to master Brooklyn by traveling to random places with a map. The narrator tries to set him straight, telling him to stay out of Red Hook, but he won't listen. "Walkin' aroun' t'roo Red Hook by himself at night an' lookin' at his map! . . . Maybe he's found out by now dat he'll neveh live long enough to know duh whole of Brooklyn."

Only the dead know Brooklyn. Did Wolfe mean that we're all stiffs here, or that the place itself is a morgue? I have to admit a good part of the borough's terrain seems taken up by cemeteries. The border between Brooklyn and Queens alone has such a concentration of cemeteries it's been called "the city of the dead." And by the time you subtract all the smaller graveyards, funeral homes, mortuary headstone firms, etc., what are you left with? A sliver for the living.

Maybe I can't help thinking this way because the neighborhood I reside in, Carroll Gardens, has an abundance of funeral parlors: Raccuglia's, Scotto's, Russo's, Pastorelli's, Cobble Hill Chapels, Cuccinella's (which specializes in foreign shipping). What saltwater taffy and casinos are to Atlantic City, burial arrangements are to Carroll Gardens. It's an old Italian neighborhood with lots of old Italians, but not enough to keep six funeral parlors thriving. I leave my house in the morning and see the functionaries in black suits running interference for limousines, holding parking spots, helping the florists make deliveries, or just standing on the street corner looking dignified.

On top of that mortuary concentration, four blocks away from me, just over the Gowanus Canal, is the South Brooklyn Casket Company. Many is the time I've walked by that casket manufacturer and brooded on the brevity of glory.

In an effort to penetrate these terminal mysteries, I phoned the number of the South Brooklyn Casket Company and asked if I might ask a few questions for a magazine article. "We're not interested in that kind of thing," a gruff voice said. My suspicions were aroused: what were they shipping in those caskets? A recent tabloid scandal had exposed funeral parlors in the tristate area hacking up corpses and selling body parts for transplants abroad. I decided to nose around.

On a warm day in March I strode up Union Street, crossed the verdigris, irenic waters of the Gowanus, and stealthily approached my target. The South Brooklyn Casket Company occupies brick warehouses on both sides of the street. Its offices are located in a slender, aluminum-sided building topped by an American flag. I saw hard-bitten men wheeling caskets and loading them onto the backs of trucks. Trying to look nonchalant, I wandered over, eavesdropping on two workers speaking in Spanish.

"Where are you taking them?" I asked one of the men.

"All over," he replied enigmatically.

There was little more to glean from him, so I headed around the corner, knowing that sometimes more can be learned from the back of a building than the front. I peered into its windows, seeing stacks of caskets polished and shiny like new sedans, champagne-colored, taupe, all the season's popular colors. I would not like to be buried in such a metallic-looking sheath. A plain pine box, thank you. Around back stood a truck with Canadian plates; two men were unloading caskets. "Are those made in Canada?" I asked.

"Yes. We drove 'em down from there this morning," said the trucker, with what I thought was a Cajun accent.

"So . . . South Brooklyn doesn't manufacture its own caskets? It just distributes other companies'?"

"No, they make 'em too."

I had nothing more to ask. My researches had led nowhere. None of it made sense. It was true, after all: I would have to wait until after I was dead to understand Brooklyn.

But there was one last hope: the Center for Thanatoptic Research. I had noticed the plaque for this morbid-sounding organization next to a big old church on Atlantic Avenue. I made an appointment by phone, but I knew not what to expect from an enterprise whose name invoked the God of Death. An altar with a stuffed black cat, presided over by a mad priestess? I rang the bell, and to my mixed relief and disappointment the door opened to reveal a sort of mail-order business, offering pamphlets and publications about coping with death, grieving stages, burial practices, and the art of gravestone rubbing.

The director was a sensible, gray-haired woman in sneakers, a former art teacher who had stumbled on this emerging thanatoptic field and, sensing the public's need for information, decided to supply it. She talked to me about the way death used to be a much more accepted visitor in Brooklynites' homes: the second-story hallway niches often found in brownstones, for instance, were put there so that the casket could be more easily maneuvered down the staircase. She had much to say about the wonders of Green-Wood Cemetery, whose artistic landscaping had inspired Olmsted and Vaux's Central Park. She led me over to her library, a wall of books on the subject of mortality, and tactfully left me alone with them.

Staring at the learned tomes, I began to feel giddy, the linoleum at my feet seemed to buckle underneath me, the book titles swirled faster and faster, I was seized by vertigo, an inner tornado, and at the conic base of the whirlwind's funnel I suddenly experienced ahead of me a clearing, a rapture, an ecstatic release such as epileptics report in the midst of an attack, and I was flooded at once with illumination, the mysteries of the universe past and present were revealed to me in a pageant at my feet, Antony and Cleopatra, Robespierre and Danton, I understood the numerology of the Kabbala, Einstein's theorem was as child's play to me, but more important, I understood Brooklyn for the first time, the way it all fit together—of course East New York could only lead to Canarsie, and Canarsie had to be next to Flatlands, it made perfect sense—and there, by the edge of the Atlantic near Coney Island, was the key to it all, the Aleph, a precinct's name so redolent and resonant with encrypted meaning I could barely bring myself to utter it . . . Gravesend! Someday soon, I knew, I would have to explore that area.

IAN McEWAN

On John Updike

FROM *The New York Review of Books*

IN HIS AUTOBIOGRAPHY *Self-Consciousness,* a "big-bellied Lutheran God" within the young John Updike looked on in contempt
as he struggled to give up cigarettes. Many years later the older
Updike, now giving up on alcohol, coffee, and salt, put into the
mouth of that God the words of Frederick the Great excoriating
his battle-shy soldiers—"Dogs, would you live forever?" But all the
life-enhancing substances were set aside, and writing became Updike's "sole remaining vice. It is an addiction, an illusory release, a
presumptuous taming of reality." In the mornings, he could write
"breezily" of what he could not "contemplate in the dark without
turning in panic to God." The plain facts of life were "unbearably
heavy, weighted as they are with our personal death. Writing, in
making the world light—in codifying, distorting, prettifying, ver-
balizing it—approaches blasphemy."

And now this masterly blasphemer, whose literary schemes and
pretty conceits touched at points on the Shakespearean, is gone,
and American letters, deprived in recent years of its giants, Bellow and Mailer, is a leveled plain, with one solitary peak guarded
by Roth. We are coming to the end of the golden age of the American novel in the twentieth century's second half. Henry Bech, Updike's remote Jewish other, never immune to an attack of status
anxiety, mused on the teeming hordes of his gifted and despised
contemporaries:

Those that didn't appear, like John Irving and John Fowles, garrulously,
Dickensianly reactionary in method seemed, like John Hawkes and John

Barth, smugly, hermetically experimental. O'Hara, Hersey, Cheever, Updike — suburbanites all living safe while art's inner city disintegrated. And that was just the Johns.

This most Lutheran of writers, driven by intellectual curiosity all his life, was troubled by science as others are troubled by God. When it suited him, he could easily absorb and be impressed by physics, biology, astronomy, but he was constitutionally unable to "make the leap of unfaith." The "weight" of personal death did not allow it, and much seriousness and dark humor derive from this tension between intellectual reach and metaphysical dread.

In a short story from 1985, "The Wallet," Mr. Fulham (who, we are told in the first line, "had assembled a nice life") experiences death terrors when he takes his grandchildren to a local cinema. While "starships did special-effects battle" Fulham's "true situation in time and space" was revealed: "a speck of consciousness now into its seventh decade, a mortal body poised to rejoin the minerals, a member of a lost civilization that once existed on a sliding continent." This "lonely possession" of his own existence, he concludes, is "sickeningly serious."

God makes no appearance in this story, but it is unlikely that an atheist could have conjured so much from the minor domestic disturbance that follows. First, a large check "in the low six figures," a return on canny investments, fails to show up in the post. Fulham makes many phone calls to the company in Houston; the matter begins to loom too large — "He slept poorly, agitated by the injustice of it." He suspects a thief, a "perpetrator," or that there is a flaw in the mindless system. He is tormented by "outrageous cosmic *unanswerableness.*"

Then, the "perpetrator" strikes again. His wallet — "a friendly adjunct to his person" — vanishes. This being Updike, its contents are minutely, satirically listed, the credit, membership, and hospital cards, the priceless clippings, photographs of family and one of a long-ago lover, the obsolete receipts. Who has not searched in vain, like Fulham, returning superstitiously to the same places, trying to re-create the movements of the careless self of yesterday? But "the wallet's non-existence rang out through the rooms like a pistol shot which leaves deafness in its wake." In despair, Fulham exclaims to his wife,

"Without that wallet, I'm nothing." His tongue had outraced his brain, but once he said it he realized this to be true: without the wallet, he was a phantom, flitting about in a house without walls.

At last, the check shows up, only after it has been canceled; the granddaughter finds the wallet, but only after the accounts have been frozen. The nights are cooler now and something has shifted in Fulham. He has had a near-death experience, a rehearsal, and now is reconciled to his end.

Like much that appears secular in Updike, this story is suffused with his religious seriousness—the very spirit that Philip Larkin, an atheist, famously acknowledged in his description of a church as being "a serious house on serious earth." It is no accident that Fulham's moments of dread come upon him in a movie house. In the opening of the major novel *In the Beauty of the Lilies*, Mary Pickford faints on the set of a D. W. Griffith movie, *The Call to Arms*, while elsewhere a clergyman is painfully losing his faith after reading a book by the atheist Robert Ingersoll and realizing "what he had long suspected, that the universe was utterly indifferent to his states of mind and as empty of divine content as a corroded kettle." He confronts "the blood-soaked selfishness of a cosmic mayhem" and leaves the ministry to become an encyclopedia salesman. And so they are linked, cinema and religion, two grand designs conjuring light out of darkness. For Updike, cinema and its brattish child television "became our religion." This was not a disapproving observation—in his youth, "it was the movies that moved me, and gave me something to live for, to live toward."

And cinema was above all, for the young Updike, an education in sexual manners, in modes of seduction, in the codes of glances and touch and all that business with cigarettes. It was there from the very beginning, in his writing, that celebrated or infamous capacity for fastidious, clinical, visually intense, painfully and hilariously honest descriptions of men and women making love. However fleeting or disastrous the coupling, the metaphysical shadows are always on the wall—the same seriousness is in play. "Nature dangles sex to keep us walking toward the cliff," Piet reflects in *Couples*. When he makes love outdoors to Georgene—"A lip of resistance, then an easeful deepness, a slipping by steps"—he is troubled that he is "under the eye of God."

The ruthless recording eye made Updike unpopular with some women readers, especially back in the salad days of Theory, when talk of the "male gaze" was the fashion. Piet notes in Foxy's nakedness "the goosebumped roughness of her buttocks, the gray unpleasantness of her shaved armpits." But in Updike as in life, bodies are rarely perfect, unlike in the movies; this is fictional realism and goosebumps do not stand in the way of the lovers' transcendent pleasure. While she fellates him "lazily," he combs her lovely hair and reflects on her "coral cunt, coral into burgundy, with its pansy-shaped M, or W, of fur"; then it comes to him that mouths are noble. "They move in the brain's court. We set our genitals mating down below like peasants, but when the mouth condescends, mind and body marry."

In his last novel, *The Widows of Eastwick,* Updike engaged playfully with his female critics through his character Sukie, the romantic novelist. She erases from a work in progress a passage about carefully buffed fingernails digging deep "into Hercule's broad, heaving back." She reminds herself that a proper romance never dwells on sexual details, for it might lose its "targeted demographic of dreamy, dissatisfied women . . . Women know the facts but don't want them spelled out."

In fact, Updike's level, unblinking gaze is not only on women, and is not confined to the physical. In *Roger's Version,* when Lambert lies to his wife to conceal an infidelity, he does so, "trusting my face, that thin-skinned traitor, to back me up." And there was never a more fallible and exposed character in modern fiction than Harry "Rabbit" Angstrom. The Rabbit tetralogy not only describes from the inside modern man's major and minor dishonesties, self-deceptions, special pleadings, and lumpish passivity, it also charts over four novels and more than thirty years a slow physical and mental deterioration accelerated by laziness, junk food, and American prosperity.

The tetralogy is Updike's masterpiece and will surely be his monument. In all its detail, homely or hard-edged, and all its arenas —work, politics, retirement, and above all sex—the metaphysical is always there, sometimes a mere gleam buried in the fold of a sentence, at other times overtly, comically. In the first of the novels, *Rabbit, Run,* when youngish Harry, the typesetter and ex–basketball player, makes love to Ruth, a small-town prostitute, their sessions

are interrupted by a gut-level theological dispute about God's existence, prompted by Sunday churchgoers in the street below. Harry,
naturally, is on the side of God— "The idea of making it while the
churches are full excites him."

Many years later, he is on the operating table, watching his own
insides on a screen ("The Rabbit Angstrom Show"), surrounded by
machines and technocratic doctors and their satellites who "mur-
murously crouch over Harry's sheeted, strategically exposed body,"
conducting a three-and-a-half-hour angioplasty following his heart
attack. The scene is rich in Updike's strengths. "The mechanically
precise dark ghost of the catheter is the worm of death within
him. Godless technology is fucking the pulsing wet tubes we inherited from the squid, the boneless sea-cunts." The experience is
intensely unpleasant— "like his chest is being cooked in a micro-
wave. Jesus." He closes his eyes a few times and attempts to pray
— "but it feels like a wrong occasion, there is too much crowding
in, of the actual material world. No old wispy Biblical God would
dare interfere." The one consolation is that his doctor is Jewish, for
Harry has a

> gentile prejudice that Jews do everything a little better than other peo-
> ple, something about all those generations crouched over the Talmud
> and watch-repair tables, they aren't as distracted as other persuasions,
> they don't expect to have as much fun. They stay off the booze and dope
> and have a weakness only . . . for broads.

Like Bellow, his only equal in this, Updike is a master of effort-
less motion— between third and first person, from the metaphorical density of literary prose to the demotic, from specific detail to
wide generalization, from the actual to the numinous, from the
scary to the comic. For his own particular purposes, Updike devised for himself a style of narration, an intense, present-tense, free
indirect style, that can leap up, whenever it wants, to a God's-eye
view of Harry, or the view of his put-upon wife, Janice, or his victimized son, Nelson. This carefully crafted artifice permits here assumptions about evolutionary theory, which are more Updike than
Harry, and comically sweeping notions of Jewry, which are more
Harry than Updike.

This at the heart of the tetralogy's achievement. Updike once
said of the Rabbit books that they were an exercise in point of view.

This was typically self-deprecating, but contains an important grain of truth. Harry's education extends no further than high school, his view is further limited by a range of prejudices and a stubborn, combative spirit, and yet he is the vehicle for a half-million-word meditation on postwar American anxiety, failure, and prosperity. A mode had to be devised to make this possible, and that involved pushing beyond the bounds of realism. In a novel like this, Updike insisted, you have to be generous and allow your characters eloquence, "and not chop them down to what you think is the right size." He was clear too that we all sense more than we can ever put into words, and was mindful of the example of Joyce and his "great attempt to capture the way we move through life."

The three Bech books, which Updike always listed with his short stories, have alliterative titles, like the tetralogy, and read now like a trilogy of a distinctive comic genius. Henry Bech is a Jewish-American writer whose career rises, fades horribly, and rises again to embrace the Nobel Prize denied his creator. In one of the final episodes, *Bech Noir*, Henry takes, rather implausibly, to murdering the critics who have offended him over a lifetime. A poisoned self-addressed envelope and a discreet shove on a crowded subway platform dispose of two with little bother. To reach another, Bech done up in cape and mask, armed with gun and silencer, climbs a fire escape with an accomplice, his current lover in a catsuit, to take the life of Orlando Cohen, an old man with emphysema, whose chaste ambition was to be "the ultimate adjudicator" of American literature and who had "refused to grant Bech a place, even a minor place, in the canon."

They find an emaciated, enfeebled Cohen breathing oxygen through a mask with a volume of Walter Benjamin's *Selected Writings* on his lap. This is comedy, high and dark, but it does not prevent the critic, minutes before his death, delivering a sharp dismissal of Bech's work for its failure to understand America. Its core, Bech had failed to grasp, was essentially Protestant. The first settlers thought the Holy Ghost had led them to a Promised Land. Fighting for air, Cohen pronounces: "The Holy Ghost . . . who the hell is that? Some pigeon, that's all . . . but that God-awful faith . . . Bech . . . when it burns out . . . it leaves a dead spot. Love it or leave it . . . a dead spot. That's where America is . . . in that dead spot."

Bech failed to find that spot, but his creator had long ago made it his subject. That dead spot was the ruined inner city of *Roger's Version*, a spoiled landscape through which a divinity professor takes a thirty-page stroll—one of the great set pieces of the entire body of work; the dead spot was the shadowy center of scores of novels and stories, in the freeways, malls, TV-addicted children, junk food, the boundless suburbs and their heartless intrigues and pursuit of ecstasy in restless, hopeful couplings, the messy divorces and their wounded children, the racial divide, the rackety politics filtered through TV screens, the national bafflement as manufacturing industries declined and the Japanese moved in with their cheaper cars.

That dead spot is probed and palpated in the ever-present metaphysics, the thwarted religious sense, or in moments when a denatured suburbanite glances up beyond the telegraph poles and wires and notices that spring is coming on and experiences a jolt of indistinct excitement that is quickly smothered; or when Harry Angstrom, waiting to receive a serve in a game of social tennis, thinks of the mounting numbers of dead in his life, and feels camaraderie for his friends, and loves the treetops around him—but cannot name a single tree, never reads a book, knows nothing, and feels his life to be threadbare.

There is in Updike always comedy or mischief in these moments of frustrated entitlement. A great writer cannot help showing us that there is something strangely comic, or antic, about the perfectly turned phrase; the precise insight into a human moment carries with it generosity and warmth, and prompts a smile of recognition. A baby "corkscrews" in its father's arms; a newly married couple look "self-cherished, like gladioli"; when gales of '60s social mayhem sweep through Harry's marital home and the house has unwanted visitors and, in the dead of night, he must make love quietly to his new mistress, Updike notes that "the rooms are quadrants of one rustling heart"—a sweetly pitched observation that finds expression in an iambic pentameter.

The Updike opus is so vast, so varied and rich, that we will not have its full measure for years to come. We have lived with the expectation of his new novel or story or essay so long, all our lives, that it does not seem possible that this flow of invention should suddenly cease. We are truly bereft that this reticent, kindly man with the ferocious work ethic and superhuman facility will write for us no more. He was intensely private, learned, generous, courtly, the kind of man who could apologize for replying to one's letter by return mail because it was the only way he could keep his desk clear.

Contrary to what his work might suggest to a literal reader, John Updike was in actual life devoted to his large family that sprawled across the generations, so why not let one of his youngest characters take the parting bow on his behalf? When Henry Bech goes up onstage in Stockholm to make his Nobel acceptance speech, he takes with him on his hip his one-year-old daughter. She wriggles impatiently through his lecture, and when at last he has finished, she reaches out for the microphone "with the curly, beslobbered fingers of one hand as if to pluck the fat metallic bud." Bech feels the warmth of her skull, he inhales "her scalp's powdery scent . . . Then she lifted her right hand, where all could see, and made the gentle clasping and unclasping that signifies bye-bye."

STEVEN PINKER

My Genome, My Self

FROM *The New York Times Magazine*

ONE OF THE PERKS of being a psychologist is access to tools that allow you to carry out the injunction to know thyself. I have been tested for vocational interest (closest match: psychologist), intelligence (above average), personality (open, conscientious, agreeable, average in extroversion, not too neurotic), and political orientation (neither leftist nor rightist, more libertarian than authoritarian). I have MRI pictures of my brain (no obvious holes or bulges) and soon will undergo the ultimate test of marital love: my brain will be scanned while my wife's name is subliminally flashed before my eyes.

Last fall I submitted to the latest high-tech way to bare your soul. I had my genome sequenced and am allowing it to be posted on the Internet, along with my medical history. The opportunity arose when the biologist George Church sought ten volunteers to kick off his audacious Personal Genome Project. The PGP has created a public database that will contain the genomes and traits of one hundred thousand people. Tapping the magic of crowd sourcing that gave us Wikipedia and Google rankings, the project seeks to engage geneticists in a worldwide effort to sift through the genetic and environmental predictors of medical, physical, and behavioral traits.

The Personal Genome Project is an initiative in basic research, not personal discovery. Yet the technological advance making it possible—the plunging cost of genome sequencing—will soon give people an unprecedented opportunity to contemplate their own biological and even psychological makeups. We have entered the era of consumer genetics. At one end of the price range you can get a complete sequence and analysis of your genome from Knome (often pronounced "know me") for $99,500. At the other you can get a sample of traits, disease risks, and ancestry data from 23andMe for $399. The science journal *Nature* listed "Personal Genomics Goes Mainstream" as a top news story of 2008.

Like the early days of the Internet, the dawn of personal genomics promises benefits and pitfalls that no one can foresee. It could usher in an era of personalized medicine, in which drug regimens are customized for a patient's biochemistry rather than juggled through trial and error, and screening and prevention measures are aimed at those who are most at risk. It opens up a niche for bottom-feeding companies to terrify hypochondriacs by turning dubious probabilities into Genes of Doom. Depending on who has access to the information, personal genomics could bring about national health insurance, leapfrogging decades of debate, because piecemeal insurance is not viable in a world in which insurers can cherry-pick the most risk-free customers, or in which at-risk customers can load up on lavish insurance.

The pitfalls of personal genomics have already made it a subject of government attention. In 2008 President Bush signed the Genetic Information Nondiscrimination Act, outlawing discrimination in employment and health insurance based on genetic data. And the states of California and New York took action against the direct-to-consumer companies, arguing that what they provide are medical tests and thus can be ordered only by a doctor.

With the genome no less than with the Internet, information wants to be free, and I doubt that paternalistic measures can stifle the industry for long (but then, I have a libertarian temperament). For better or for worse, people will want to know about their genomes. The human mind is prone to essentialism—the intuition that living things house some hidden substance that gives them their form and determines their powers. Over the past century, this essence has become increasingly concrete. Growing out of the early, vague idea that traits are "in the blood," the essence became identified with the abstractions discovered by Gregor Mendel called genes, and then with the iconic double helix of DNA. But DNA has long been an invisible molecule accessible only to a white-coated priesthood. Today, for the price of a flat-screen TV, people can read their essence as a printout detailing their very own A's, C's, T's, and G's.

A firsthand familiarity with the code of life is bound to confront us with the emotional, moral, and political baggage associated with the idea of our essential nature. People have long been familiar with tests for heritable diseases, and the use of genetics to trace ancestry—the new *Roots*—is becoming familiar as well. But we are only beginning to recognize that our genome also contains information about our temperaments and abilities. Affordable genotyping may offer new kinds of answers to the question "Who am I?" —to ruminations about our ancestry, our vulnerabilities, our character, and our choices in life.

Over the years I have come to appreciate how elusive the answers to those questions can be. During my first book tour fifteen years ago, an interviewer noted that the paleontologist Stephen Jay Gould had dedicated his first book to his father, who took him to see the dinosaurs when he was five. What was the event that made me become a cognitive psychologist who studies language? I was dumbstruck. The only thing that came to mind was that the human mind is uniquely interesting and that as soon as I learned you could study it for a living, I knew that that was what I wanted to do. But that response would not just have been charmless; it would also have failed to answer the question. Millions of people are exposed to cognitive psychology in college but have no interest in making a career of it. What made it so attractive to *me*?

As I stared blankly, the interviewer suggested that perhaps it was because I grew up in Quebec in the 1970s when language, our preeminent cognitive capacity, figured so prominently in debates about the future of the province. I quickly agreed—and silently vowed to come up with something better for the next time. Now I say that my formative years were a time of raging debates about the political implications of human nature, or that my parents subscribed to a Time-Life series of science books, and my eye was caught by the one called *The Mind*, or that one day a friend took me to hear a lecture by the great Canadian psychologist D. O. Hebb, and I was hooked. But it is all humbug. The very fact that I had to think so hard brought home what scholars of autobiography and memoir have long recognized. None of us know what made us what we are, and when we have to say something, we make up a good story.

An obvious candidate for the real answer is that we are shaped by our genes in ways that none of us can directly know. Of course genes can't pull the levers of our behavior directly. But they affect the wiring and workings of the brain, and the brain is the seat of our drives, temperaments, and patterns of thought. Each of us is dealt a unique hand of tastes and aptitudes, like curiosity, ambition, empathy, a thirst for novelty or for security, a comfort level with the social or the mechanical or the abstract. Some opportunities we come across click with our constitutions and set us along a path in life.

This hardly seems radical—any parent of more than one child will tell you that babies come into the world with distinct personalities. But what can anyone say about how the baby got to be that way? Until recently, the only portents on offer were traits that ran in the family, and even they conflated genetic tendencies with family traditions. Now, at least in theory, personal genomics can offer a more precise explanation. We might be able to identify the actual genes that incline a person to being nasty or nice, an egghead or a doer, a sad sack or a blithe spirit.

Looking to the genome for the nature of the person is far from innocuous. In the twentieth century, many intellectuals embraced the idea that babies are blank slates that are inscribed by parents and society. It allowed them to distance themselves from toxic doctrines like that of a superior race, the eugenic breeding of a better species, or a genetic version of the Twinkie Defense in which individuals or society could evade responsibility by saying that it's all in the genes. When it came to human behavior, the attitude toward genetics was "Don't go there." Those who did go there found themselves picketed, tarred as Nazis and genetic determinists, or, in the case of the biologist E. O. Wilson, doused with a pitcher of ice water at a scientific conference.

Today, as the lessons of history have become clearer, the taboo is fading. Though the twentieth century saw horrific genocides inspired by Nazi pseudoscience about genetics and race, it also saw horrific genocides inspired by Marxist pseudoscience about the malleability of human nature. The real threat to humanity comes from totalizing ideologies and the denial of human rights, rather than a curiosity about nature and nurture. Today it is the humane democracies of Scandinavia that are hotbeds of research in behavioral genetics, and two of the groups who were historically most victimized by racial pseudoscience—Jews and African Americans —are among the most avid consumers of information about their genes.

Nor should the scare word "determinism" get in the way of understanding our genetic roots. For some conditions, like Huntington's disease, genetic determinism is simply correct: everyone with the defective gene who lives long enough will develop the condition. But for most other traits, any influence of the genes will be probabilistic. Having a version of a gene may change the odds, making you more or less likely to have a trait, all things being equal, but as we shall see, the actual outcome depends on a tangle of other circumstances as well.

With personal genomics in its infancy, we can't know whether it will deliver usable information about our psychological traits. But evidence from old-fashioned behavioral genetics—studies of twins, adoptees, and other kinds of relatives—suggests that those genes are in there somewhere. Though once vilified as fraud-infested crypto-eugenics, behavioral genetics has accumulated sophisticated methodologies and replicable findings, which can tell us how much we can ever expect to learn about ourselves from personal genomics.

To study something scientifically, you first have to measure it, and psychologists have developed tests for many mental traits. And contrary to popular opinion, the tests work pretty well: they give a similar measurement of a person every time they are administered, and they statistically predict life outcomes like school and job performance, psychiatric diagnoses, and marital stability. Tests for intelligence might ask people to recite a string of digits backward, define a word like "predicament," identify what an egg and a seed have in common, or assemble four triangles into a square. Personality tests ask people to agree or disagree with statements like "Often I cross the street in order not to meet someone I know," "I often was in trouble in school," "Before I do something I try to consider how my friends will react to it," and "People say insulting and vulgar things about me." People's answers to a large set of these questions tend to vary in five major ways: openness to experience, conscientiousness, extroversion, agreeableness (as opposed to antagonism), and neuroticism. The scores can then be compared with those of relatives who vary in relatedness and family backgrounds.

The most prominent finding of behavioral genetics has been summarized by the psychologist Eric Turkheimer: "The nature-nurture debate is over . . . All human behavioral traits are heritable." By this he meant that a substantial fraction of the variation among individuals within a culture can be linked to variation in their genes. Whether you measure intelligence or personality, religiosity or political orientation, television watching or cigarette smoking, the outcome is the same. Identical twins (who share all their genes) are more similar than fraternal twins (who share half their genes that vary among people). Biological siblings (who share half those genes too) are more similar than adopted siblings (who share no more genes than do strangers). And identical twins separated at birth and raised in different adoptive homes (who share their genes but not their environments) are uncannily similar.

Behavioral geneticists like Turkheimer are quick to add that many of the differences among people *cannot* be attributed to their genes. First among these are the effects of culture, which cannot be measured by these studies because all the participants come from the same culture, typically middle-class European or American. The importance of culture is obvious from the study of history and anthropology. The reason that most of us don't challenge each other to duels or worship our ancestors or chug down a nice warm glass of cow urine has nothing to do with genes and everything to do with the milieu in which we grew up. But this still leaves the question of why people in the same culture differ from one another.

Behavioral geneticists will point to data showing that even within a single culture, individuals are shaped by their environments. This is another way of saying that a large fraction of the differences among individuals in any trait you care to measure do not correlate with differences among their genes. But a look at these nongenetic causes of our psychological differences shows that it's far from clear what this "environment" is.

Behavioral genetics has repeatedly found that the "shared environment"—everything that siblings growing up in the same home have in common, including their parents, their neighborhood, their home, their peer group, and their school—has less of an influence on the way they turn out than their genes. In many studies, the shared environment has no measurable influence on the adult at all. Siblings reared together end up no more similar than siblings reared apart, and adoptive siblings reared in the same family end up not similar at all. A large chunk of the variation among people in intelligence and personality is not predictable from any obvious feature of the world of their childhood.

Think of a pair of identical twins you know. They are probably highly similar, but they are certainly not indistinguishable. They clearly have their own personalities, and in some cases one twin can be gay and the other straight, or one schizophrenic and the other not. But where could these differences have come from? Not from their genes, which are identical. And not from their parents or siblings or neighborhood or school either, which were also, in most cases, identical. Behavioral geneticists attribute this mysterious variation to the "nonshared" or "unique" environment, but that is just a fudge factor introduced to make the numbers add up to 100 percent.

No one knows what the nongenetic causes of individuality are. Perhaps people are shaped by modifications of genes that take place after conception, or by haphazard fluctuations in the chemical soup in the womb or the wiring up of the brain or the expression of the genes themselves. Even in the simplest organisms, genes are not turned on and off like clockwork but are subject to a lot of random noise, which is why genetically identical fruit flies bred in controlled laboratory conditions can end up with unpredictable differences in their anatomy. This genetic roulette must be even more significant in an organism as complex as a human, and it tells us that the two traditional shapers of a person, nature and nurture, must be augmented by a third one, brute chance.

The discoveries of behavioral genetics call for another adjustment to our traditional conception of a nature-nurture cocktail. A common finding is that the effects of being brought up in a given family are sometimes detectable in childhood, but that they tend to peter out by the time the child has grown up. That is, the reach of the genes appears to get stronger as we age, not weaker. Perhaps our genes affect our environments, which in turn affect ourselves. Young children are at the mercy of parents and have to adapt to a world that is not of their choosing. As they get older, however, they can gravitate to the microenvironments that best suit their natures. Some children naturally lose themselves in the library or the local woods or the nearest computer; others ingratiate themselves with the jocks or the goths or the church youth group. Whatever genetic quirks incline a youth toward one niche or another will be magnified over time as they develop the parts of themselves that allow them to flourish in their chosen worlds. Also magnified are the accidents of life (catching or dropping a ball, acing or flubbing a test), which, according to the psychologist Judith Rich Harris, may help explain the seemingly random component of personality variation. The environment, then, is not a stamping machine that pounds us into a shape but a cafeteria of options from which our genes and our histories incline us to choose.

All this sets the stage for what we can expect from personal genomics. Our genes are a big part of what we are. But even knowing the totality of genetic predictors, there will be many things about ourselves that no genome scan — and for that matter, no demographic checklist — will ever reveal. With these bookends in mind, I rolled up my sleeve, drooled into a couple of vials, and awaited the results of three analyses of my DNA.

The output of a complete genome scan would be a list of six billion A's, C's, G's, and T's — a multigigabyte file that is still prohibitively expensive to generate and that, by itself, will always be perfectly useless. That is why most personal genomics ventures are starting with smaller portions of the genome that promise to contain nuggets of interpretable information.

The Personal Genome Project is beginning with the exome: the 1 percent of our genome that is translated into strings of amino acids that assemble themselves into proteins. Proteins make up our physical structure, catalyze the chemical reactions that keep us alive, and regulate the expression of other genes. The vast majority of heritable diseases that we currently understand involve tiny differences in one of the exons that collectively make up the exome, so it's a logical place to start.

Only a portion of my exome has been sequenced by the PGP so far, none of it terribly interesting. But I did face a decision that will confront every genome consumer. Most genes linked to disease nudge the odds of developing the illness up or down a bit, and when the odds are increased, there is a recommended course of action, like more frequent testing or a preventive drug or a lifestyle change. But a few genes are perfect storms of bad news: high odds of developing a horrible condition that you can do nothing about. Huntington's disease is one example, and many people whose family histories put them at risk (like Arlo Guthrie, whose father, Woody, died of the disease) choose not to learn whether they carry the gene.

Another example is the apolipoprotein E gene (APOE). Nearly a quarter of the population carries one copy of the E4 variant, which triples their risk of developing Alzheimer's disease. Two percent of people carry two copies of the gene (one from each parent), which increases their risk fifteenfold. James Watson, who with Francis Crick discovered the structure of DNA and who was one of the first two humans to have his genome sequenced, asked not to see which variant he had.

As it turns out, we know what happens to people who do get the worst news. According to preliminary findings by the epidemiologist Robert C. Green, they don't sink into despair or throw themselves off bridges; they handle it perfectly well. This should not be terribly surprising. All of us already live with the knowledge that we have the fatal genetic condition called mortality, and most of us cope using some combination of denial, resignation, and religion. Still, I figured that my current burden of existential dread is just about right, so I followed Watson's lead and asked for a line-item veto of my APOE gene information when the PGP sequencer gets to it.

The genes analyzed by a new company called Counsyl are more actionable, as they say in the trade. Their "universal carrier screen" is meant to tell prospective parents whether they carry genes that put their potential children at risk for more than a hundred serious diseases like cystic fibrosis and alpha thalassemia. If both parents have a copy of a recessive disease gene, there is a one-in-four chance that any child they conceive will develop the disease. With this knowledge they can choose to adopt a child instead or to un-

dergo *in vitro* fertilization and screen the embryos for the dangerous genes. It's a scaled-up version of the Tay-Sachs test that Ashkenazi Jews have undergone for decades.

I have known since 1972 that I am clean for Tay-Sachs, but the
Counsyl screen showed that I carry one copy of a gene for familial dysautonomia, an incurable disorder of the autonomic nervous
system that causes a number of unpleasant symptoms and a high
chance of premature death. A well-meaning colleague tried to console me, but I was pleased to gain the knowledge. Children are not
in my cards, but my nieces and nephews, who have a 25 percent
chance of being carriers, will know to get tested. And I can shut the
door to whatever wistfulness I may have had about my childless-
ness. The gene was not discovered until 2001, well after the choice
confronted me, so my road not taken could have led to tragedy.
But perhaps that's the way you think if you are open to experience
and not too neurotic.

Familial dysautonomia is found almost exclusively among Ashkenazi Jews, and 23andMe provided additional clues to that ancestry
in my genome. My mitochondrial DNA (which is passed intact
from mother to offspring) is specific to Ashkenazi populations and
is similar to ones found in Sephardic and Oriental Jews and in
Druze and Kurds. My Y chromosome (which is passed intact from
father to son) is also Levantine, common among Ashkenazi, Sephardic, and Oriental Jews and also sprinkled across the eastern
Mediterranean. Both variants arose in the Middle East more than
two thousand years ago and were probably carried to regions in Italy by Jewish exiles after the Roman destruction of Jerusalem, then
to the Rhine Valley in the Middle Ages and eastward to the Pale of
Settlement in Poland and Moldova, ending up in my father's father and my mother's mother a century ago.

It's thrilling to find yourself so tangibly connected to two millennia of history. And even this secular, ecumenical Jew experienced
a primitive tribal stirring in learning of a deep genealogy that co-
incides with the handing down of traditions I grew up with. But my
blue eyes remind me not to get carried away with delusions about
a Semitic essence. Mitochondrial DNA, and the Y chromosome, do
not literally tell you about "your ancestry" but only half of your
ancestry a generation ago, a quarter two generations ago, and so
on, shrinking exponentially the further back you go. In fact, since

the further back you go the more ancestors you theoretically have (eight great-grandparents, sixteen great-great-grandparents, and so on), at some point there aren't enough ancestors to go around, everyone's ancestors overlap with everyone else's, and the very concept of personal ancestry becomes meaningless. I found it just as thrilling to zoom outward in the diagrams of my genetic lineage and see my place in a family tree that embraces all of humanity.

As fascinating as carrier screening and ancestry are, the really new feature offered by 23andMe is its genetic report card. The company directs you to a Web page that displays risk factors for fourteen diseases and ten traits, and links to pages for an additional fifty-one diseases and twenty-one traits for which the scientific evidence is more iffy. Curious users can browse a list of markers from the rest of their genomes with a third-party program that searches a wiki of gene-trait associations that have been reported in the scientific literature. I found the site user-friendly and scientifically responsible. This clarity, though, made it easy to see that personal genomics has a long way to go before it will be a significant tool of self-discovery.

The two biggest pieces of news I got about my disease risks were a 12.6 percent chance of getting prostate cancer before I turn eighty compared with the average risk for white men of 17.8 percent, and a 26.8 percent chance of getting type 2 diabetes compared with the average risk of 21.9 percent. Most of the other outcomes involved even smaller departures from the norm. For a blessedly average person like me, it is completely unclear what to do with these odds. A one-in-four chance of developing diabetes should make any prudent person watch his weight and other risk factors. But then so should a one-in-five chance.

It became all the more confusing when I browsed for genes beyond those on the summary page. Both the PGP and the genome browser turned up studies that linked various of my genes to an *elevated* risk of prostate cancer, deflating my initial relief at the lowered risk. Assessing risks from genomic data is not like using a pregnancy-test kit with its bright blue line. It's more like writing a term paper on a topic with a huge and chaotic research literature. You are whipsawed by contradictory studies with different sample sizes, ages, sexes, ethnicities, selection criteria, and levels of statistical significance. Geneticists working for 23andMe sift through the journals and make their best judgments of which associations are solid. But these judgments are necessarily subjective, and they can quickly become obsolete now that cheap genotyping techniques have opened the floodgates to new studies.

Direct-to-consumer companies are sometimes accused of peddling "recreational genetics," and there's no denying the horoscopelike fascination of learning about genes that predict your traits. Who wouldn't be flattered to learn that he has two genes associated with higher IQ and one linked to a taste for novelty? It is also strangely validating to learn that I have genes for traits that I already know I have, like light skin and blue eyes. Then there are the genes for traits that seem plausible enough but make the wrong prediction about how I live my life, like my genes for tasting the bitterness in broccoli, beer, and brussels sprouts (I consume them all), for lactose intolerance (I seem to tolerate ice cream just fine), and for fast-twitch muscle fibers (I prefer hiking and cycling to basketball and squash). I also have genes that are nothing to brag about (like average memory performance and lower efficiency at learning from errors), ones whose meanings are a bit baffling (like a gene that gives me "typical odds" for having red hair, which I don't have), and ones whose predictions are flat-out wrong (like a high risk of baldness).

For all the narcissistic pleasure that comes from poring over clues to my inner makeup, I soon realized that I was using my knowledge of myself to make sense of the genetic readout, not the other way around. My novelty-seeking gene, for example, has been associated with a cluster of traits that includes impulsivity. But I don't think I'm particularly impulsive, so I interpret the gene as the cause of my openness to experience. But then it may be like that baldness gene, and say nothing about me at all.

Individual genes are just not very informative. Call it Geno's Paradox. We know from classic medical and behavioral genetics that many physical and psychological traits are substantially heritable. But when scientists use the latest methods to fish for the responsible genes, the catch is paltry.

Take height. Though health and nutrition can affect stature, height is highly heritable: no one thinks that Kareem Abdul-Jabbar just ate more Wheaties growing up than Danny DeVito. Height should therefore be a target-rich area in the search for genes, and in 2007 a genomewide scan of nearly sixteen thousand people turned up a dozen of them. But these genes collectively accounted for just 2 *percent* of the variation in height, and a person who had most of the genes was barely an inch taller, on average, than a person who had few of them. If that's the best we can do for height, which can be assessed with a tape measure, what can we expect for more elusive traits like intelligence or personality?

Geno's Paradox entails that apart from carrier screening, personal genomics will be more recreational than diagnostic for some time to come. Some reasons are technological. The affordable genotyping services don't actually sequence your entire genome but follow the time-honored scientific practice of looking for one's keys under the lamppost because that's where the light is best. They scan for half a million or so spots on the genome where a single nucleotide (half a rung on the DNA ladder) is likely to differ from one person to the next. These differences are called Single Nucleotide Polymorphisms, or SNPs (pronounced "snips"), and they can be cheaply identified en masse by putting a dollop of someone's DNA on a device called a microarray or SNP chip. A SNP can be a variant of a gene, or can serve as a signpost for variants of a gene that are nearby.

But not all genetic variation comes in the form of these one-letter typos. A much larger portion of our genomes varies in other ways. A chunk of DNA may be missing or inverted or duplicated, or a tiny substring may be repeated different numbers of times—say, five times in one person and seven times in another. These variations are known to cause diseases and differences in personality, but unless they accompany a particular SNP, they will not turn up on a SNP chip.

As sequencing technology improves, more of our genomic variations will come into view. But determining what those variants *mean* is another matter. A good day for geneticists is one in which they look for genes that have nice big effects and that are found in many people. But remember the minuscule influence of each of the genes that affects stature. There may be hundreds of other such genes, each affecting height by an even smaller smidgen, but it is hard to discern the genes in this long tail of the distribution amid the cacophony of the entire genome. And so it may be for the hundreds or thousands of genes that make you a teensy bit smarter or duller, calmer or more jittery.

Another kind of headache for geneticists comes from gene variants that do have large effects but that are unique to you or to some tiny fraction of humanity. These, too, are hard to spot in genome-wide scans. Say you have a unique genetic variant that gives you big ears. The problem is that you have other unique genes as well. Since it would be literally impossible to assemble a large sample of people who do and don't have the crucial gene and who do and don't have big ears, there is no way to know which of your proprietary genes is the culprit. If we understood the molecular assembly line by which ears were put together in the embryo, we could identify the gene by what it does rather than by what it correlates with. But with most traits, that's not yet possible—not for ears, and certainly not for a sense of humor or a gift of gab or a sweet disposition. In fact, the road to discovery in biology often goes in the other direction. Biologists discover the genetic pathways that build an organ by spotting genes that correlate with different forms of it and then seeing what they do.

So how likely is it that future upgrades to consumer genomics kits will turn up markers for psychological traits? The answer depends on why we vary in the first place, an unsolved problem in behavioral genetics. And the answer may be different for different psychological traits.

In theory, we should hardly differ at all. Natural selection works like compound interest: a gene with even a 1 percent advantage in the number of surviving offspring it yields will expand geometrically over a few hundred generations and quickly crowd out its less fecund alternatives. Why didn't this winnowing leave each of us with the best version of every gene, making each of us as vigorous, smart, and well adjusted as human physiology allows? The world would be a duller place, but evolution doesn't go out of its way to keep us entertained.

It's tempting to say that society as a whole prospers with a mixture of tinkers, tailors, soldiers, sailors, and so on. But evolution selects among genes, not societies, and if the genes that make tinkers outreproduce the genes that make tailors, the tinker genes will become a monopoly. A better way of thinking about genetic diversity is that if everyone were a tinker, it would pay to have tailor genes, and the tailor genes would start to make an inroad, but then as society filled up with tailor genes, the advantage would shift back to the tinkers. A result would be an equilibrium with a certain proportion of tinkers and a certain proportion of tailors. Biologists call this process balancing selection: two designs for an organism are equally fit, but in different physical or social environments, including the environments that consist of other members of the species. Often the choice between versions of such a trait is governed by a single gene, or a few adjacent genes that are inherited together. If instead the trait were controlled by many genes, then during sexual reproduction those genes would get all mixed up with the genes from the other parent, who might have the alternative version of the trait. Over several generations the genes for the two designs would be thoroughly scrambled, and the species would be homogenized.

The psychologists Lars Penke, Jaap Denissen, and Geoffrey Miller argue that personality differences arise from this process of balancing selection. Selfish people prosper in a world of nice guys, until they become so common that they start to swindle one another, whereupon nice guys who cooperate get the upper hand, until there are enough of them for the swindlers to exploit, and so on. The same balancing act can favor rebels in a world of conformists and vice versa, or doves in a world of hawks.

The optimal personality may also depend on the opportunities and risks presented by different environments. The early bird gets the worm, but the second mouse gets the cheese. An environment that has worms in some parts but mousetraps in others could select for a mixture of go-getters and nervous nellies. More plausibly, it selects for organisms that sniff out what kind of environment they are in and tune their boldness accordingly, with different individuals setting their danger threshold at different points.

But not all variation in nature arises from balancing selection. The other reason that genetic variation can persist is that rust never sleeps: new mutations creep into the genome faster than natural selection can weed them out. At any given moment, the population is laden with a portfolio of recent mutations, each of whose days are numbered. This Sisyphean struggle between selection and mutation is common with traits that depend on many genes, because there are so many things that can go wrong.

Penke, Denissen, and Miller argue that a mutation-selection standoff is the explanation for why we differ in intelligence. Unlike personality, where it takes all kinds to make a world, with intelligence, smarter is simply better, so balancing selection is unlikely. But intelligence depends on a large network of brain areas, and it thrives in a body that is properly nourished and free of diseases and defects. Many genes are engaged in keeping this system going, and so there are many genes that, when mutated, can make us a little bit stupider.

At the same time there aren't many mutations that can make us a whole lot smarter. Mutations in general are far more likely to be harmful than helpful, and the large, helpful ones were low-hanging fruit that were picked long ago in our evolutionary history and entrenched in the species. One reason for this can be explained with an analogy inspired by the mathematician Ronald Fisher. A large twist of a focusing knob has some chance of bringing a microscope into better focus when it is far from the best setting. But as the barrel gets closer to the target, smaller and smaller tweaks are needed to bring any further improvement.

The Penke/Denissen/Miller theory, which attributes variation in personality and intelligence to different evolutionary processes, is consistent with what we have learned so far about the genes for those two kinds of traits. The search for IQ genes calls to mind the cartoon in which a scientist with a smoldering test tube asks a colleague, "What's the opposite of Eureka?" Though we know that genes for intelligence must exist, each is likely to be small in effect, found in only a few people, or both. In a recent study of six thousand children, the gene with the biggest effect accounted for less than one-quarter of an IQ point. The quest for genes that underlie major disorders of cognition, like autism and schizophrenia, has been almost as frustrating. Both conditions are highly heritable, yet no one has identified genes that cause either condition across a wide range of people. Perhaps this is what we should expect for a high-maintenance trait like human cognition, which is vulnerable to many mutations.

The hunt for personality genes, though not yet Nobel-worthy, has had better fortunes. Several associations have been found between personality traits and genes that govern the breakdown, recycling, or detection of neurotransmitters (the molecules that seep from neuron to neuron) in the brain systems underlying mood and motivation.

Dopamine is the molecular currency in several brain circuits associated with wanting, getting satisfaction, and paying attention. The gene for one kind of dopamine receptor, DRD4, comes in several versions. Some of the variants (like the one I have) have been associated with "approach related" personality traits like novelty seeking, sensation seeking, and extroversion. A gene for another kind of receptor, DRD2, comes in a version that makes its dopamine system function less effectively. It has been associated with impulsivity, obesity, and substance abuse. Still another gene, COMT, produces an enzyme that breaks down dopamine in the prefrontal cortex, the home of higher cognitive functions like reasoning and planning. If your version of the gene produces less COMT, you may have better concentration but might also be more neurotic and jittery.

Behavioral geneticists have also trained their sights on serotonin, which is found in brain circuits that affect many moods and drives, including those affected by Prozac and similar drugs. SERT, the serotonin transporter, is a molecule that scoops up stray serotonin for recycling, reducing the amount available to act in the brain. The switch for the gene that makes SERT comes in long and short versions, and the short version has been linked to depression and anxiety. A 2003 study made headlines because it suggested that the gene may affect a person's resilience to life's stressors rather than giving them a tendency to be depressed or content across the board. People who had two short versions of the gene (one from each parent) were likely to have a major depressive episode only if they had undergone traumatic experiences; those who had a more placid history were fine. In contrast, people who had two long versions of the gene typically failed to report depression regardless of their life histories. In other words, the effects of the gene are sensitive to a person's environment. Psychologists have long known that some people are resilient to life's slings and arrows and others are more fragile, but they had never seen this interaction played out in the effects of individual genes.

Still other genes have been associated with trust and commitment, or with a tendency to antisocial outbursts. It's still a messy science, with plenty of false alarms, contradictory results, and tiny effects. But consumers will probably learn of genes linked to personality before they see any that are reliably connected to intelligence.

Personal genomics is here to stay. The science will improve as efforts like the Personal Genome Project amass huge samples, the price of sequencing sinks, and biologists come to a better understanding of what genes do and why they vary. People who have grown up with the democratization of information will not tolerate paternalistic regulations that keep them from their own genomes, and early adopters will explore how this new information can best be used to manage our health. There are risks of misunderstandings, but there are also risks in much of the flimflam we tolerate in alternative medicine, and in the hunches and folklore that many doctors prefer to evidence-based medicine. And besides, personal genomics is just too much fun.

At the same time, there is nothing like perusing your genetic data to drive home its limitations as a source of insight into yourself. What should I make of the nonsensical news that I am "probably light-skinned" but have a "twofold risk of baldness"? These diagnoses, of course, are simply peeled off the data in a study: 40 percent of men with the C version of the rs2180439 SNP are bald, compared with 80 percent of men with the T version, and I have the T. But something strange happens when you take a number representing the proportion of people in a sample and apply it to a single individual. The first use of the number is perfectly respectable as an input into a policy that will optimize the costs and benefits of treating a large similar group in a particular way. But the second use of the number is just plain weird. Anyone who knows me can confirm that I'm not 80 percent bald, or even 80 percent likely to be bald; I'm 100 percent likely not to be bald. The most charitable interpretation of the number when applied to me is, "If you knew nothing else about me, your subjective confidence that I am bald, on a scale of 0 to 10, should be 8." But that is a statement about your mental state, not my physical one. If you learned more clues about me (like seeing photographs of my father and grandfathers), that number would change, while not a hair on my head would be different. Some mathematicians say that "the probability of a single event" is a meaningless concept.

Even when the effect of some gene is indubitable, the sheer

complexity of the self will mean that it will not serve as an oracle on what the person will do. The gene that lets me taste propylthiouracil, 23andMe suggests, might make me dislike tonic water, coffee, and dark beer. Unlike the tenuous genes linked to personality or intelligence, this one codes for a single taste-bud receptor, and I don't doubt that it lets me taste the bitterness. So why hasn't it stopped me from enjoying those drinks? Presumably it's because adults get a sophisticated pleasure from administering controlled doses of aversive stimuli to themselves. I've acquired a taste for Beck's Dark; others enjoy saunas, rock climbing, thrillers, or dissonant music. Similarly, why don't I conform to type and exploit those fast-twitch muscle fibers (thanks, ACTN3 genes!) in squash or basketball, rather than wasting them on hiking? A lack of coordination, a love of the outdoors, an inclination to daydream, all of the above? The self is a byzantine bureaucracy, and no gene can push the buttons of behavior by itself. You can attribute the ability to defy our genotypes to free will, whatever that means, but you can also attribute it to the fact that in a hundred-trillion-synapse human brain, any single influence can be outweighed by the product of all of the others.

Even if personal genomics someday delivers a detailed printout of psychological traits, it will probably not change everything, or even most things. It will give us deeper insight about the biological causes of individuality, and it may narrow the guesswork in assessing individual cases. But the issues about self and society that it brings into focus have always been with us. We have always known that people are liable, to varying degrees, to antisocial temptations and weakness of the will. We have always known that people should be encouraged to develop the parts of themselves that they can ("a man's reach should exceed his grasp") but that it's foolish to expect that anyone can accomplish anything ("a man has got to know his limitations"). And we know that holding people responsible for their behavior will make it more likely that they behave responsibly. "My genes made me do it" is no better an excuse than "We're depraved on account of we're deprived."

Many of the dystopian fears raised by personal genomics are simply out of touch with the complex and probabilistic nature of genes. Forget about the hyperparents who want to implant math genes in their unborn children, the *Gattaca* corporations that scan people's

DNA to assign them to castes, the employers or suitors who hack into your genome to find out what kind of worker or spouse you'd make. Let them try; they'd be wasting their time.

The real-life examples are almost as futile. When the connection between the ACTN3 gene and muscle type was discovered, parents and coaches started swabbing the cheeks of children so they could steer the ones with the fast-twitch variant into sprinting and football. Carl Foster, one of the scientists who uncovered the association, had a better idea: "Just line them up with their classmates for a race and see which ones are the fastest." Good advice. The test for a gene can identify one of the contributors to a trait. A measurement of the trait itself will identify all of them: the other genes (many or few, discovered or undiscovered, understood or not understood), the way they interact, the effects of the environment, and the child's unique history of developmental quirks.

It's our essentialist mindset that makes the cheek swab feel as if it is somehow a deeper, truer, more authentic test of the child's ability. It's not that the mindset is utterly misguided. Our genomes truly are a fundamental part of us. They are what make us human, including the distinctively human ability to learn and create culture. They account for at least half of what makes us different from our neighbors. And though we can change both inherited and acquired traits, changing the inherited ones is usually harder. It is a question of the most perspicuous level of analysis at which to understand a complex phenomenon. You can't understand the stock market by studying a single trader, or a movie by putting a DVD under a microscope. The fallacy is not in thinking that the entire genome matters, but in thinking that an individual gene will matter, at least in a way that is large and intelligible enough for us to care about.

So if you are bitten by scientific or personal curiosity and can think in probabilities, by all means enjoy the fruits of personal genomics. But if you want to know whether you are at risk for high cholesterol, have your cholesterol measured; if you want to know whether you are good at math, take a math test. And if you really want to know yourself (and this will be the test of how much you do), consider the suggestion of François de La Rochefoucauld: "Our enemies' opinion of us comes closer to the truth than our own."

RON RINDO

Gyromancy

FROM *The Gettysburg Review*

Gyromancy / noun. [Old & mod. French *gyromancie*.] *Hist.* Divination by inference from the point at which a person walking round and round a marked circle fell down from dizziness.

— *Shorter Oxford English Dictionary*

THE EXTERNAL DETAILS OF this story are well known: On December 23, 1888, during the first of three unspecified "attacks" manifested over several months while he lived and painted in Arles, a village in Provence, Vincent van Gogh sliced off the lower half of his left ear and presented it to a prostitute before being admitted to the local hospital. A second attack occurred on February 4, 1889, which returned him to the hospital, and a third came in early March, which kept him there. Frightened by Van Gogh's odd behavior, the people of Arles had circulated a petition demanding his continued confinement. Distraught and bewildered by his condition, and uncertain if or when another attack might occur, in May 1889, Van Gogh committed himself to the Saint-Paul-de-Mausole asylum for epileptics and lunatics in nearby Saint-Rémy, from which he created many of his most dazzling paintings in a stunning new style.

A month into his voluntary commitment, he wrote to his brother, Theo, "As for me, my health is good, and as for my brain, that will be, let us hope, a matter of time and patience." His good health did not last. Wracked by a far more serious attack that lasted from early July until mid-August, Van Gogh wrote to Theo in September that he feared "a [yet] more violent attack may forever destroy my ability to paint," noting, with understandable gloom, "But I cannot live, since I have this dizziness so often, except in a fourth or fifth rate condition." Between December 1889 and late April 1890, he endured three more attacks, leaving him depressed, disoriented, and exhausted. In May 1890, he left the asylum in Saint-Rémy to take a room in Auvers-sur-Oise under the care of a new physician, Dr. Gachet. But then on July 27, Van Gogh wandered into the French countryside and shot himself in the chest with a pistol. He died of his wound on July 29, with Theo, who had been summoned from Paris, by his side. He was thirty-seven years old.

For over one hundred years, the dominant medical explanation for this narrative has been that Van Gogh suffered from temporal lobe epilepsy and cycloid psychosis. Indeed, his physical and psychiatric symptoms seemed to warrant both diagnoses, first made in 1889 by Dr. Peyron at the Saint-Rémy asylum, and corroborated, posthumously, by many other physicians. But on July 25, 1990, an article appeared in the *Journal of the American Medical Association* arguing that Van Gogh's symptoms may have been caused not by epilepsy or madness, but by Ménière's disease, a chronic condition of the inner ear resulting in recurrent attacks of severe, disabling vertigo. Writing from the International Ménière's Disease Research Institute and the Colorado Neurologic Institute, I. K. Arenberg, L. F. Countryman, L. H. Bernstein, and G. E. Shambaugh Jr. reviewed 796 letters Van Gogh wrote between 1884 and his death in 1890. These letters, they argue, "reveal a man constantly in control of his reason and suffering from severe, repeated attacks of disabling vertigo, not a seizure disorder." They note that Ménière's description of his syndrome was not well known in the 1880s and was often "misdiagnosed as epilepsy well into the 20th century." Art historians were thus confronted by a potential new theory to explain the swirling textures and frenetic sense of movement in many of Van Gogh's late paintings, and biographers had new cause to reexamine art history's most famous act of self-mutilation.

I suddenly had a heartening connection to someone who perhaps would have recognized the symptoms of my own most miserable hours. When I look at the vibrating stars and vertiginous brushwork of *The Starry Night*, Van Gogh's best-known canvas, painted at Saint-Rémy in June 1889, I see something gloriously beautiful and original but also strangely familiar: a landscape, town, and night sky that refuse to remain still. Art historians have noted that the scene may be a composite—two different views of Saint-Rémy as seen from the asylum, transformed by Van Gogh's startling imagination, and, I would argue, enlivened not from without but from within, by the pulsating perceptions and spinning sensations of vertigo.

Though young children seem to find milder versions of the sensation intensely pleasurable, on the severity scale of human suffering, uncontrolled rotary vertigo—the nauseating illusion that everything is ceaselessly spinning—is listed second behind chronic, excruciating pain. Severe pain and vertigo could not be more different, so in many ways this opinion reminds me of Robert Frost's poem "Fire and Ice," in which Frost concludes that as a means of ending all life on earth, either option would suffice. Even so, if asked whether I would rather endure excruciating pain or suffer from vertigo for several hours, I would probably choose vertigo. In other words, I would choose ice over fire. But it would not be an easy decision.

Human beings who have suffered horrific pain—patients of surgery in the days before anesthetics, such as Abigail Smith, the adult daughter of John and Abigail Adams, who endured a mastectomy performed by four surgeons in a twenty-five-minute operation in the Adamses' bedroom in 1811—visit a landscape most of us will never encounter. With the advent of anesthesia and the widespread availability of powerful opiates such as morphine and codeine, few human beings will ever know the agony of Abigail Smith. Many, however—40 percent of American adults, by most estimates—will, at least once, experience the spins. Of those, about 5 percent will endure chronic vertigo, recurring episodes of symptoms so debilitating the sufferers are rendered helpless for hours or days. The worst of these cases, Van Gogh's likely among them, might be bedridden or housebound for months, invalids at the mercy of vestibular systems gone awry.

Some cases, like mine, will be comparatively mild, striking with some warning, leaving one in a perpetual state of spinning and nausea for hours at a time before abating. The episode will last, at most, four to six weeks as the symptoms recede with the help of medication, and then a few months, a year, or far longer might pass before the vertigo strikes again.

My first attack came when I was in my late twenties. Newly married and in graduate school, and living in a small, second-floor apartment on the east side of Milwaukee, I had come down with what I thought was an infection in my right ear. I couldn't hear well. The fluid inside crackled whenever I chewed. I also had tinnitus, a constant, high-pitched ringing that seemed to come from somewhere in the middle of my head. Moreover, I felt lightheaded for days. Standing up rapidly from a sitting position would result in a strange, fluttering sensation that lasted five or ten seconds, as if I were seeing the world through rapidly blinking eyelids, accompanied by the sensation of falling off a cliff in a dream.

That afternoon, walking home to my apartment, I felt as if the sidewalk were dropping away from me with each step. I entered the apartment and walked to my desk, and as I bent over to set my backpack on the floor, instantly the world around me began to spin wildly. The sensation panicked me. My heart pounding, I lurched back toward the door, listed to the right, then bumped into a chair, the bookshelf, the wall. Because the floor seemed to be moving, walking became almost impossible, crawling in a straight line nearly so. Having never experienced anything like this complete disorientation, I feared I was having a stroke.

I found the door and burst into the hallway in search of a neighbor who might help me, looking perhaps like someone who had had too much to drink. Sweat covered my face and soaked into my hair and my shirt, and I had to fight to keep from vomiting. It was as if I were walking through a large tube that kept rolling clockwise beneath my feet. Everything on the vertical plane spun as well, from right to left, like a counterclockwise slide show of the same images. If I stared at a single object—a doorknob, for example—it looked as if the same doorknob were on every card in a deck of cards and someone was flicking rapidly through the deck. Sliding my right shoulder along the wall, closing my eyes as much as I could, which was the only way I could keep from falling, I approached the door of my nearest neighbor, a kindly older woman named Betty, and knocked. As I stood waiting with my head against the doorframe and my eyes closed, miraculously the spinning began to slow. After ten or fifteen seconds with my head held perfectly still, it stopped altogether.

Betty greeted me with some alarm. As I tried to explain what had just happened, she listened politely and nodded, said that she herself had dizzy spells from time to time. Perhaps, she suggested, my blood pressure was low. When she asked me if I wanted her to call an ambulance, I said no, I thought I would be all right. I carefully walked back to my apartment, feeling exhausted, lightheaded, nauseated, and frightened. I ended up walking a few blocks to the emergency room of the nearest hospital, where I explained my symptoms to the unconcerned young doctor who examined me.

"So you think you had a stroke, huh?" he asked, barely concealing a smile. "Maybe," I said. He shook his head and smiled. "You didn't have a stroke. You had vertigo." He told me to take decongestants to try to clear the fluid from my ear, and he gave me a prescription for Antivert, a brand name of the drug meclazine, which would help to control the vertigo if it returned. I didn't realize then how important meclazine would become in my life for the next ten or twelve years.

To maintain level movement through space, airplanes, spacecraft, and ships employ a gyroscope or gyrocompass, an instrument consisting of a wheel mounted inside a ring with an axis free to turn in any direction. It looks something like a top shaped like the rings of Saturn mounted inside a round wire cage. No matter which direction a ship is tossed by the sea, the gyroscope retains a level orientation. To maintain our own sense of balance, human beings have a vestibular system that consists of an intricate network of nerves, tiny bones, and a pair of fluid-filled vestibular labyrinths, one within each inner ear, which are about the size of large, cooked macaroni noodles. Each labyrinth comprises the vestibule, the cochlea, and the three tiny, semicircular canals of the inner ear: the horizontal, posterior, and superior canal. These canals, which are set at right angles to each other as if located on the x, y, and z planes of a three-dimensional graph, contain fluid and tiny hairs that act as sensors and function like gyroscopes to detect motion and help us maintain balance no matter which direction our head is positioned. All three canals are linked to the utricle, which contains tiny crystals of calcium carbonate that are attached to sensors that detect gravity and motion.

When this vestibular system malfunctions, vertigo is often the uncomfortable result. The system can go awry for many different reasons, from rather mundane causes such as temporomandibular joint (TMJ) disorders, ear infections, or migraine headaches, to tumors and more exotic-sounding conditions such as benign paroxysmal positional vertigo (BPPV), which occurs when the calcium carbonate crystals loosen and float freely in the vestibular fluid, and labyrinthitis, a swelling in the inner ear likely caused by a virus or a blow to the head. The symptoms of vestibular malfeasance— vertigo, nausea, tinnitus, nystagmus (rapid movement of the eyes from side to side), and a feeling of fullness in the affected ear— are usually the same regardless of the diagnosis. The primary difference is that, in most instances, once the condition is identified and treated, the vertigo disappears, almost always for good.

Not so in the case of Ménière's disease, also sometimes referred to as endolymphatic hydrops (the medical term for an increase of hydraulic pressure within the inner ear, thought to be the cause of the symptoms). Identified by the French ear specialist Dr. Prosper Ménière in 1861, Ménière's disease is distinguished by similar symptoms—periodic, usually severe episodes of rotary vertigo, with accompanying nausea and vomiting, diaphoresis (sweating), tinnitus, and fluctuating hearing loss, with pressure and sometimes pain in the affected ear—with two important distinctions. First, these symptoms return following weeks, months, or even years of spontaneous remission. Second, there is a progressive loss of hearing in the affected ear after each subsequent attack. Clinical diagnosis is made based largely upon this recurrence of symptoms, though certain tests, such as transtympanic electrocochleography and electronstagmography, can help to confirm the condition.

At its worst, in my thirties, I would have two or three such attacks every year, each lasting from many days to many weeks. Over the past decade—I am now forty-nine—I have had far fewer episodes, though they have become more severe. Each attack begins with pressure and pain in my right ear, which develop over the course of several days, and a growing sense of lightheadedness. I can move my lower jaw from side to side and hear the fluid in my ear crackling. I might roll over in bed and experience a flash of disorientation, four or five slow, pulsing spins, before my brain settles and adjusts to its new position. I might also be awakened at night by unusual sounds coming from inside my head. Sometimes the noise is like a small explosion, or like the rush of the ocean against the beach. At other times it is uncannily like the sound of a fetus's beating heart, amplified *in utero* at the obstetrician's office. Occasionally the sound seems so real, so certain to have emanated from the exterior world, that I am tempted to wake my wife to ask if she, too, had heard it. But over time I have learned not to do so, because the noise is an illusion, no matter how lifelike it seems.

If decongestants and Dramamine or Antivert don't help, and my symptoms progress, looking down at the floor or up from a sitting position will result in a warm sensation, almost like an electric impulse, arcing from ear to ear over the top of my skull or across the back of my brain stem. The most advanced sign of impending vertigo is a slowly increasing pulsing, a strobelike flashing behind my eyes. These flashes, which are accompanied by the feeling that I am falling, typically last five or six seconds. When they strike, if I hold my head still, I can often stop the onset of spinning, at least temporarily. And if the medications work, and I am careful and attentive for ten to fifteen days—moving my head very slowly, taking time to lie down and gradually rise again, turning over in bed as little as possible—I can forestall a severe attack of vertigo altogether. I will experience brief moments of spinning that last fifteen or twenty seconds, but nothing worse. But sometimes, even when I take every precaution, a full-fledged attack strikes.

Recently, I was coping with the usual set of preliminary symptoms for about a week. On Tuesday, February 19, 2008, at 6:30 in the morning, I rolled to throw my arm over my wife in bed and instantly our bedroom began to spin. I returned to my back, hoping to reverse the process and forestall the symptoms, but too late. Once the merry-go-round gets started, I have no choice but to ride awhile. I can tell when the attack will be a bad one, when the spinning is likely to continue, on and off, for hours, and a palpable distress, bordering on panic, fills me.

Doctors make a distinction between subjective and objective vertigo. Subjective vertigo is when you feel as if *you* are spinning. A drunken person who gets the spins has subjective vertigo. He can trick his brain into stopping them by lowering a foot from his spinning bed to the floor. (Having been in that position on an occasion or two, I can attest that this technique works surprisingly well.) Objective vertigo occurs when you feel stable but the external world seems to be moving. At its worst, when vertigo strikes me, as it did that morning, I experience both. Closing my eyes helps to alleviate the effects of objective vertigo, but the subjective vertigo remains, making walking or moving in any coordinated way nearly impossible. Within one or two minutes of that Tuesday episode, my T-shirt and hair were soaked through with sweat. I got to my feet, stood with my head and one shoulder pressed tightly against the wall, and kept my eyes closed, the only position in which I might eventually find relief—if I could hold it long enough without vomiting.

When people ask me what an attack feels like, I urge them to imagine a severe case of the stomach flu or seasickness while being dizzy and also riding a rapidly spinning amusement-park ride. Add the high-pitched whine of a tinny siren in the ears, and the soaking sweats usually associated with a high fever, and there are the typical set of symptoms of a Ménière's attack. It is not painful at all in the way we understand pain, unless the ear aches, and it sometimes does, but it is a devastatingly miserable episode, perhaps even more debilitating than pain. Your sense of hearing waxes and wanes—sounds seem to arrive from a distance, or up from the bottom of a well. Wracked by nausea and soaked in sweat, your body is of no use to you as an instrument of pleasure or locomotion. Because you must close your eyes to avoid seeing the spinning world, you are rendered temporarily sightless. Worst of all is the state of your head. Because your spinning brain is so addled, you are incapable of reasoning, concentrating, or sleeping. Everything, including your inner life, spins into the vortex. Even daydreaming, that most simple and constant of human pleasures, is almost impossible. Consciousness itself, the steady stream of thought and memory, the touchstone of identity, is numbed until the distress of vertigo ends.

That Tuesday morning, my vertigo came and went in cycles of fifteen or twenty minutes for about three hours. I wretched each time the spins resumed, but because I had not eaten for over twelve hours, my stomach was empty. I had no Antivert so I took Dramamine, which, if I can keep it down, not only reduces the spinning but sedates my brain—puts me, finally, to sleep. When I awoke an hour or so later, the spinning had stopped, though the blockage in my ear and the tinnitus remained. My brain and body felt exhausted.

For the next three days, I was weak, lightheaded, occasionally dizzy, unbalanced, and disoriented when walking. In some ways, it was like living in a funhouse, with all its crooked floors and unusual mirrors. Because of an influenza outbreak in our city, I couldn't get in to see a doctor for an Antivert prescription, so I held another attack at bay with Dramamine and stillness, moving my head as little as possible. Finally, on Friday afternoon three days later, the pressure in my ear started to decrease a bit. I heard the soft crackling from time to time, even as I sat still. I had taken a twelve-hour dose of Sudafed, though I don't know if the pseudoephedrine had anything to do with the abatement of symptoms. My wife, Jenna, and I were scheduled to meet a group of friends for a dinner party at a local restaurant that night at six. They were Jenna's closest friends, and she wanted to go, and I felt as if I could handle it. On the drive into town, three times I felt the pulsing, the flash of warm-up spinning, behind my eyes. Beads of sweat formed on my forehead, but I kept my head still and the feeling passed. Inside the restaurant, seated at a long table with seven other people, I moved as little as possible and conversed while holding my head and torso stock-still.

Vertigo struck anyway. Without warning, the scene at the restaurant began to spin, rushing from right to left across my field of vision. Sweating and nausea followed, and for four hellish hours thereafter the world again spun uncontrollably around me. Jenna brought the car around to the restaurant entrance, and friends held each of my arms and guided me to it. Before departing, Jenna placed a plastic grocery sack in my hands. I didn't need it until three miles from our driveway, when the potholes of our country road seemed to toss the car so violently, my head felt as if it were spinning in every direction. I vomited the rest of the way home. At times, the spinning was so severe that I felt almost as if I were spinning upside down, a disabling, estranging, and frightening illusion.

Once at home, I spent the next hour in the bathroom and two more after that reclined in a chair with my eyes tightly closed. The spinning would pause briefly, a respite so welcome it nearly brought me to tears, but then it would return again without warning. The spinning came and went, came and went, until it slowed and finally, around 10:30 or 11:00 P.M., subsided altogether.

Several days later, I finally got in to see the doctor, who wrote me a prescription for Antivert, twenty-five milligrams, three times a day, which got me through the rest of the episode. It is now April 7. Forty-seven days have passed since the initial attack. The illusive sensations of movement have ceased. I have been able to wrestle and shoot baskets with my youngest son, jog, and roll over in bed without symptoms. And yesterday, accompanied by a light fluttering in both perception and consciousness, the final bit of fullness in my inner ear suddenly cleared. My ear felt almost the way it does when pilots reduce cabin pressure in a descending airplane: I was coming down for a landing, my feet finally on solid, unmoving ground. Outside, the sun was shining and migrating geese were calling. I felt the exuberance of a return to good health, the joy that always comes to me following the end of any protracted illness.

Though I am fully recovered, the attack did not come without permanent consequence. The hearing loss in my right ear continues to worsen, though not yet to the degree that it affects my day-to-day living. If anything, I have come to accept the benefits of partial deafness, particularly late at night, when my older children are still up watching television or conversing with friends on their cell phones. I put my left ear against the pillow and fall asleep, blissfully unaware of the noise.

I am hopeful that many months or years will pass before disabling vertigo arrives again. I will refill my Antivert prescription in the meantime, and I will leave a few pills scattered in various places—the house, my car, my office at work, my fly-fishing box, my wallet. They are distinctively shaped, like tiny eyes the color of butter, not easily mistaken for anything else. The peace of mind this provides is enhanced by the knowledge that even if things get worse for me, sturdier medical intervention is available. During the last episode, my physician offered to prescribe a sedative, noting that many of them, including diazepam (Valium), had proven extremely effective in controlling severe vertigo for many people. I thanked him but declined. I told him I would save that backup for a moment of desperation, when I truly needed it. He replied that if medication no longer alleviates my Ménière's symptoms, surgery is an effective option, though of last resort, since it usually entails the permanent loss of hearing in the surgically treated ear. It is, therefore, unlikely I will ever have to resort to a pistol on a warm July afternoon.

Which is my way of saying that nothing else — no meclazine, no diazepam, no surgical option — was available to Vincent van Gogh. Each time Ménière's strikes me, I imagine how frightened, how disoriented he must have been. From the outside, I am sure, with the exception of nystagmus and the excessive sweating brought on by the nausea — which I believe Van Gogh's caretakers regularly mistook for a fever — he must have looked stable, a body as still as someone at rest. But inside his head and brain was a swirling chaos clouded with dread and misery. If he got up from bed to try to make his way down the street, his uncertain stumbling and delirious sense of himself in space would no doubt cause strangers to believe he suffered from some mental disease. They would, perhaps, cross to the other side of the road.

In our dreams and nightmares, we sometimes experience flying, moving fast, jumping high, falling. As a young man I used to dream of dunking a basketball, something I could never do in my conscious life, defying gravity with the ease of an NBA-caliber athlete. Ménière's provides a similar sense of motion, but with nightmarish rather than dreamlike consequences. The sensory deprivation and sensory illusions are horrific and disorienting in their scale and duration. One's senses of hearing, vision, and touch are rendered not only unreliable but the cause of suffering; no longer are they the windows through which the beauty of the world enters the brain and heart. And without the steady reassurance of a safely meandering consciousness, one's very sense of humanity, even one's sanity, can easily seem under attack.

Gyromancy is an old occult practice of divination in which the participant either walks around or spins inside a circle whose circumference contains the letters of the alphabet or some other series of prophetic codes or messages. The "victim" spins until she is so dizzy that she falls down, and others mark the letter or code upon which the body has landed. Once able to stand, the participant begins to spin inside the circle again until she falls a second time. This continues until she can no longer go on, or until the prophetic message spelled out by her repeated falling is revealed.

The Ménière's sufferer is like an unwilling participant in this divination game, though instead of letters of the alphabet, he is surrounded by the places, the people, and the activities of his daily life—his home and family, his place of work, his weekend chores and hobbies. The spinning might begin at any time, and without the intervention of powerful medication, regardless of the strength of his will, the quality of his health, or the sturdiness of his body, it will bring him down somewhere in the circle, again and again.

When I imagine Vincent van Gogh in France during the last year of his life, alone and far from home, connected to his dear brother Theo only by that stream of letters, I am both awed by his courage and certain of his anguish and bewilderment. Arles, Saint-Rémy, and Auvers have become a gyromantic circle, with Vincent spinning in the center, clawing at the pain and crackling in his whistling ear, soaked in sweat, and staggering clumsily until he falls, again and again. During each attack he is disoriented, weakened by recurring nausea, for weeks unable to reason, to sleep well, to think clearly or even daydream, certainly unable to paint. He cannot be blamed for believing himself mad. The ringing and strange noises in his ear cannot be heard by others. The world that for him continuously pulses and spins is still and stable to his neighbors. His disrupted consciousness is invisible to everyone, yet it has made him unrecognizable, even to himself.

When confronted by chronic illness, human beings often leap to metaphors of struggle or warfare. They say, "I'm going to fight it," or "I'm going to beat this thing." And this is perhaps a healthy and necessary stance when confronted with an illness that might kill. But chronic disease can also become part of identity, worming its way into the sense of self, imagination, and daydreams. Once there it can evoke small transformations. While it diminishes in one respect, it can, ironically, elevate in another, even when, in the end, it defeats the will to live.

Of course I cannot, finally, know for certain that Van Gogh had *essaying* Ménière's disease, or for that matter any of the other conditions physicians have at one time or another ascribed to him—epilepsy, psychosis, bipolar disorder, digitalis intoxication, thujone poisoning, acute intermittent porphyria, and so forth. But when I see the undeniable sense of motion in his finest late paintings— *The Olive Trees, Self-Portrait, The Starry Night,* all painted in 1889—I am comfortable in my belief that Van Gogh transformed the nightmares of Ménière's disease into works of art that have dazzled millions around the world. Like so many of them, I own a print of *The Starry*

Night. It hangs on the wall above the bed where my wife and I sleep. Sometimes the moon shines upon it while we dream. And sometimes I lie on my back beneath it, soaked in sweat, nauseated, my brain pummeled by the illusion that the earth is trying to spin me off its belly into space. I can open my eyes, then, and see the night sky Van Gogh created. Even in the midst of my worst hours, I find some comfort there.

• Does he side-step risks of meditation on illness?

    – opens it w/ Van Gogh rather than starting w/ self

    – balance horizontal & vertical using research & white space

    – uses concrete images to help us understand (macaroni noodles)

DAVID SEDARIS

Guy Walks into a Bar Car

FROM *The New Yorker*

IN THE GOLDEN AGE of American travel, the platforms of train stations were knee deep in what looked like fog. You see it all the time in black-and-white movies, these low-lying eddies of silver. I always thought it was steam from the engines, but now I wonder if it didn't come from cigarettes. You could smoke everywhere back then: in the dining car, in your sleeping berth. Depending on your preference, it was either absolute heaven or absolute hell.

I know there was a smoking car on the Amtrak I took from Raleigh to Chicago in 1984, but seven years later it was gone. By then if you wanted a cigarette your only option was to head for the bar. It sounds all right in passing, romantic even — "the bar on the Lake Shore Limited" — but in fact it was rather depressing. Too bright, too loud, and full of alcoholics who commandeered the seats immediately after boarding and remained there, marinating like cheap kebabs, until they reached their destinations. At first, their voices might strike you as jolly: the warm tones of strangers becoming friends. Then the drinkers would get sloppy and repetitive, settling, finally, on that cross-eyed mush that passes for alcoholic sincerity.

On the train I took from New York to Chicago in early January of 1991, one of the drunks pulled down his pants and shook his bare bottom at the woman behind the bar. I was thirty-four, old enough to know better, yet I laughed along with everyone else. The trip was interminable — almost nineteen hours, not counting any delays — but nothing short of a derailment could have soured my good mood. I was off to see the boyfriend I'd left behind when I moved to New York. We'd known each other for six years, and though we'd broken up more times than either of us could count, there was the hope that this visit might reunite us. Then he'd join me for a fresh start in Manhattan, and all our problems would disappear.

It was best for both of us that it didn't work out that way, though of course I couldn't see it at the time. The trip designed to bring us back together tore us apart for good, and it was a considerably sorrier me that boarded the Limited back to New York. My train left Union Station in the early evening. The late-January sky was the color of pewter, and the ground beneath it — as flat as rolled-out dough — was glazed with slush. I watched as the city receded into the distance, and then I went to the bar car for a cigarette. Of the dozen or so drunks who'd staggered on board in Chicago, one in particular stood out. I've always had an eye for ruined-looking men, and that's what attracted me to this guy — I'll call him Johnny Ryan — the sense that he'd been kicked around. By the time he hit thirty, a hardness would likely settle about his mouth and eyes, but as it was — at twenty-nine — he was right on the edge, a screw-top bottle of wine the day before it turns to vinegar.

It must have been he who started the conversation, as I'd never have had the nerve. Under different circumstances, I might have stammered hello and run back to my seat, but my breakup convinced me that something major was about to happen. The chance of a lifetime was coming my way, and in order to accept it I needed to loosen up, to stop being so "rigid." That was what my former boyfriend had called me. He'd thrown in "judgmental" while he was at it, another of those synonyms for "no fun at all." The fact that it stung reaffirmed what I had always suspected: it was all true. No one was duller, more prudish and set in his ways, than I was.

Johnny didn't strike me as gay, but it was hard to tell with alcoholics. Like prisoners and shepherds, many of them didn't care who they had sex with, the idea being that what happens in the dark stays in the dark. It's the next morning you have to worry about — the name-calling, the slamming of doors, the charge that you somehow cast a spell. I must have been desperate to think that such a person would lead me to a new life. Not that Johnny was bad company — it's just that the things we had in common were all so depressing. Unemployment, for instance. My last job had been as an elf at Macy's.

"Personal assistant" was how I phrased it, hoping he wouldn't ask for whom.

"Uh—Santa?"

His last job had involved hazardous chemicals. An accident at Thanksgiving had caused boils to rise on his back. A few months before that, a tankard of spilled benzene had burned all the hair off his arms and hands. This only made him more attractive. I imagined those smooth pink mitts of his opening the door to the rest of my life.

"So are you just going to stand here smoking all night?" he asked.

Normally, I waited until nine o'clock to start drinking, but "What the heck," I said. "I'll have a beer. Why not?" When a couple of seats opened up, Johnny and I took them. Across the narrow carriage, a black man with a bushy mustache pounded on the Formica tabletop. "So a nun goes into town," he said, "and sees a sign reading, 'Quickies—Twenty-five Dollars.' Not sure what it means, she walks back to the convent and pulls aside the mother superior. 'Excuse me,' she asks, 'but what's a quickie?'"

"And the old lady goes, 'Twenty-five dollars. Just like in town.'"

As the car filled with laughter, Johnny lit a fresh cigarette. "Some comedian," he said. I don't know how we got onto the subject of gambling—perhaps I asked if he had a hobby.

"I'll bet on sporting events, on horses and greyhounds—hell, put two fleas on the table and I'll bet over which one can jump the highest. How about you?"

Gambling to me is what a telephone pole might be to a groundhog. He sees that it's there but doesn't for the life of him understand why. Friends have tried to explain the appeal, but still I don't get it. Why take chances with money?

Johnny had gone to Gamblers Anonymous, but the whining got on his nerves, and he quit after his third meeting. Now, he confessed, he was on his way to Atlantic City, where he hoped to clean up at the blackjack tables.

"All right," called the black man on the other side of the carriage. "I've got another one. What do you have if you have nuts on a wall?" He lit a cigarette and blew out the match. "Walnuts!"

A red-nosed woman in a decorative sweatshirt started to talk, but the black fellow told her that he wasn't done yet. "What do you have if you have nuts on your chest?" He waited a beat. "Chestnuts! What do you have when you have nuts on your chin?" He looked from face to face. "A dick in your mouth!"

"Now, that's good," Johnny said. "I'll have to remember that."

"I'll have to remind you," I told him, trembling a little at my forwardness. "I mean . . . I'm pretty good at holding on to jokes."

As the black man settled down, I asked Johnny about his family. It didn't surprise me that his mother and father were divorced. Each of them was fifty-four years old, and each was currently living with someone much younger. "My dad's girlfriend—fiancée, I guess I should call her—is no older than me," Johnny said. "Before losing my job, I had my own place, but now I'm living with them. Just, you know, until I get back on my feet."

I nodded.

"My mom, meanwhile, is a total mess," he said. "Total pothead, total motormouth, total perfect match for her asshole thirty-year-old boyfriend."

Nothing in this guy's life sounded normal to me. Take food: He could recall his mother rolling joints on the kitchen counter, but he couldn't remember her cooking a single meal, not even on holidays. For dinner, they'd eat takeout hamburgers or pizzas, sometimes a sandwich slapped together over the sink. Johnny didn't cook, either. Neither did his father or his future stepmother. I asked what was in their refrigerator, and he said, "Ketchup, beer, mixers—what else?" He had no problem referring to himself as an alcoholic. "It's just a fact," he said. "I have blue eyes and black hair, too. Big deal."

"Here's a clean one," the black man said. "A fried-egg sandwich walks into a bar and orders a drink. The bartender looks him up and down, then goes, 'Sorry, we don't serve food here.'"

"Oh, that's old," one of his fellow drunks said. "Not only that but it's supposed to be a hamburger, not a fried-egg sandwich."

"It's supposed to be *food* is what it's supposed to be," the black man told him. "As to what that food is, I'll make it whatever the hell I want to."

"Amen," Johnny said, and the black man gave him a thumbs-up.

His next joke went over much better. "What did the leper say to the prostitute? 'Keep the tip.'"

I pictured what looked like a mushroom cap resting in the palm of an outstretched hand. Then I covered my mouth and laughed so hard that beer trickled out of my nose. I was just mopping it up when the last call was announced, and everyone raced to the counter to stock up. Some of the drinkers would be at it until morning, when the bar reopened, while others would find their seats and sleep for a while before returning.

As for Johnny, he had a fifth of Smirnoff in his suitcase. I had two Valiums in mine, and, because I have never much cared for sedatives, the decision to share them came easily. An hour later, it was agreed that we needed to smoke some pot. Each of us was holding, so the only question was where to smoke it—and how to get there from the bar. Since taking the Valium, drinking six beers, and following them with straight vodka, walking had become a problem for me. I don't know what it took to bring down Johnny, but he wasn't even close yet. That's what comes with years of socking it away—you should be unconscious, but instead you're up and full of bright ideas. "I think I've got a place we can go to," he said.

I'm not sure why he chose the women's lounge rather than the men's. Perhaps it was closer, or maybe there was no men's lounge. One way or the other, even now, almost twenty years later, it shames me to think of it. The idea of holing up in a bathroom, of hogging the whole thing just so that you can hang out with someone who will never, under any circumstances, return your interest, makes me cringe. Especially given that this—the "dressing room," it was called—was Amtrak's one meager attempt to recapture some glamour. It amounted to a small chamber with a window—a space not much bigger than a closet. There was an area to sit while brushing your hair or applying makeup, and a mirror to look into while you did it. A second, inner door led to a sink and toilet, but we kept that shut and installed ourselves on the carpeted floor.

Johnny had brought our plastic cups from the bar, and, after settling in, he poured us each a drink. I felt boneless, as if I'd been filleted, yet still I managed to load the pipe and hold my lighter to the bowl. Looking up through the window, I could see the moon, which struck me, in my half-conscious state, as flat and unnaturally bright, a sort of glowing Pringle.

"Do you think we can turn that overhead light off?" I asked.

"No problem, Chief."

It was he who brought up the subject of sex. One moment, I was asking if his mom gave him a discount on his drugs, and the next thing I knew he was telling me about this woman he'd recently had sex with. "A fatty," he called her. "A bloodsucker." Johnny also told me that the older he got, the harder it was to get it up. "I'll be totally into it, and then it's, like, 'What the fuck?' You know?"

"Oh, definitely."

He poured more vodka into his plastic cup and swirled it around, as if it were a fine cognac that needed to breathe. "You get into a lot of fights?" he asked.

"Arguments?"

"No," he said. "I mean with your fists. You ever punch people?"

I relit the pipe and thought of the dustup my former boyfriend and I had had before I left. It was the first time since the fifth grade that I'd hit someone not directly related to me, and it left me feeling like a grade A moron. This had a lot to do with my punch, which was actually more of a slap. To make it worse, I'd then slipped on the icy sidewalk and fallen into a bank of soft gray snow.

There was no need to answer Johnny's fistfight question. The subject had been raised for his benefit rather than mine, an excuse to bemoan the circumference of his biceps. Back when he was boxing, the one on the right had measured seventeen and a half inches. "Now it's less than fourteen," he told me. "I'm shrinking before my very fucking eyes."

"Well, can't you fatten it back up somehow?" I asked. "You're young. I mean, just how hard can it be to gain weight?"

"The problem isn't gaining weight, it's gaining it in the right place," Johnny said. "Two six-packs a day might swell my stomach, but it's not doing shit for my arms."

"Maybe you could lift the cans for a while before opening them," I offered. "That should count for something, shouldn't it?"

Johnny flattened his voice. "You're a regular comedian, aren't you? Keep it up and maybe you can open for that asshole in the bar." A minute of silence and then he relit the pipe, took a hit, and passed it my way. "Look at us," he said, and he let out a long sigh. "A couple of first-class fucking losers."

I wanted to defend myself, or at least point out that we were in *second* class, but then somebody knocked on the door. "Go away,"

Johnny said. "The bathroom's closed until tomorrow." A minute later, there came another knock, this one harder, and before we could respond a key turned and a conductor entered. It wouldn't have worked to deny anything: the room stunk of pot and cigarette smoke. There was the half-empty bottle of vodka, the plastic cups turned on their sides. Put a couple of lampshades on our heads and the picture would have been complete.

I suppose that the conductor could have made some trouble — confiscated our dope, had us arrested at the next stop — but instead he just told us to take a hike, no easy feat on a train. Johnny and I parted without saying good night, I staggering off to my seat, and he going, I assumed, to his. I saw him again the following morning, back in the bar car. Whatever spell had been cast the night before was broken, and he was just another alcoholic starting his day with a shot and a chaser. As I ordered a coffee, the black man told a joke about a witch with one breast.

"Give it a rest," the woman in the decorative sweatshirt said.

I smoked a few cigarettes and then returned to my seat, nursing what promised to be a two-day headache. While slumped against the window, trying unsuccessfully to sleep, I thought of a trip to Greece I'd taken in August of 1982. I was twenty-four that summer, and flew by myself from Raleigh to Athens. A few days after arriving, I was joined by my father, my brother, and my older sister, Lisa. The four of us traveled around the country, and when they went back to North Carolina I took a bus to the port city of Patras. From there I sailed to Brindisi, Italy, wondering all the while why I hadn't returned with the rest of my family. In theory it was wonderful — a European adventure. I was too self-conscious to enjoy it, though, too timid, and it stymied me that I couldn't speak the language.

A bilingual stranger helped me buy a train ticket to Rome, but on the return to Brindisi I had no one but myself to rely on. The man behind the counter offered me three options, and I guess I said yes to the one that meant "No seat for me, thank you. I would like to be packed as tightly as possible amongst people with no access to soap or running water."

It was a common request, at least among the young and foreign. I heard French, Spanish, German, and a good many languages I couldn't quite identify. What was it that sounded like English played backward? Dutch? Swedish? If I found the crowd intimidating, it had more to do with my insecurity than with the way anyone treated me. I suppose the others seemed more deserving than I did, with their faded bandannas and goatskin bags sagging with wine. While I was counting the days until I could go back home, they seemed to have a real talent for living.

When I was a young man, my hair was dark brown and a lot thicker than it is now. I had one continuous eyebrow instead of two separate ones, and this made me look as if I sometimes rode a donkey. It sounds odd to say it—conceited, even—but I was cute that August when I was twenty-four. I wouldn't have said so at the time, but reviewing pictures taken by my father in Athens, I think, That was me? Really? Looks-wise, that single month constituted my moment, a peak from which the descent was both swift and merciless.

It's only three hundred and fifty miles from Rome to Brindisi, but, what with the constant stopping and starting, the train took forever. We left, I believe, at around 8:30 P.M., and for the first few hours everyone stood. Then we sat with our legs crossed, folding them in a little bit tighter when one person and then another decided to lie down. As my fellow passengers shifted position, I found myself pushed toward the corner, where I brushed up against a fellow named Bashir.

Lebanese, he said he was, en route to a small Italian university, where he planned to get a master's in engineering. Bashir's English was excellent, and in a matter of minutes we formed what passes between wayfarers in a foreign country as a kind of automatic friendship. More than a friendship, actually—a romance. Coloring everything was this train, its steady rumble as we passed through the dark Italian countryside. Bashir was—how to describe him? It was as if someone had coaxed the eyes out of Bambi and resettled them, half asleep, into a human face. Nothing hard or ruined-looking there; in fact, it was just the opposite—angelic, you might call him, pretty.

What was it that he and I talked about so intently? Perhaps the thrill was that we *could* talk, that our tongues, flabby from lack of exercise, could flap and make sounds in their old familiar way. Three hours into our conversation, he invited me to get off the train in his college town and spend some time, as much as I liked, in the apartment that was waiting for him. It wasn't the offer you'd make to a backpacker but something closer to a proposal. "Be with me" was the way I interpreted it.

At the end of our car was a little room, no more than a broom closet, really, with a barred window in it. It must have been 4 A.M. when two disheveled Germans stepped out, and we moved in to take their place. As would later happen with Johnny Ryan, Bashir and I sat on the floor, the state of which clearly disgusted him. Apart from the fact that we were sober and were pressed so close that our shoulders touched, the biggest difference was that our attraction was mutual. The moment came when we should have kissed—you could practically hear the surging strings—but I was too shy to make the first move, and so, I guess, was he. Still, I could feel this thing between us, not just lust but a kind of immediate love, the sort that, like instant oatmeal, can be realized in a matter of minutes and is just as nutritious as the real thing. We'll kiss . . . now, I kept thinking. Then, OK . . . now. And on it went, more tortuous by the second.

The sun was rising as we reached his destination, the houses and church spires of this strange city—a city I could make my own— silhouetted against the weak morning sky. "And so?" he asked. I don't remember my excuse, but it all came down to cowardice. For what, really, did I have to return to? A job pushing a wheelbarrow on Raleigh construction sites? A dumpy one-bedroom next to the IHOP?

Bashir got off with his three big suitcases and became a perennial lump in my throat, one that rises whenever I hear the word "Lebanon" or see its jittery outline on the evening news. Is that where you went back to? I wonder. Do you ever think of me? Are you even still alive?

Given the short amount of time we spent together, it's silly how often, and how tenderly, I think of him. All the way to Penn Station, hung over from my night with Johnny Ryan, I wondered what might have happened had I taken Bashir up on his offer. I imagined our apartment overlooking a square: the burbling fountain, the drawings of dams and bridges piled neatly on the desk.

When you're young, it's easy to believe that such an opportunity will come again, maybe even a better one. Instead of a Lebanese guy in Italy, it might be a Nigerian one in Belgium, or maybe a Pole in Turkey. You tell yourself that if you traveled alone to Europe this summer you could surely do the same thing next year and the year after that. Of course, you don't, though, and the next thing you know you're an aging, unemployed elf, so desperate for love that you spend your evening mooning over a straight alcoholic.

The closer we got to New York the more miserable I became. Then I thought of this guy my friend Lili and I had borrowed a ladder from a few months earlier, someone named Hugh. I'd never really trusted people who went directly from one relationship to the next, so after my train pulled into Penn Station, and after I'd taken the subway home, I'd wait a few hours, or maybe even a full day, before dialing his number and asking if he'd like to hear a joke.

- Tradition of Thurber & White (dry humor, satire)

- Embellishing = caricature for humor to throw light on absurd [he says he isn't going to call it fiction, if 98% is true & 2% is embellished]

How is oratory like essay? recursive; conversational

VOICE = IDENTITY
often kill or lose one
side or the other

Discourse Conflict   race, gender, class
→ lose ability to move back & forth (the
tragic mulatto.)

ZADIE SMITH

Speaking in Tongues

FROM *The New York Review of Books*

How does obama fit? politicians vs. artists?
→ artists = parameters of what is going on
→ trying to break down ideology of monomyth
↳ is it about language or politics   > like Borges

The following is based on a lecture given at the New York
Public Library in December 2008.

conversational

1

HELLO. This voice I speak with these days, this English voice with its rounded vowels and consonants in more or less the right place—this is not the voice of my childhood. I picked it up in college, along with the unabridged *Clarissa* and a taste for port. Maybe this fact is only what it seems to be—a case of bald social climbing—but at the time I genuinely thought *this* was the voice of lettered people, and that if I didn't have the voice of lettered people I would never truly be lettered. A braver person, perhaps, would have stood firm, teaching her peers a useful lesson by example: not all lettered people need be of the same class, nor speak identically. I went the other way. Partly out of cowardice and a constitutional eagerness to please, but also because I didn't quite see it as a straight swap, of this voice for that.

My own childhood had been the story of this and that combined, of the synthesis of disparate things. It never occurred to me that I was leaving the London district of Willesden for Cambridge. I thought I was *adding* Cambridge to Willesden, this new way of talking to that old way. Adding a new kind of knowledge to a different kind I already had. And for a while, that's how it was: at home, during the holidays, I spoke with my old voice, and in the old voice seemed to feel and speak things that I couldn't express in college, and vice versa. I felt a sort of wonder at the flexibility of the thing. Like being alive twice.

But flexibility is something that requires work if it is to be maintained. Recently my double voice has deserted me for a single one, reflecting the smaller world into which my work has led me. Willesden was a big, colorful, working-class sea; Cambridge was a smaller, posher pond, and almost univocal; the literary world is a puddle. This voice I picked up along the way is no longer an exotic garment I put on like a college gown whenever I choose — now it is my only voice, whether I want it or not. I regret it; I should have kept both voices alive in my mouth. They were both a part of me. But how the culture warns against it! As George Bernard Shaw delicately put it in his preface to the play *Pygmalion,* "many thousands of [British] men and women . . . have sloughed off their native dialects and acquired a new tongue."

Few, though, will admit to it. Voice adaptation is still the original British sin. Monitoring and exposing such citizens is a national pastime, as popular as sex scandals and libel cases. If you lean toward the Atlantic with your high-rising terminals you're a sellout; if you pronounce borrowed European words in their original style — even if you try something as innocent as *parmigiano* for "parmesan" — you're a fraud. If you go (metaphorically speaking) down the British class scale, you've gone from cockney to "mockney," and can expect a public tarring and feathering; to go the other way is to perform an unforgivable act of class betrayal. Voices are meant to be unchanging and singular. There's no quicker way to insult an expat Scotsman in London than to tell him he's lost his accent. We feel that our voices are who we are, and that to have more than one, or to use different versions of a voice for different occasions, represents, at best, a Janus-faced duplicity, and at worst, the loss of our very souls.

Whoever changes their voice takes on, in Britain, a queerly tragic dimension. They have betrayed that puzzling dictum "To thine own self be true," so often quoted approvingly as if it represented the wisdom of Shakespeare rather than the hot air of Polonius. "*What's to become of me? What's to become of me?*" wails Eliza Doolittle, realizing her middling dilemma. With a voice too posh for the flower girls and yet too redolent of the gutter for the ladies in Mrs. Higgins's drawing room.

*

But Eliza—patron saint of the tragically double-voiced—is worthy of closer inspection. The first thing to note is that both Eliza and *Pygmalion* are entirely didactic, as Shaw meant them to be. "I delight," he wrote, "in throwing [*Pygmalion*] at the heads of the wiseacres who repeat the parrot cry that art should never be didactic. It goes to prove my contention that art should never be anything else."

He was determined to tell the unambiguous tale of a girl who changes her voice and loses her self. And so she arrives like this:

> Don't you be so saucy. You ain't heard what I come for yet. Did you tell him I come in a taxi? . . . Oh, we are proud! He ain't above giving lessons, not him: I heard him say so. Well, I ain't come here to ask for any compliment; and if my moneys not good enough I can go elsewhere . . . Now you know, don't you? I'm come to have lessons, I am. And to pay for em too: make no mistake . . . I want to be a lady in a flower shop stead of selling at the corner of Tottenham Court Road. But they wont take me unless I can talk more genteel.

And she leaves like this:

> I can't. I could have done it once; but now I can't go back to it. Last night, when I was wandering about, a girl spoke to me; and I tried to get back into the old way with her; but it was no use. You told me, you know, that when a child is brought to a foreign country, it picks up the language in a few weeks, and forgets its own. Well, I am a child in your country. I have forgotten my own language, and can speak nothing but yours.

By the end of his experiment, Professor Higgins has made his Eliza an awkward, in-between thing, neither flower girl nor lady, with one voice lost and another gained, at the steep price of everything she was and everything she knows. Almost as an afterthought, he sends Eliza's father, Alfred Doolittle, to his doom, too, securing a three-thousand-a-year living for the man on the condition that Doolittle lecture for the Wannafeller Moral Reform World League up to six times a year. This burden brings the philosophical dustman into the close, unwanted embrace of what he disdainfully calls "middle class morality." By the time the curtain goes down, both Doolittles find themselves stuck in the middle, which is, to Shaw, a comi-tragic place to be, with the emphasis on the tragic. What are they fit for? What will become of them?

How persistent this horror of the middling spot is, this dread of the interim place! It extends through the specter of the tragic mulatto, to the plight of the transsexual, to our present anxiety—disguised as genteel concern—for the contemporary immigrant, tragically split, we are sure, between worlds, ideas, cultures, voices—whatever will become of them? Something's got to give—one voice must be sacrificed for the other. What is double must be made singular.

But this, the apparent didactic moral of Eliza's story, is undercut by the fact of the play itself, which is an orchestra of many voices, simultaneously and perfectly rendered, with no shade of color or tone sacrificed. Higgins's Harley Street high-handedness is the equal of Mrs. Pierce's lower-middle-class gentility, Pickering's kindhearted aristocratic imprecision every bit as convincing as Arthur Doolittle's Nietzschean Cockney-by-way-of-Wales. Shaw had a wonderful ear, able to reproduce almost as many quirks of the English language as Shakespeare. Shaw was in possession of a gift he wouldn't, or couldn't, give Eliza: he spoke in tongues.

It gives me a strange sensation to turn from Shaw's melancholy Pygmalion story to another, infinitely more hopeful version, written by the new president of the United States of America. Of course, his ear isn't half bad either. In *Dreams from My Father,* the new president displays an enviable facility for dialogue, and puts it to good use, animating a cast every bit as various as the one James Baldwin—an obvious influence—conjured for his own many-voiced novel *Another Country.* Obama can do young Jewish male, black old lady from the South Side, white woman from Kansas, Kenyan elders, white Harvard nerds, black Columbia nerds, activist women, churchmen, security guards, bank tellers, and even a British man called Mr. Wilkerson, who on a starry night on safari says credibly British things like, "I believe that's the Milky Way." This new president doesn't just speak *for* his people. He can *speak* them. It is a disorienting talent in a president; we're so unused to it. I have to pinch myself to remember who wrote the following well-observed scene, seemingly plucked from a comic novel:

> "Man, I'm not going to any more of these bullshit Punahou parties."
> "Yeah, that's what you said the last time . . ."
> "I mean it this time . . .. These girls are A-1, USDA-certified racists. All

of 'em. White girls. Asian girls—shoot, these Asians worse than the whites. Think we got a disease or something."

"Maybe they're looking at that big butt of yours. Man, I thought you were in training."

"Get your hands out of my fries. You ain't my bitch, nigger . . . buy your own damn fries. Now what was I talking about?"

"Just 'cause a girl don't go out with you doesn't make her a racist."

This is the voice of Obama at seventeen, as remembered by Obama. He's still recognizably Obama; he already seeks to unpack and complicate apparently obvious things ("Just 'cause a girl don't go out with you doesn't make her a racist"); he's already gently cynical about the impassioned dogma of other people ("Yeah, that's what you said the last time"). And he has a sense of humor ("Maybe they're looking at that big butt of yours"). Only the voice is different: he has made almost as large a leap as Eliza Doolittle. The conclusions Obama draws from his own Pygmalion experience, however, are subtler than Shaw's. The tale he tells is not the old tragedy of gaining a new, false voice at the expense of a true one. The tale he tells is all about addition. His is the story of a genuinely many-voiced man. If it has a moral it is that each man must be true to his selves, plural.

For Obama, having more than one voice in your ear is not a burden, or not solely a burden—it is also a gift. And the gift is of an interesting kind, not well served by that dull publishing-house title *Dreams from My Father: A Story of Race and Inheritance* with its suggestion of a simple linear inheritance, of paternal dreams and aspirations passed down to a son, and fulfilled. *Dreams from My Father* would have been a fine title for John McCain's book *Faith of My Fathers,* which concerns exactly this kind of linear masculine inheritance, in his case from soldier to soldier. For Obama's book, though, it's wrong, lopsided. He corrects its misperception early on, in the first chapter, while discussing the failure of his parents' relationship, characterized by their only son as the end of a dream. "Even as that spell was broken," he writes, "and the worlds that they thought they'd left behind reclaimed each of them, I *occupied the place* where their dreams had been."

To *occupy* a dream, to exist in a dreamed space (conjured by both father and mother), is surely a quite different thing from simply *inheriting* a dream. It's more interesting. What did Pauline Kael

call Cary Grant? "The Man from Dream City." When Bristolian Ar-
chibald Leach became suave Cary Grant, the transformation happened in his voice, which he subjected to a strange, indefinable
manipulation, resulting in that heavenly sui generis accent, neither
West Country nor posh, American nor English. It came from nowhere; *he* came from nowhere. Grant seemed the product of a collective dream, dreamed up by moviegoers in hard times, as it sometimes feels voters have dreamed up Obama in hard times. Both
men have a strange reflective quality, typical of the self-created
man—we see in them whatever we want to see. "Everyone wants to
be Cary Grant," said Cary Grant. "Even I want to be Cary Grant."
It's not hard to imagine Obama having that same thought, back-
stage at Grant Park, hearing his own name chanted by the hopeful
multitude. *Everyone wants to be Barack Obama. Even I want to be Barack Obama.*

> beyond monomyth → is what
> is that what Amer,
> ② really is?

But I haven't described Dream City. I'll try to. It is a place of many
voices, where the unified singular self is an illusion. Naturally,
Obama was born there. So was I. When your personal multiplicity
is printed on your face, in an almost too obviously thematic manner, in your DNA, in your hair, and in the neither this nor that
beige of your skin—well, anyone can see you come from Dream
City. In Dream City everything is doubled, everything is various.
You have no choice but to cross borders and speak in tongues.
That's how you get from your mother to your father, from talking
to one set of folks who think you're not black enough to another
who figure you insufficiently white. It's the kind of town where the
wise man says "I" cautiously, because "I" feels like too straight and
singular a phoneme to represent the true multiplicity of his experience. Instead, citizens of Dream City prefer to use the collective
pronoun "we."

Throughout his campaign Obama was careful always to say "we."
He was noticeably wary of "I." By speaking so, he wasn't simply
avoiding a singularity he didn't feel, he was also drawing us in with
him. He had the audacity to suggest that, even if you can't see it
stamped on their faces, most people come from Dream City, too.
Most of us have complicated back stories, messy histories, multiple
narratives.

It was a high-wire strategy, for Obama, this invocation of our collective human messiness. His enemies latched on to its imprecision, emphasizing the exotic, un-American nature of Dream City, this ill-defined place where you could be from Hawaii and Kenya, Kansas and Indonesia, all at the same time, where you could jive talk like a street hustler and orate like a senator. What kind of a crazy place is that? But they underestimated how many people come from Dream City, how many Americans, in their daily lives, conjure contrasting voices and seek a synthesis between disparate things. Turns out, Dream City wasn't so strange to them.

Or did they never actually see it? We now know that Obama spoke of *Main Street* in Iowa and of *sweet potato pie* in northwest Philly, and it could be argued that he succeeded because he so rarely misspoke, carefully tailoring his intonations to suit the sensibility of his listeners. Sometimes he did this within one speech, within one line: "We worship an awesome God in the blue states, and we don't like federal agents poking around our libraries in the red states." *Awesome God* comes to you straight from the pews of a Georgia church; *poking around* feels more at home at a kitchen table in South Bend, Indiana. The balance was perfect, cunningly counterpoised and never accidental. It's only now that it's over that we see him let his guard down a little, on *60 Minutes,* say, dropping in that culturally, casually black construction "Hey, I'm not stupid, *man,* that's why I'm president," something it's hard to imagine him doing even three weeks earlier. To a certain kind of mind, it must have looked like the mask had slipped for a moment.

Which brings us to the single-voiced Obamanation crowd. They rage on in the blogs and on the radio, waiting obsessively for the mask to slip. They have a great fear of what they see as Obama's doubling ways. "He says one thing but he means another"—this is the essence of the fear campaign. He says he's a capitalist, but he'll spread your wealth. He says he's a Christian, but really he's going to empower the Muslims. And so on and so forth. These are fears that have their roots in an anxiety about voice. *Who is he?* people kept asking. *I mean, who is this guy, really?* He says *sweet potato pie* in Philly and *Main Street* in Iowa! When he talks to us, he sure *sounds* like us—but behind our backs he says we're clinging to our religion, to our guns. And when Jesse Jackson heard that Obama had lectured a black church congregation about the epidemic of absent black fathers, he experienced this, too, as a tonal betrayal;

Obama was "talking down to black people." In both cases, there was the sense of a double-dealer, of someone who tailors his speech to fit the audience, who is not *of* the people (because he is able to look at them objectively) but always above them.

The Jackson gaffe, with its Oedipal violence ("I want to cut his nuts out"), is especially poignant because it goes to the heart of a generational conflict in the black community, concerning what we will say in public and what we say in private. For it has been a point of honor among the civil rights generation that any criticisms or negative analyses of our community, expressed, as they often are, by white politicians, without context, without real empathy or understanding, should not be repeated by a black politician when the white community is listening, even if (*especially* if) the criticism happens to be true (more than half of all black American children live in single-parent households). Our business is our business. Keep it in the family; don't wash your dirty linen in public; stay unified. (Of course, with his overheard gaffe, Jackson unwittingly broke his own rule.)

Until Obama, black politicians had always adhered to these unwritten rules. In this way, they defended themselves against those two bogeymen of black political life: the Uncle Tom and the House Nigger. The black politician who played up to, or even simply echoed, white fears, desires, and hopes for the black community was in danger of earning these epithets—even Martin Luther King was not free from such suspicions. Then came Obama, and the new world he had supposedly ushered in, the postracial world, in which what mattered most was not blind racial allegiance but factual truth. It was felt that Jesse Jackson was sadly out of step with this new postracial world: even his own son felt moved to publicly repudiate his "ugly rhetoric." But Jackson's anger was not incomprehensible, nor his distrust unreasonable. Jackson lived through a bitter struggle, and bitter struggles deform their participants in subtle, complicated ways. The idea that one should speak one's cultural allegiance first and the truth second (and that this is a sign of authenticity) is precisely such a deformation.

Right up to the wire, Obama made many black men and women of Jackson's generation suspicious. How can the man who passes between culturally black and white voices with such flexibility, with such ease, be an honest man? How *will* the man from Dream City keep it real? Why won't he speak with a clear and unified voice? These were genuine questions for people born in real cities at a time when those cities were implacably divided, when the black movement had to yell with a clear and unified voice, or risk not being heard at all. And then he won. Watching Jesse Jackson in tears in Grant Park, pressed up against the varicolored American public, it seemed like he, at least, had received the answer he needed: only a many-voiced man could have spoken to that many people.

A clear and unified voice. In that context, this business of being biracial, of being half black and half white, is awkward. In his memoir, Obama takes care to ridicule a certain black girl called Joyce — a composite figure from his college days who happens also to be part Italian and part French and part Native American and is inordinately fond of mentioning these facts, and who likes to say:

> I'm not black . . . I'm *multiracial* . . . Why should I have to choose between them? . . . It's not white people who are making me choose . . . No—it's *black people* who always have to make everything racial. *They're* the ones making me choose. *They're* the ones who are telling me I can't be who I am.

He has her voice down pat and so condemns her out of her own mouth. For she's the third bogeyman of black life, the tragic mulatto, who secretly wishes she "passed," always keen to let you know about her white heritage. It's the fear of being mistaken for Joyce that has always ensured that I ignore the box marked "biracial" and tick the box marked "black" on any questionnaire I fill out, and call myself unequivocally a black writer and roll my eyes at anyone who insists that Obama is not the first black president but the first biracial one. But I also know in my heart that it's an equivocation; I know that Obama has a double consciousness, is black and, at the same time, white, as I am, unless we are suggesting that one side of a person's genetics and cultural heritage cancels out or trumps the other.

But to mention the double is to suggest shame at the singular. Joyce insists on her varied heritage because she fears and is ashamed of the singular black. I suppose it's possible that subconsciously I am also a tragic mulatto, torn between pride and shame. In my conscious life, though, I cannot honestly say I feel proud to be white and ashamed to be black or proud to be black and ashamed to be white. I find it impossible to experience either pride or shame over accidents of genetics in which I had no active part. I understand how those words got into the racial discourse, but I can't sign up to them. I'm not proud to be female either. I am not even proud to be human—I only love to be so. As I love to be female and I love to be black, and I love that I had a white father.

It's telling that Joyce is one of the few voices in *Dreams from My Father* that is truly left out in the cold, outside of the expansive sympathy of Obama's narrative. She is an entirely didactic being, a demon Obama has to raise up, if only for a page, so everyone can watch him slay her. I know the feeling. When I was in college I felt I'd rather run away with the Black Panthers than be associated with the Joyces I occasionally met. It's the Joyces of this world who "talk down to black folks." And so to avoid being Joyce, or being seen to be Joyce, you unify, you speak with one voice.

And the concept of a unified black voice is a potent one. It has filtered down, these past forty years, into the black community at all levels, settling itself in that impossible injunction "keep it real," the original intention of which was unification. We were going to unify the concept of Blackness in order to strengthen it. Instead we confined and restricted it. To me, the instruction "keep it real" is a sort of prison cell, two feet by five. The fact is, it's too narrow. I just can't live comfortably in there. "Keep it real" replaced the blessed and solid genetic fact of Blackness with a flimsy imperative. It made Blackness a quality each individual black person was constantly in danger of losing. And almost anything could trigger the loss of one's Blackness: attending certain universities, an impressive variety of jobs, a fondness for opera, a white girlfriend, an interest in golf. And of course, any change in the voice. There was a popular school of thought that maintained the voice was at the very heart of the thing; fail to keep it real there and you'd never see your Blackness again.

How absurd that all seems now. And not because we live in a postracial world—we don't—but because the reality of race has diversified. Black reality has diversified. It's black people who talk like me, and black people who talk like Lil Wayne. It's black conservatives and black liberals, black sportsmen and black lawyers, black computer technicians and black ballet dancers and black

[handwritten margin note: deft use of humor while maintaining tone]

truck drivers and black presidents. We're all black, and we all love to be black, and we all sing from our own hymn sheet. We're all surely black people, but we may be finally approaching a point of human history where you can't talk up or down to us anymore, but only *to* us. *He's talking down to white people*—how curious it sounds the other way round! In order to say such a thing one would have to think collectively of white people, as a people of one mind who speak with one voice—a thought experiment in which we have no practice. But it's worth trying. It's only when you play the record backward that you hear the secret message.

3

For reasons that are obscure to me, those qualities we cherish in our artists we condemn in our politicians. In our artists we look for the many-colored voice, the multiple sensibility. The apogee of this is, of course, Shakespeare: even more than for his wordplay we cherish him for his lack of allegiance. *Our* Shakespeare sees always both sides of a thing, he is black and white, male and female—he is Everyman. The giant lacunae in his biography are merely a convenience; if any new facts of religious or political affiliation were ever to arise we would dismiss them in our hearts anyway. Was he, for example, a man of Rome or not? He has appeared, to generations of readers, not of one religion but of both—in truth, beyond both. Born into the middle of Britain's fierce Catholic-Protestant culture war, how could the bloody absurdity of those years not impress upon him a strong sense of cultural contingency?

It was a war of ideas that began for Will—as it began for Barack—in the dreams of his father. For we know that John Shakespeare, a civic officer in Protestant times, oversaw the repainting of medieval frescoes and the destruction of the rood loft and altar in Stratford's own fine Guild Chapel, but we also know that in the rafters of the Shakespeare home John hid a secret Catholic "Spiritual Testament," a signed profession of allegiance to the old faith. A strange experience, to watch one's own father thus divided, professing one thing in public while practicing another in private. John Shakespeare was a kind of equivocator: it's what you do when you're in a corner, when you can't be a Catholic and a loyal Englishman at the same time. When you can't be both black and white. Sometimes in

like an essayist

a country ripped apart by dogma, those who wish to keep their heads—in both senses—must learn to split themselves in two.

And this we *still* know, here, at a four-hundred-year distance. No one can hope to be president of these United States without professing a committed and straightforward belief in two things: the existence of God and the principle of American exceptionalism. But how many of them equivocated, and who, in their shoes, would not equivocate, too?

Fortunately, Shakespeare was an artist and so had an outlet his father didn't have—the many-voiced theater. Shakespeare's art, the very medium of it, allowed him to do what civic officers and politicians can't seem to: speak simultaneous truths. (Is it not, for example, experientially true that one can both believe and *not* believe in God?) In his plays he is woman, man, black, white, believer, heretic, Catholic, Protestant, Jew, Muslim. He grew up in an atmosphere of equivocation, but he lived in freedom. And he offers us freedom: to pin him down to a single identity would be an obvious diminishment, both for Shakespeare and for us. Generations of critics have insisted on this irreducible multiplicity, though they have each expressed it different ways, through the glass of their times. Here is Keats's famous attempt, in 1817, to give this quality a name: "At once it struck me, what quality went to form a Man of Achievement especially in Literature and which Shakespeare possessed so enormously—I mean *Negative Capability,* that is when man is capable of being in uncertainties, Mysteries, doubts, without any irritable reaching after fact and reason."

And here is Stephen Greenblatt doing the same, in 2004: "There are many forms of heroism in Shakespeare, but ideological heroism—the fierce, self-immolating embrace of an idea or institution—is not one of them."

For Keats, Shakespeare's many voices are quasi-mystical, as suited the Romantic thrust of Keats's age. For Greenblatt, Shakespeare's negative capability is sociopolitical at root. Will had seen too many wild-eyed martyrs, too many executed terrorists, too many wars on the Catholic terror. He had watched men rage absurdly at rood screens and write treatises in praise of tables. He had seen men disemboweled while still alive, their entrails burned before their eyes, and all for the preference of a Latin Mass over a common prayer or vice versa. He understood what fierce, singular certainty creates and what it destroys. In response, he made himself a diffuse, uncertain thing, a mass of contradictory, irresolvable voices that speak truth plurally. Through the glass of 2009, "negative capability" looks like the perfect antidote to "ideological heroism."

From our politicians, though, we still look for ideological heroism, despite everything. We consider pragmatists to be weak. We call men of balance naive fools. In England, we once had an insulting name for such people: trimmers. In the mid-1600s, a trimmer was any politician who attempted to straddle the reviled middle ground between Cavalier and Roundhead, Parliament and the Crown; to call a man a trimmer was to accuse him of being insufficiently committed to an ideology. But in telling us of these times, the nineteenth-century English historian Thomas Macaulay draws our attention to Halifax, great statesman of the Privy Council, set up to mediate between Parliament and Crown as London burned. Halifax proudly called himself a trimmer, assuming it, Macaulay explains, as

> a title of honour, and vindicat[ing], with great vivacity, the dignity of the appellation. Everything good, he said, trims between extremes. The temperate zone trims between the climate in which men are roasted and the climate in which they are frozen. The English Church trims between the Anabaptist madness and the Papist lethargy. The English constitution trims between the Turkish despotism and Polish anarchy. Virtue is nothing but a just temper between propensities any one of which, if indulged to excess, becomes vice.

Which all sounds eminently reasonable and Aristotelian. And Macaulay's description of Halifax's character is equally attractive: "His intellect was fertile, subtle, and capacious. His polished, luminous, and animated eloquence . . . was the delight of the House of Lords . . . His political tracts well deserve to be studied for their literary merit."

In fact, Halifax is familiar—he sounds like the man from Dream City. This makes Macaulay's caveat the more striking:

> Yet he was less successful in politics than many who enjoyed smaller advantages. Indeed, those intellectual peculiarities which make his writings valuable frequently impeded him in the contests of active life. For

he always saw passing events, not in the point of view in which they commonly appear to one who bears a part in them, but in the point of view in which, after the lapse of many years, they appear to the philosophic historian.

To me, this is a doleful conclusion. It is exactly men with such intellectual peculiarities that I have always hoped to see in politics. But maybe Macaulay is correct: maybe the Halifaxes of this world make, in the end, better writers than politicians. A lot rests on how this president turns out—but that's a debate for the future. Here I want instead to hazard a little theory, concerning the evolution of a certain type of voice, typified by Halifax, by Shakespeare, and very possibly the president. For the voice of what Macaulay called "the philosophic historian" is, to my mind, a valuable and particular one, and I think someone should make a proper study of it. It's a voice that develops in a man over time; my little theory sketches four developmental stages.

The first stage in the evolution is contingent and cannot be contrived. In this first stage, the voice, by no fault of its own, finds itself trapped between two poles, two competing belief systems. And so this first stage necessitates the second: the voice learns to be flexible between these two fixed points, even to the point of equivocation. Then the third stage: this native flexibility leads to a sense of being able to "see a thing from both sides." And then the final stage, which I think of as the mark of a certain kind of genius: the voice relinquishes ownership of itself, develops a creative sense of disassociation in which the claims that are particular to it seem no stronger than anyone else's. There it is, my little theory—I'd rather call it a story. It is a story about a wonderful voice, occasionally used by citizens, rarely by men of power. Amidst the din of the 2008 culture wars it proved especially hard to hear.

In this lecture I have been seeking to tentatively suggest that the voice that speaks with such freedom, thus unburdened by dogma and personal bias, thus flooded with empathy, might make a good president. It's only now that I realize that in all this utilitarianism I've left joyfulness out of the account, and thus neglected a key constituency of my own people, the poets! Being many-voiced may be a complicated gift for a president, but in poets it is a pure delight in need of neither defense nor explanation. Plato banished them from his uptight and annoying republic so long ago that they have lost all their anxiety. They are fancy-free.

"I am a Hittite in love with a horse," writes Frank O'Hara.

> I don't know what blood's
> in me I feel like an African prince I am a girl walking
>   downstairs
> in a red pleated dress with heels I am a champion taking a
>   fall
> I am a jockey with a sprained ass-hole I am the light mist
>   in which a face appears
> and it is another face of blonde I am a baboon eating a
>   banana
> I am a dictator looking at his wife I am a doctor eating a
>   child
> and the child's mother smiling I am a Chinaman climbing a
>   mountain
> I am a child smelling his father's underwear I am an Indian
> sleeping on a scalp
>   and my pony is stamping in the
>   birches,
> and I've just caught sight of the Nina, the Pinta and the
>   Santa Maria.
>   What land is this, so free?

Frank O'Hara's republic is of the imagination, of course. It is the only land of perfect freedom. Presidents, as a breed, tend to dismiss this land, thinking it has nothing to teach them. If this new president turns out to be different, then writers will count their blessings, but with or without a president on board, writers should always count their blessings. A line of O'Hara's reminds us of this. It's carved on his gravestone. It reads: "Grace to be born and live as variously as possible."

But to live variously cannot simply be a gift, endowed by an accident of birth; it has to be a continual effort, continually renewed. I felt this with force the night of the election. I was at a lovely New York party, full of lovely people, almost all of whom were white, liberal, highly educated, and celebrating with one happy voice as the states turned blue. Just as they called Iowa my phone rang and a strident German voice said: "Zadie! Come to Harlem! It's vild here.

I'm in za middle of a crazy reggae bar—it's so vonderful! Vy not come now!"

I mention he was German only so we don't run away with the idea that flexibility comes only to the beige, or gay, or otherwise marginalized. Flexibility is a choice, always open to all of us. (He was a writer, however. Make of that what you will.)

But wait: all the way uptown? A crazy reggae bar? For a minute I hesitated, because I was at a lovely party having a lovely time. Or was that it? There was something else. In truth, I thought: But I'll be ludicrous, in my silly dress, with this silly posh English voice, in a crowded bar of black New Yorkers celebrating. It's amazing how many of our cross-cultural and cross-class encounters are limited not by hate or pride or shame, but by another equally insidious, less discussed emotion: embarrassment. A few minutes later, I was in a taxi and heading uptown with my Northern Irish husband and our half-Indian, half-English friend, but that initial hesitation was ominous; the first step on a typical British journey. A hesitation in the face of difference, which leads to caution before difference and ends in fear of it. Before long, the only voice you recognize, the only life you can empathize with, is your own. You will think that a novelist's screwy leap of logic. Well, it's my novelist credo and I believe it. I believe that flexibility of voice leads to a flexibility in all things. My audacious hope in Obama is based, I'm afraid, on precisely such flimsy premises.

It's my audacious hope that a man born and raised between opposing dogmas, between cultures, between voices, could not help but be aware of the extreme contingency of culture. I further audaciously hope that such a man will not mistake the happy accident of his own cultural sensibilities for a set of natural laws, suitable for general application. I even hope that he will find himself in agreement with George Bernard Shaw when he declared, "Patriotism is, fundamentally, a conviction that a particular country is the best in the world because you were born in it." But that may be an audacious hope too far. We'll see if Obama's lifelong vocal flexibility will enable him to say proudly with one voice, "I love my country," while saying with another voice, "It is a country like other countries." I hope so. He seems just the man to demonstrate that between those two voices there exists no contradiction and no equivocation but rather a proper and decent human harmony.

S. FREDERICK STARR

Rediscovering Central Asia

FROM *The Wilson Quarterly*

IN A.D. 998, TWO YOUNG MEN living nearly two hundred miles apart, in present-day Uzbekistan and Turkmenistan, entered into a correspondence. With verbal jousting that would not sound out of place in a twenty-first-century laboratory, they debated eighteen questions, several of which resonate strongly even today.

Are there other solar systems out among the stars, they asked, or are we alone in the universe? In Europe, this question was to remain open for another five hundred years, but to these two men it seemed clear that we are not alone. They also asked if the earth had been created whole and complete, or if it had evolved over time. Time, they agreed, is a continuum with no beginning or end. In other words, they rejected creationism and anticipated evolutionary geology and even Darwinism by nearly a millennium. This was all as heretical to the Muslim faith they professed as it was to medieval Christianity.

Few exchanges in the history of science have so boldly leapt into the future as this one, which occurred a thousand years ago in a region now regarded as a backwater. We know of it because a few copies of it survived in manuscript and were published almost a millennium later. Twenty-six-year-old Abu al-Rayhan al-Biruni, or al-Biruni (973–1048), hailed from near the Aral Sea and went on to distinguish himself in geography, mathematics, trigonometry, comparative religion, astronomy, physics, geology, psychology, mineralogy, and pharmacology. His counterpart, Abu Ali Sina, or Ibn Sina (c. 980–1037), was from the stately city of Bukhara, the great seat of learning in what is now Uzbekistan. He made his mark in medicine, philosophy, physics, chemistry, astronomy, theology, clinical pharmacology, physiology, ethics, and even music. When eventually Ibn Sina's great *Canon of Medicine* was translated into Latin, it triggered the start of modern medicine in the West. Together, the two are regarded as among the greatest scientific minds between antiquity and the Renaissance.

Most today know these argumentative geniuses, if at all, as Arabs. This is understandable, since both wrote in Arabic (as well as Persian). But just as a Japanese writing in English is not an Englishman, a Central Asian writing in Arabic is not an Arab. In fact, both men were part of a huge constellation of ethnically Persian or Turkic geniuses in mathematics, astronomy, medicine, geology, linguistics, political science, poetry, architecture, and practical technology— all of whom were from what today we call Central Asia. Between 800 and 1100 this pleiad of Central Asian scientists, artists, and thinkers made their region the intellectual epicenter of the world. Their influence was felt from East Asia and India to Europe and the Middle East.

Today, this is hard to imagine. This vast region of irrigated deserts, mountains, and steppes between China, Pakistan, Iran, Russia, and the Caspian Sea is easily dismissed as a peripheral zone, the "back yard" of one or another great power. In impoverished Afghanistan, traditionally considered the heart of Central Asia, U.S. forces are fighting a backward-looking and ignorant Taliban. The main news in America from the rest of Central Asia is that the Pentagon is looking for bases there from which to provision the Afghan campaign. In China, the region is seen chiefly as a semicolonial source of oil, natural gas, gold, aluminum, copper, and uranium. The Russian narrative, meanwhile, dwells on Moscow's geopolitical competition there with the West and, increasingly, China. By and large, most people abroad ignore the land of Ibn Sina and al-Biruni, dismissing it as an inconvenient territory to be crossed while getting somewhere else.

Given the dismal plight of these lands in the modern era, who can be surprised at this? Beginning a century and a half ago, Russia colonized much of the region, while Britain turned Afghanistan into a buffer to protect its Indian colonies from Russia. China eventually absorbed a big chunk to the east, now known as Xinjiang, the "New Territory." Ancient traditions of learning had long since died out, and while the Soviets revived literacy, they suppressed free thought in both the secular and religious spheres. A new day for the region began with the creation of five independent states after the collapse of the Soviet Union in 1991, and with the establishment of a new and more modern government in Afghanistan after 9/11. Eighteen years on, all of the new states have preserved their sovereignty and Afghanistan is clinging to life. But several of the region's countries remain destitute, and even the most successful ones are riddled with corruption and still dependent on authoritarian forms of rule. As William Faulkner reminded us in his speech accepting the Nobel Prize in 1950, there is a big difference between *surviving* and *prevailing*. Is the best hope of these lands merely to work their way back up to zero? Or can they possibly reclaim some of the luster of their glorious past, and prevail?

And glorious it was. It is hard to know where to begin in enumerating the intellectual achievements of Central Asians a millennium ago. In mathematics, it was Central Asians who first accepted irrational numbers, identified the different forms of cubic equations, invented trigonometry, and adapted and disseminated the decimal system and Hindu numerals (called "Arabic" numbers in the West). In astronomy, they estimated the earth's diameter to a degree of precision unmatched until recent centuries and built several of the largest observatories before modern times, using them to prepare remarkably precise astronomical tables.

In chemistry, Central Asians were the first to reverse reactions, to use crystallization as a means of purification, and to measure specific gravity and use it to group elements in a manner anticipating Dmitri Mendeleev's periodic table of 1871. They compiled and added to ancient medical knowledge, hugely broadened pharmacology, and passed it all to the West and to India. And in technology, they invented windmills and hydraulic machinery for lifting water that subsequently spread westward to the Middle East and Europe and eastward to China.

But wasn't this the great age of Arab science and learning centered at the Caliphate in Baghdad? True enough. There were brilliant Arab scientists such as the polymath and founder of ophthalmology Ibn al-Haytham (c. 965–1040). But as the Leipzig scholar Heinrich Suter first showed a century ago, many, if not most, of those "Arab" scientists were in fact either Persian or Turkic and hailed originally from Central Asia. This is true of the mathematician and astronomer Mukhammad ibn Musa al-Khorezmi (c. 780–850), who was from the same Khorezm region of the Uzbekistan-Turkmenistan border area as al-Biruni, hence "al-Khorezmi." Algorithms, one of his many discoveries, still bear his name in distorted form, while our term "algebra" comes directly from the title of his celebrated book on mathematics. Similarly, Abu Nasr al-Farabi (c. 872–961), known in the West as Alfarabius, whose innovative analyses of the ethics of Aristotle surpassed all those of Western thinkers except Thomas Aquinas, was a Turk from what is now Kazakhstan, not an Arab.

The extraordinarily important role of Central Asian intellectuals in Baghdad is less surprising when one bears in mind that the Abbassid Caliphate was actually founded by Central Asians. True, the caliphs themselves were Arabs who had settled in the East, but in the process they had "gone native" and embraced the Persian and Turkic world in which they found themselves. One caliph, al-Ma'mun, refused for years after his appointment in A.D. 818 to leave Central Asia, ruling the Muslim world instead from the splendid oasis city of Merv in what is now Turkmenistan. When he eventually moved to Baghdad he brought with him, along with his Turkic soldiers, the more open and ecumenical values of Central Asia, with their blend of influences from the Persian and Turkic cultures.

The movement from Central Asia to the Middle East recalls the ancient brain drain from the centers of Greek learning to Rome. The difference is that even as some Central Asian scientists and scholars were moving to Baghdad, Arab intellectuals were also being attracted to the great centers in Central Asia. In a kind of reverse brain drain, the extraordinarily enlightened city of Gurganj (where al-Biruni lived), in what is now Turkmenistan, became a magnet for Arab scientists, as did the well-financed and opulent court at Ghazni in eastern Afghanistan. Nor did all Central Asians who had been lured to Baghdad choose to stay there.

What territories should we include in this "Central Asia" that produced such a flowering of genius? Certainly all of the five "stans" that gained independence in 1991: Kazakhstan, Kyrgyzstan, Uzbekistan, Tajikistan, and Turkmenistan. No less central to this flowering of the intellect were the great cities of what is now Afghanistan: Balkh, Herat, and others. Add also modern Iran's northeastern province of Khorasan, whose capital city, Nishapur, produced long ranks of innovators during those bounteous years. The boundaries of this "zone of genius" also extend across what is now the western border of China to embrace the ancient city of Kashgar and several other great centers that have always fallen within the cultural orbit of Central Asia.

It is one thing to draw a circle on the map, but quite another to explain why this region—call it Greater Central Asia—should have produced such a cultural flowering. Booming cities provided the setting for cultural life. A traveling Arab marveled at what he called the "land of a thousand cities" in what is now Afghanistan, Tajikistan, and Uzbekistan. The ruins of mighty Balkh, once the capital of this region, still spread for miles and miles across the plain west of modern Mazar-i-Sharif in Afghanistan. In its heyday Balkh was larger than Paris, Rome, Beijing, or Delhi. Like all the great regional centers, it had running water, baths, and majestic palaces—and solidly built homes of sun-dried brick for non–palace dwellers.

It was also richer, thanks to continental trade. Merchants from Balkh and other Central Asian commercial centers journeyed to the Middle East, Europe, China, and deep into India. Traders from those lands brought goods to the sprawling commercial entrepôts in Greater Central Asia. Since slavery thrived throughout the Muslim world and beyond, the bazaars also included large slave markets. Gold, silver, and bronze currency from these thriving hubs of commerce traveled all the way to Gotland in Sweden and to Korea and Sri Lanka.

Central Asia lay at the junction of all the routes connecting the great cultures of the Eurasian landmass. This network of routes, today often called the Silk Road, in its heyday transported a huge variety of goods in every direction. Glass blowing spread from the Middle East to China via Central Asia, while papermaking and sericulture (the production of silk) went from China westward. But the Central Asians were not passive transmitters. For half a millennium, Middle Easterners and Europeans esteemed Samarqand paper as the best anywhere, and the treasures of more than one medieval cathedral in Europe consist of silk manufactured in the Fergana Valley of what is now mainly Uzbekistan.

Traders also carried religions. Greek settlers in the wake of Alexander the Great (356–23 B.C.) brought the cults of Athena, Hercules, and Aphrodite to their new cities in Afghanistan. Then Buddhism found fertile soil across the region, and spread from there to China, Japan, and Korea. Along the way, Buddhist artists picked up from immigrant Greeks the idea of depicting the Buddha in sculpture. About the same time, Jewish communities were formed, Syrian Christian bishoprics established, and Manichean communities founded across the region. In a stratum beneath all these religions lay the region's core faith, Zoroastrianism, with its emphasis on the struggle of good and evil, redemption, and heaven and hell. Zoroaster, who probably lived in the sixth or seventh century B.C., came from the region of Balkh, but his religion spread westward, eventually to Babylon, where Jews encountered it and fell under its influence. From Judaism its concepts spread first to Christianity and then to Islam.

So when Islam arrived with the Arab armies in the late seventh century, it encountered a population that was expert in what we might today call comparative religion and philosophical analysis. Many Central Asians converted, but others did not, at least not until after the period of cultural effervescence had passed. Muslim or not, they were expert codifiers, and one of them, Muhammad ibn Ismail al-Bukhari (A.D. 810–70), brought together and analyzed the hadiths (sayings) of Muhammad, the compilation becoming regarded as Islam's second most holy book after the Qur'an. Secular ideas also wafted back and forth across the region. The astronomer al-Khorezmi wrote a book comparing the utility of Indian numerals (and the concept of zero) with all other contenders, while others mined Indian geometry, astronomy, and even calendar systems for good ideas. Earlier Central Asians had tested various alphabets, including ones from Syria and India. Several local languages opted for an alphabet deriving from Aramaic, the language Jesus spoke. It is hard to imagine a more intellectually open region anywhere.

What distinguished Central Asians from both the Arabs and the Chinese is that they were polyglots. They considered it normal to live amid a bewildering profusion of languages and alphabets, and managed somehow to master whichever ones they needed at the time. Thus, when the Arab armies arrived bearing a new religion, it was natural that at least some officials and intellectuals would learn the Arabs' strange language to see what it offered. Traders soon thereafter began arriving with writings newly translated from classical Greek. Often the work of Christian Arabs, these translations suddenly opened challenging new ideas in philosophy and science to Central Asians. In due course, they were to master and even go beyond their ancient Greek mentors.

The flowering of Greater Central Asia was thus a product of "location, location, location," both with respect to the trade-based prosperity that it generated and to the welter of religions and ideas that came on the back of that trade. But trade alone would not have given rise to the intellectual awakening that occurred, for not all trade unleashes genius. Perhaps it is best to think of trade as a necessary condition for intellectual takeoff, but not a sufficient one.

How important was religion to this explosion of creativity? For many, Islam was the crucial factor. When al-Bukhari embarked on his life-work of scholarship he was doubtless moved by deep piety, as were scores of other great thinkers. Al-Farabi never doubted that his research into the basis of ethics would strengthen formal religion. Others agreed with al-Farabi but insisted that free inquiry and research should guide religion, not vice versa, and certainly not be constrained by it. Still others were outright skeptics who dismissed religion as fine for the mass of society but a farce for intellectuals. This was the view of Omar Khayyám (1048–1123), the brilliant mathematician who is known today mainly for his poetry, a collection of which was introduced to the West in the nineteenth century as the *Rubáiyát of Omar Khayyám*.

All this adds up to the possibility that intellectual boldness owed less to what religion did than to what it did not do. This is important, given the struggle that existed at times between religion and science in the West. But one senses that someone like al-Farabi, who tossed off a major study on musical theory in addition to all his other works, needed neither permission nor encouragement to treat the whole world as his oyster.

Pinpointing the causes of Central Asia's golden age is all the more difficult because the great minds who gave the age its brilliance were such a diverse lot. A few came from wealthy landed families and could live off their estates, while others, such as Ibn

Sina and al-Biruni, won appointments to lucrative high offices. But they were exceptions. Most of the thinkers were full-time scientists, scholars, and intellectuals, or at least aspired to be. With no universities or academies of science to support them, this was no easy undertaking. Even if they assembled a few paying students, the resulting income never provided enough to sustain them. And so, by default, they relied on the patronage of rulers.

Here was one of Central Asia's great strengths. To be sure, a would-be scientist could strike out for Baghdad in hopes of joining the House of Wisdom, an academy of sciences established by the Central Asia–born caliph al-Ma'mun. But there were many local rulers and courts throughout the region, just as there were also in Persia, to the west. All gave a respectful nod to Baghdad but considered themselves functionally independent. Each of these rulers was a kind of caliph in his own right, ruling in a thoroughly authoritarian manner and defending his territory with a large army of Turks. But they also promoted trade, collected taxes, built splendid capitals, and, significantly, spent fortunes on the arts and sciences. One such court was at Gurganj, where al-Biruni worked. Another was at the already ancient walled city of Samarqand, where between 850 and 1000 the Samanid dynasty maintained a magnificent library, intense salons where savants discussed the Great Questions, and a lively social world centered on music and poetry.

There was nothing kind and gentle about some of these rulers; nor were all of them sophisticated as patrons of the arts and sciences. From his capital in eastern Afghanistan, Mahmud of Ghazna (971–1030) ruled an empire stretching from India to the heart of modern Iran. Mahmud was ruthless and viewed culture more as an adornment than a necessity. Yet he successfully engaged al-Biruni, who proceeded to write the first comprehensive study of India and Hinduism in any language. Mahmud also patronized the great poet Abolqasem Ferdowsi, whose grand panorama of pre-Muslim Persia, the *Shahnameh* (c. 1000), influenced troubadours as far away as France and remains a classic of world literature.

The last great explosion of cultural energy in Central Asia occurred under the Seljuk Turks, beginning about 1037 and continuing for more than a century. From their eastern capitals at Merv in modern Turkmenistan and Nishapur near the present-day Iranian-Afghan border, they encouraged innovators in many fields. Among their achievements was the invention of a way to cover large spaces with double domes. One of their earliest efforts can still be seen rising from the desolation of their ruined capital at Merv. Following a circuitous route that led through Filippo Brunelleschi's dome at the Cathedral of Florence to St. Nicholas's Cathedral in St. Petersburg, this innovation eventually defined the cupola of the U.S. Capitol in Washington.

Why did the great age of Central Asia fade? The most common explanation blames the waning of the intellectual whirlwind on the Mongol invasion, which Genghis Khan launched from the Mongolian heartland in 1218. It is true that the Mongol invaders sacked most of the magnificent cities of Central Asia, but three objections undermine this thesis. First, all but a few of the cities quickly revived, thanks to trade and commerce. Second, far from isolating the region, the Mongol conquest increased contacts between Greater Central Asia and both Europe and the rest of Asia. This happened because the conquering Mongols abolished borders and tariffs within their vast empire. When Marco Polo passed through Afghanistan en route to China in the thirteenth century, he did so with a single "patent," or visa. To the extent that cross-cultural contact was an essential ingredient of intellectual vitality, it flourished under the Mongols.

Third, even if the Mongols had set out to suppress free thought in 1221 (they did not), there would have been no need for them to do so. A full century earlier, much of the cultural energy that had crackled across the length and breadth of Central Asia for hundreds of years had dissipated. True, at Merv in the twelfth century there were still a dozen libraries, one of them with twelve thousand volumes, and there were more than fifty doctors in Bukhara. But as early as 1100, the focus of intellectual life had shifted from bold sallies into vast and unknown territories to the preparation of compendiums of earlier studies and careful treatises on safer, more limited subjects. A sure sign that the formerly bright flame had diminished is the fact that most of the surviving manuscripts from this period are either copies of earlier writings or commentaries on them, not original works.

If the "Whodunit?" question does not point to the Mongols, what caused the decline? Most of Central Asia's great ancient cities today present a picture of gaunt ruins baking silently in the desert sun, the bleakness relieved only by occasional tufts of sage. Viewing them, one is tempted to blame the cultural downturn on climate change or some other ecological shift. But most studies of the region's ecological history conclude that the climate during the boom years was nearly identical to what it is today, and that the main change was the decay of the irrigation systems that were once the region's glory.

Looking beyond the Mongols and ecology, at least four factors contributed to the region's decline. First, and perhaps foremost, nothing endures forever. The golden age of classical Athens lasted barely a century before the city slipped into a lesser silver age. Few of the Renaissance cities remained at a peak of cultural creativity for more than a century and a half. It is natural and inevitable that decline should set in after a high point.

In the case of Central Asia, even more than with the Arabs to the west, the mighty stimulus for original thinking had been the challenge of mastering and assimilating vast and unfamiliar bodies of thought, from ancient Greece, the Middle East, and India. By 1100 this had been accomplished, and no comparably huge body of new learning presented itself thereafter. The European Renaissance should have provided such a stimulus, of course, but by that time the great trade routes that had connected civilizations had seen better days and Central Asia's isolation and decline was becoming entrenched.

Second, religions, like the cultures of which they are a part, go through cycles, beginning in dynamism, self-confidence, and experimentation and then hardening into orthodoxy. In Central Asia, this had already occurred with both Zoroastrianism and Buddhism. In the case of Islam, the greatest flowering of creative thought started early, between 800 and 1100. The hardening into orthodoxy also began early, but did not reach its apex until around 1100. Even then, there remained a few isolated outposts that stayed intellectually vital for another century or so. But in Persian and Turkic Central Asia, as in the Arab heartland and in Persia proper, the demands of a steadily rigidifying Muslim orthodoxy gradually narrowed the sphere in which free thought and humanism could be exercised.

Beyond these "morphological" realities that contributed to the withering of free intellectual life in Greater Central Asia, a third and much more specific factor was at work: the Sunni-Shia split within the Muslim faith. This fundamental division dates to the first generation after Muhammad's death in A.D. 632. By the time of the rise of the first Caliphate in Damascus, the Sunnis were firmly in charge throughout the Muslim world except in Egypt, where the Fatimids, a Shiite dynasty, flourished from 968 to 1171. But even before the fall of the Fatimids, the Shiite faithful were being hounded eastward, shifting the core zone of confessional conflict to Persia and Central Asia. As this occurred, the reigning Sunni rulers across the region tightened their grip on all who might be suspected of schismatic leanings. Many of the great innovators, such as Ibn Sina, had come from Shiite families. Now anyone like him was suspect.

Needless to say, the change hit the freethinkers particularly hard, but it affected no less the mainline Sunnis. Two figures from the town of Tus on the western fringe of Central Asia in what is now eastern Iran epitomized this new direction. The first, Nizam al-Mulk (1018–92), was a highly gifted administrator and also one of the best political scientists of the era. Al-Mulk's teachers had introduced him to works by the best minds of the Central Asian renaissance. But by the time he was appointed vizier of the Seljuk Empire, the battle against Shiite dissidence was at full tilt. Fearing deviance on every side, al-Mulk proposed to establish a network of schools, or madrassas, that would instill orthodox Sunni Islam and turn young men into well-informed loyalists of the faith. Graduates would reject not only the Shiite schism but any other forms of thought that might be suspected of deviance from orthodoxy.

The second transformative figure, Abu Hamid Muhammad ibn Muhammad al-Ghazali (1058–1111), a philosopher and theologian, launched a frontal attack on the dangers posed by the unrestrained exercise of reason. The title of his most famous work tells it all: *The Incoherence of the Philosophers* (i.e., scientists). Like the Grand Inquisitor in Feodor Dostoevsky's *Brothers Karamazov,* al-Ghazali intimately knew his enemy, in this case Aristotelian empiricism, which had attracted the best minds of the region. Attacking Aristotle, he attacked all contemporary rationalists, and to devastating effect.

Together, al-Mulk and al-Ghazali lowered the curtain on inde-

pendent thought that had been raised in Central Asia for three
centuries. Yet Central Asians responded with their typical creativity. With outer forms of the faith hardened and rigidified, they
evinced a fresh interest in individual spirituality. Their highly personal system for achieving a mystical experience of God required
no books, hierarchies, or mosques, and was called Sufism. Central
Asians were acquainted with many forms of such mystical and private worship, thanks to their contacts with Hindu India and their
rich local traditions of Buddhism, Syrian Christianity, and even Judaism, which had thrived in the region's trade centers. How mystical currents within these faiths contributed to Sufism is much
debated, but one thing is clear: even though the first Sufis had
been Arabs, Central Asia became Sufism's heartland. Several of the
first and greatest Sufi movements arose there and spread thence
throughout the Muslim world. Today Sufi poems by Rumi, Attar,
and others have gained a New Age following, but in their own era
they represented a turning inward and away from the civic realm.

Central Asia by no means disappeared from the world's view after 1100. In the fourteenth century, Timur, known in the West as
Tamerlane, conquered the world from Delhi to the eastern shore
of the Mediterranean and then assembled learned scientists and
writers in his rebuilt capital of Samarqand. A century later, Babur
sprang from the Fergana Valley and went on to found the Mughal
dynasty in India. A gifted writer, Babur followed the old Central
Asian practice of gathering creative talent to his court.

Yet Central Asia never regained the intellectual luster it had possessed in the centuries between 800 and 1100. High local tariffs
killed the golden goose that had given birth to prosperity and in-
tercultural contact. Religious orthodoxy stifled the region's most
original thinkers. As the decline set in, Central Asia gradually
ceased to be central to the high culture of all Eurasia and sank into
the status of a remote and dusty boondocks.

From this descent into obscurity it was an easy step to Dan Rather's coverage of Afghanistan and the region in the immediate wake
of 9/11. Donning a bush jacket and filming at dawn and dusk, he
presented the region as inaccessible, backward, exotic, marginal,
and threatening—in short, the end of the world. Ibn Sina, al-
Biruni, and scores of other world-class geniuses from the region
might just as well never have lived.

Even though the Central Asia of Rather's depiction was and is an evocative image, it carries some bothersome implications. On the one hand, it conjures up a place where the best the United States and the world community can hope for is to limit the damage arising from it. This means destroying whatever threatens us and then getting out. The problem is that the thinking behind such an approach can then become self-fulfilling: a place we judged to be hopeless becomes truly so, and even more threatening than before. The fact that Central Asia and Afghanistan are situated between four—and possibly soon five—nuclear powers does not help matters.

Fortunately, this prevailing image of backwardness is not the whole story. Since the region emerged from Soviet and Taliban rule, the ancient continental trade routes have begun to revive. Indians and Koreans flying to Europe stop off there. Half a dozen countries and as many international financial institutions are busily building a network of highways that will eventually link Europe, China, India, and the Middle East. The fact that this is occurring without central direction means that its extent has largely gone unnoticed. But the road-building has now reached the level of an unstoppable force. The opening of routes between Europe and China and across Afghanistan toward the Arabian Sea, India, and Southeast Asia and linking the Middle East, China, and India will, in the coming decade, transform the entire Eurasian landmass. Little that is emerging is absolutely new. Indeed, anyone interested in knowing what the new transport configuration will look like might start by examining the trade routes of the golden era.

Similarly, the opening of Central Asia between 1991 and 2001 is beginning to transform the region intellectually. Tens of thousands of the region's students have gone to study at the best universities abroad. In an act of enlightenment worthy of their predecessors a millennium ago, the governments of Kazakhstan and Uzbekistan have paid for these young people to acquire the most modern knowledge and bring it back home. They return with a passion for reconnecting their region with the global world of ideas. Within the next decade, these young men and women will assume leadership roles in their societies and in the region as a whole. It is hard to imagine that they will consider the prevailing corruption to be normal, or accept Soviet-style controls over their ideas. Even in Afghanistan the National University, the recently established American University, and thousands of lower schools are opening new prospects to the rising generation.

These young people quite reasonably ask, "Who are we?" Answers pour in from every side. Many in the Middle East and even in the West, from the White House down, tell them they are Muslims, defined mainly by the faith in which they were raised. Alternatively, some experts smugly invoke the notions of tribal or clan heritage to explain what they consider the region's hopelessly retrograde politics. Meanwhile, local patriots hail their various national ethnic identities—Kyrgyz, Tajik, or Uzbek—each of which, they insist, is absolutely unique and like no other.

These proposed identities may have some basis in reality. But all run the risk of narrowing the horizons of the emerging generation and limiting their expectations of themselves. The attraction of some young people to fundamentalist religious organizations or narrowly nationalistic groups is also a cause for concern. But Central Asians have ready at hand a meaningful past that lifts up the individual, defines each person in terms of reason and wisdom, and places that person in the mainstream of global developments. This is the great tradition that for three hundred years made their region the center of the world of intellect. Why shouldn't Central Asians and their friends abroad place this remarkable heritage, rather than some narrowly religious or national ideology, as the lodestone of their policies today?

This means focusing more of our support and theirs on reopening the great continental transport routes, instituting freer borders, lowering tariffs, and reducing meddling from the governments. Free trade must also extend to the world of ideas. This means creating the unfettered intellectual space that enabled Ibn Sina and al-Biruni to hypothesize on evolution rather than creationism and even to contemplate the existence of other worlds. Though they each lived under a different government, nobody intercepted their mail and nobody censured their heretical thoughts. In fact, rulers competed to become their patrons and to support their work.

Would this happen today in Central Asia? Several governments in the region are glad to talk of unfettered continental trade but bridle at the prospect of an unfettered exchange of ideas. Yet in every country in the region, there are distinguished champions of the kind of intellectual openness that will give rise to modern Ibn Sinas and al-Birunis. With the emergence of the new generation, increasing numbers of these people are in government. The idea of a fresh flowering of Central Asia may seem a distant prospect, but it is not impossible, especially if Central Asians become more familiar with their rich heritage and draw from it relevant lessons for the present.

If this is the challenge to inhabitants of the region today, the challenge to their international partners is to treat the regional states as sovereign countries, not as culturally inert objects to be shoved around on a chessboard. It is not enough to view them simply as a "zone of [our] special interest," as Vladimir Putin's government does; as a source of raw materials, as the Chinese do; or as a fueling stop en route to Kabul, as the United States does. The better alternative is to acknowledge that somewhere in the DNA of these peoples is the capacity to manage great empires and even greater trading zones, to interact as equals with the other centers of world culture, and to use their unique geographical position to become a link and bridge between civilizations. Such an awareness will raise expectations on all sides, and encourage the region's international partners to view it as more than the object of a geopolitical game.

This, too, won't be easy, but acquiring a deeper knowledge of Central Asia's past is an essential place to begin.

JOHN H. SUMMERS

Gettysburg Regress

FROM The New Republic

LAST WINTER, I was walking with my wife along Seminary Ridge on the Gettysburg battlefield when an odd detail drew into sight: piles of felled trees, stacked alongside a road. The cuts smelled as fresh as the trees looked strong. What happened to them? we wondered. I grew up in Gettysburg, and my mother still lives in the shadow of Lutheran Theological Seminary, low in the lap of the ridge it names. Seminary Ridge is one of a string of ridges surrounding the town; General Robert E. Lee stood there on July 2 and 3, 1863. The woods atop the ridge had made it a sublime place to stroll for as long as I could remember—until that winter walk, which ended with a logging truck lumbering by.

Asking around, I learned that parts of the battlefield were in "rehabilitation." In the hope of providing visitors with an authentic historical experience, the National Park Service was seeking to restore some of Gettysburg's landscapes to their condition when the Union and Confederate armies clashed on them. And so the trees that once crowned Devil's Den—from whose crevices Confederate sharpshooters picked off Union soldiers—were missing also. Hundreds of acres of woodland, actually, were gone or going. (In July 1863, the battlefield contained 898 acres of woodland; since that time, the number has grown to roughly 2,000.) The "rehabilitation," many and varied in its activities, has also rebuilt fences, replanted orchards, and demolished large buildings, including a car dealership. The goal, as NPS regional director Don Barger told the *Christian Science Monitor* in April 2008, is to make visitors "almost feel the bullets . . . That is what you want to have happen in a battlefield."

The project likely delights the reenactors who troop to Gettysburg every year in pursuit of authenticity, as well as those tourists who expect less to encounter history during their battlefield trip than to experience it. Academic historians also appear to approve. University of Virginia professor Gary Gallagher, who advised a recent project at the battlefield, cheers in the current issue of *Civil War Times* that "there has never been a better time to visit Gettysburg." Those who might object to the removal of the trees, he says, are "people who don't understand the difference between a historic park and Yosemite." Rehabilitation has something for everyone: it flatters the left's suspicion of cultural authority, its invitation to ordinary Americans to participate in their history, even as it honors conservatism's fetish for an unchanged, historically correct past. Indeed, Gettysburg, the jewel of America's battlefields, is one of several currently targeted for rehabilitation, including Vicksburg and Antietam.

As a historian, I can appreciate the impulse to restore. But my wife, Anna, felt foul about my explanation of salvation-through-improvement, and together we ruminated on her instinctual reaction at Seminary Ridge: Did those trees really have to go? The more we thought about this question, the more the whole project troubled us. Those trees weighed in our concern, to be sure. But we began to believe we saw something larger, a distinctive pattern of thought sweeping across the battlefield, working in sympathy with the changing expectations Americans apply to their history.

In the Gettysburg Address—delivered just over four months after the battle's conclusion—President Lincoln cautioned that "we cannot dedicate, we cannot consecrate, we cannot hallow this ground. The brave men, living and dead, who struggled here, have consecrated it, far above our poor power to add or detract." In this season of Lincoln, it seems worth asking whether rehabilitating Gettysburg to its original state is really a process of adding or detracting—and whether the managers of our battlefields are, in their quest for maximum authenticity, cheating visitors out of something more important.

In high school in the late 1980s, I worked at the Gettysburg battlefield, imparting names, dates, and locations that were, by and large, irrelevant to the moral history of the war. Which was fine with me. I loaded the customers onto the fleet of blue and gray double-decker buses, climbed to the top, and took my seat at the rear, where I sunned myself avidly. The problem I grappled with most earnestly on these pleasure grounds was how to pry visiting adolescent girls from their fathers. As for the matter of North versus South, I felt, perhaps along with the sunglass-sporting tourists, that I might have gone either way.

The main destinations then were no more inspired than my tours. A few family attractions conveyed some slight educational matter—the Electric Map, National Civil War Wax Museum, Lincoln Train Museum, Hall of Presidents—and, lying beyond town, there were diversions such as the Land of Little Horses. The entertainments were neither authentic nor inauthentic. They were kitsch, lacking any clear point of view; and, as they were pointless, so they were also harmless.

Today's drive to refurbish Gettysburg, more ambitious in every respect, has not stinted on inspiration—or controversy. A $135 million Museum and Visitor Center, which opened in the spring of 2008, has lately grabbed headlines thanks to allegations of ethical impropriety. (Questions are swirling about why two firms—one run by the head of the Gettysburg Foundation, the Park Service's partner in building the new center; the other run by his son—were selected to do work at the battlefield.) Less attention, however, has been trained on the ongoing effort to rehabilitate parts of the battlefield to their July 1863 states. This effort marks the latest chapter in a contest between dueling conceptions of Gettysburg—the battlefield as unchanging relic and the battlefield as living memorial.

In April 1864, the Pennsylvania legislature chartered the Gettysburg Battlefield Memorial Association (GBMA). It had taken burial gangs until March of that year to complete the bulk of their work and inter most of the Union dead in Soldiers' National Cemetery. And not until 1873 were the Confederate dead removed from mass graves and reburied in Richmond and Raleigh, Charleston and Savannah. The GBMA made some efforts in the direction of restoration—repositioning cannons, for example—and its founder argued for maintaining the July 1863 appearance of some key aspects of the battlefield. At the same time, he urged the construction of monuments, while his organization's charter called for it to commemorate the carnage with "works of art and taste." In 1866, the legislature empowered the GBMA to plant trees at the site. By 1895, when the Department of War assumed jurisdiction and created the Gettysburg National Military Park, the GBMA held title to 600 acres of land from which it had carved 17 miles of roads. In its first decade of administration, the War Department added more than 800 acres of land, planted nearly 17,000 additional trees, and improved roads. The commemorative work of boosters and government officials utterly transformed the battlefield.

Administrative control over the land migrated from the War Department to the Department of the Interior and the National Park Service in 1933; and developments surrounding the battlefield continued to reflect tension between the two conceptions of Gettysburg. On the one hand, New Deal officials issued a six-year general plan that identified a desire to return the land to its July 1863 appearance. Barns were restored, fences and walls rebuilt. Using workers from the Civilian Conservation Corps, the Park Service pared away overgrowth for the sake of an authentic view at Little Round Top. Yet in other respects the site continued to migrate away from its 1863 appearance. In 1938, at the battle's seventy-fifth anniversary, President Roosevelt came to dedicate the Eternal Light Peace Memorial, whose torch—situated above a granite and limestone monument—was meant to symbolize domestic unity while Europe rearmed. Fewer than two thousand Gettysburg veterans attended the ceremony, and their average age was over ninety. Perhaps they exercised something of a check on the drive for authenticity: one can see how wishing for an authentic battle experience in the presence of these survivors—who did not have the experience of the battle so much as they were had by it—might have been considered tasteless.

Eventually, however, the veterans died off, and, as told in Jim Weeks's *Gettysburg: Memory, Market, and an American Shrine* and Harlan Unrau's *Administrative History: Gettysburg National Military Park and Gettysburg National Cemetery, Pennsylvania*, the idea of rehabilitation continued to inform new plans for the park. In the late 1950s, President Eisenhower—whose farm was near the battlefield—egged on the campaign to restore Gettysburg. "I think it is a pity this one piece of terrain is not kept so that youngsters can see it nearly like it was in 1863," the president told *Parade* magazine.

Rehabilitation was a major initiative in the National Park Service's 1999 General Management Plan, thanks to John Latschar, the park's current superintendent. Last summer, Latschar explained to the *Gettysburg Magazine* how he could tell, soon after arriving in 1994, that a comprehensive program was needed to rescue the battlefield from the encroachments of time. "I'd been here a couple of weeks maybe and they scheduled my tour and I went out with a retired Marine colonel who's one of our best guides," he said. "He carried with him a stack of historic photographs that was probably three-quarters of an inch thick. I thought, what's he need all these for? But what he needed them for was to explain the course of the battle. Because so much of what the commanders could see in 1863 was obscured by vegetation that had grown up. And it was at that moment, I can remember thinking to myself, something's got to be done about this."

Is it possible to return vast tracts of land to their appearance in 1863? On the Park Service's website, Latschar explains that he is drawing on maps, participant reports of the battle, diaries, and newspaper accounts for a description of the battlefield's original condition. If that sounds straightforward, consider how little anyone knows for certain about the site's prewar appearance. Very few photographs of the Gettysburg outdoors from before the battle exist. William Frassanito's *Early Photography at Gettysburg*, published in 1995, identified M. S. Converse's map as the lone relatively detailed one available in July 1863, and the Converse map did not portray woods, hills, ridges, and other topographical features. General G. K. Warren and his team of military engineers made a sweeping survey of the battlefield in 1868 and 1869, then revised the map in 1873. But even the Warren map, the most authoritative made after the battle, has gaps and errors. "It is my cumulative observation," writes Frassanito, "that the finished product of 1873 more accurately reflects the appearance of the battlefield in 1869 than in 1863."

The scale and complexity of the carnage at Gettysburg has made it difficult to understand much about it. The approximately 1,328 markers and monuments scattered about the grounds are a stellar collection of public sculpture, but, individually and as a whole, they reflect "a constructed view of a certain version of the past, rather than a factual description of some historical truth," according to Thomas Desjardin's *These Honored Dead: How the Story of Gettysburg Shaped American Memory.* Many of these iron, bronze, and stone structures were placed in the 1880s, and most excluded the Confederates. Apocrypha that still surrounds Little Round Top and other areas originated not in the infallible testimony of eyewitnesses but in remembrances blurred, biased, or invented. Desjardin argues convincingly that "there is no 'what really happened' at Gettysburg; only a mountain of varying, often contradictory accounts that are seldom in accord, all tainted in some way or other by memory, bias, politics, ego, or a host of other factors."

Nobody learned the practical limits of such research faster than the battle's first historian, John Bachelder, who received $50,000 from Congress in 1880 to write a history of the event. In spite of the numerous interviews Bachelder conducted with eyewitnesses and participants soon after the battle and in subsequent years, he never produced the history for which he was paid. Flaws found in his maps, plus the intractable conflicts he found in the collective memory, defeated his attempt to make the story cohere. Soldiers and commanders alike said they found their experience incomprehensible, their vision clouded by fields curtained in smoke. General Abner Doubleday wrote to Bachelder in this chastened spirit five years after the congressional appropriation: "It is difficult in the excitement of battle to see every thing going on around us for each has his own part to play and that absorbs his attention to the exclusion of every thing else. People are very much mistaken when they suppose because a man is in a battle, he knows all about it."

Much of what we think we know about Gettysburg is knowledge gained at a remove beyond the experience of the battle. Paul Philippoteaux and his team painted the Gettysburg Cyclorama in 1884 from ten photographs by William Tipton, photos that depicted the battlefield as it was in 1882, not 1863. Photographers like Mathew Brady, Alexander Gardner, and the Tyson brothers, Charles and Isaac, circulated the earliest images of the battlefield. At Antietam, Gardner had supplied many urban newspaper readers with their first glimpses of dead soldiers. At Gettysburg, he captured images before the burials finished. How easy it is to forget, in light of his achievement, that neither Gardner nor anyone else photographed the battle itself.

But suppose the evidence was overwhelming. Suppose an abundance of available pictures, eyewitness accounts both reliable and comprehensive, and maps could guide history's eye with flawless accuracy. The question would still remain: Why should battlefield visitors want to "almost feel the bullets"?

Earlier generations of tourists brought more modest expectations. In 1869, the Katalysine Springs Hotel opened in Gettysburg on the heels of news that a medicinal spring had been discovered west of town. The hotel offered three hundred guests use of a billiard room and bowling alley, as well as a cupola that provided a panoramic view of the battlefield. This vantage point, high above the grounds, became very popular. In 1878, a private developer constructed an observatory on East Cemetery Hill, which also offered a panoramic view. The War Department raised five steel observation towers overlooking the battlefield. In 1974, a developer erected a tower more than three hundred feet high over the strenuous objections of preservationists.

Latschar demolished this structure (the National Tower, as it was called by its owner) in 2000—a key symbolic moment in his drive for rehabilitation. The towers enforce a moral distance between the seer and the scene. Accordingly, the early ones sprung up when memory of the suffering at Gettysburg was still raw. But towers also impede the ability of visitors to experience the battle; and experience is what today's battlefield managers aim to provide.

To truly experience what it was like to be at Gettysburg, we would need to lie with soldiers as they bled to death, groaning in pain; rotting corpses with missing limbs; streams running red; winds swarming with flies; air smelling of burning horseflesh. As we cannot know the precise cartography of the battlefield, or the movements of every soldier, or the location of every tree, so we should not try to leap backward into authenticity, or expect to become an eyewitness to history simply by showing up. The arrogance laid up around this expectation is astonishing. At Gettysburg, as elsewhere, the parties of preservation, restoration, and rehabilitation seek to transport us forward into the past by scrubbing off the blemishes of time. But, in offering the illusion of authentic experience, inviting us to "almost feel the bullets," they promise both too much and too little: they forget that historical suffering must be regarded from a distance if tragedy is to make us humble—or even be understood at all.

If a battlefield is not a locus of authentic experience, then what is it? A shrine? A classroom? The trees may teach us something yet. As flesh decayed at Gettysburg, it fertilized the earth for new vegetation. What the Park Service calls "non-historic trees"—that is, trees that grew after 1863—once were seedlings. Since then, in the changefulness of the seasons, they have formed a palimpsest, offering the closest we may come to communing with the lost souls of the battle. "As he gazed around him the youth felt a flash of astonishment at the blue, pure sky and the sun gleaming on the trees and fields," Stephen Crane wrote in *The Red Badge of Courage.* "It was surprising that Nature had gone tranquilly on with her golden processes in the midst of so much devilment."

Most of us, like my wife Anna on Seminary Ridge, intuit the connective tissues of trees and grief. That humans plant trees on gravesites is a spiritual fact of great and ancient significance. Homer signals a transition from war to peace by telling how Odysseus, returning home, found his father tending a young fruit tree. Ovid, in *Metamorphoses,* tells of Cyparissus "begging the gods to . . . let him grieve forever" after he accidentally kills a stag: "As his lifeblood drained away with never-ending tears, his limbs began to take a greenish cast; and the soft hair that used to cluster on his snow-white brow became a bristling crest. The boy was now a rigid tree with frail and spiring crown that gazes on the heavens and the stars." The trees on Seminary Ridge were a standing reminder of the pity and terror of tragedy. Those who run Gettysburg would grasp this—if only they were less obsessed with authenticity and more inclined toward history.

JOHN EDGAR WIDEMAN

Fatheralong*

FROM *Harper's Magazine*

LOUIS TILL, the father of Emmett Till, the fourteen-year-old Chicago boy murdered in Mississippi in 1955, one year after the Supreme Court's school desegregation decision, is the first father I think about when I am asked to comment on the alleged failure of black males to assume properly the responsibilities of fatherhood. I also think about Freud, about the global crisis demanding a metamorphosis of family that's not new, not black. President Barack Obama, who addressed such issues earlier and eloquently in his *Dreams from My Father* (1995), is clearly the catalyst of the present discussions as he works to apply his personal insights and experiences to a national dilemma. I'm moved by his honest explorations of fatherhood, his witness. The world is a troubled, dangerous place, at best. Unfairly dangerous for young Americans in free fall, growing up too fast or not growing at all, deprived of the love, guidance, positive example, the material, intellectual, and moral support of fathers negotiating the perils with them.

Louis Till's Non-Battle Casualty Report lists his rank as PVT, his serial number as 36392273, lists the Date of Casualty as July 2, his Reporting Theatre as MTO, the Mediterranean Theatre of Operations, lists his Arm or Service as TC, the Transportation Command, a noncombat unit to which nearly every colored soldier in the segregated U.S. Army was assigned, lists the Place of Casualty as Italy, and leaves blank, except for an asterisk, the space in which Type of Casualty should be listed. Mrs. Mamie Till's name (misspelled

---

*The word I heard as a child when the church sang "Farther Along."

"Mammie") appears on the Battle Casualty Report, but it does not mention Till's son, Emmett.

The first time Mamie Till knew her husband had been hanged in Italy by the United States Army was in the fall of 1955, not long after their son Emmett was murdered, about a dozen years after she'd seen Louis Till last in Chicago. The telegram she had received from the army on July 13, 1945, composed of selected facts from the Non-Battle Casualty Report, informed her that her husband, Private Louis Till, had died of willful misconduct, but omitted "sol died in non-battle status" and "judicial asphixiation," words typed into a confidential footnote below the official report. Although Mrs. Till was assisted by a lawyer, her attempt to investigate the circumstances surrounding the death of her husband and the father of her only child had been stymied by the government's terminal unresponsiveness, the very same government that ordered its colored soldiers to serve in what amounted to a separate, second-class army of conscripted laborers.

The government that at its highest levels chose to break its own rules and violate the rights of Private Louis Till by sending his confidential service record, which included a transcript of his court-martial (CM288642), to lawyers defending the kidnappers and killers of his son Emmett. Driven by their desire to repair the public image of a state that was being drubbed nationwide by press coverage of Emmett Till's murder, the Mississippi arch-segregationist senators James Eastland and John Stennis are likely the ones who obtained and leaked Louis Till's papers, as only officials with their rank and clout could demand and receive, from the army's adjutant general, a soldier's classified service record. A Colonel Ralph K. Johnson, TJAG (the judge advocate general), on October 14, 1955, did the dirty work of signing off on the release and penciling out the word CONFIDENTIAL stamped on the cover and pages of the Record of Trial by General Courts Martial, dated February 17, 1945.

In November 1955, approximately six weeks after a trial that found two World War II veterans—J. W. Milam and his brother-in-law Roy Bryant—not guilty of murdering Emmett Till, a trial that the Cleveland *Post and Call* derided ("Mississippi Jungle Law Frees Slayers of Child") and the Greenwood, Mississippi, *Morning Star* complimented ("Fair Trial Was Credit to Mississippi"), the state of Mississippi, compelled by the testimony of a sheriff during the trial that Milam and Bryant admitted to him they had taken Emmett Till from his great-uncle Moses Wright's home, sought indictments against the two men for kidnapping. Parties unknown leaked to the press that Emmett Till's father, Mamie Till's husband, Louis, far from being the martyred war hero portrayed in northern papers during the trial, had been hanged by the U.S. Army for committing rape and murder.

This revelation of the crimes of the father doomed any chance that jurors in Sumner, Mississippi, would indict the killers of Louis Till's son for any wrongdoing whatever. Instead of what measure of comfort she might have felt if the court had punished her son's murderers, Mamie Bradley Till found herself watching in dismay as Emmett Till's already dead and brutalized body was tarred, feathered, and lynched again for the father's sins, her fourteen-year-old boy stigmatized, scorned as rotten fruit from a rotten tree.

The novelist Chester Himes, expressing the despair shared by many of his fellow citizens, published a letter in the *New York Post* on September 25, 1955, in which he wrote, "The real horror comes when your dead brain must face the fact that we as a nation don't want it to stop. If we wanted to, we would. So let us all share the guilt, those in New York as well as those in Sumner, Mississippi."

As a father, Louis Till didn't have much time to spend with his son. Emmett Till was born in July of 1941 (a month after I was born), and Louis Till (like my father) went off to war in a segregated army in 1942, returning to Chicago only once, one AWOL night before the army came and knocked on Mamie's door in the morning and hauled him back. A ring Louis Till purchased in Casablanca and had engraved with his initials and the date May 25, 1943, was included among the personal effects Mamie Till received from the army after she was notified of his death. This silver ring, cached in Emmett Till's jewelry box or occasionally worn on his finger, padded by tape until his finger grew thick enough the last year of his life to keep it in place, may have been the most intimate link between father and son, an irony, since the ring also served to identify Emmett Till's battered, bloated, disfigured body when it was pulled from the Tallahatchie River.

What kind of father did Emmett Till imagine when he wore the silver ring. Looking down at the ring encircling his own dark finger, did Louis Till ever think about a son bearing his name, Till, wearing the ring one day.

While his sentence of death by hanging was receiving its mandatory review by the Judge Advocate General's Division, Louis Till was confined in the Disciplinary Training Center, a United States military prison in Metato, near Pisa. The poet Ezra Pound, facing a capital sentence himself, on charges of treasonous radio broadcasts, was Till's fellow prisoner, the only civilian in a population of 3,600 mostly colored inmates. The Pisan Cantos, written during Pound's internment in the DTC, imagine Louis Till as Outis, Greek for "no one," "nobody," the wanderer of the *Odyssey*, as Zeus the lusty ram, Till's sign, the Chinese ideogram "M4," "a man upon whom the sun has gone down" (Canto LXXIV: 170–178, edited by Richard Sieburth).

If Louis Till had been around to school Emmett about the perils of the South, about how white men treat black boys down south and up north, would Emmett have returned to Chicago safely on the City of New Orleans train from his trip to visit relatives in Money, Mississippi, started up public school in the fall, earned good grades, maybe even have become successful and rich, eluding the fate of his father. Or does his father's fate draw Emmett like a fluttering moth to its flame, Emmett flying backward and forward at once, like the African sankofa bird flies, because part of the father's fate is not to be around to advise and supervise and support the son, the fate of father and son to be divided always. A cycle of predictable missings and absence eternally renewed. A flicker of wings igniting, quickly extinguished, then darkness.

Race is myth. When we stop talking about race, stop believing in race, it will disappear. Except for its career historically and in people's memories as the antithesis of human freedom, the embodiment of inequality and injustice that remained far too long a toxic, unresolved paradox in nations proclaiming themselves free. In a raceless society color wouldn't disappear. Difference wouldn't disappear. Africa wouldn't disappear. In post-race America "white" people would disappear. That is, no group could assume as birthright and identity a privileged, supernaturally ordained superiority at the top of a hierarchy of other groups, a supremacy that bestows upon their particular kind the right perpetually to rule and regulate the lives of all other kinds. This idea, this belief in "whiteness," whether the belief is expressed in terms of color, ethnicity, nationality, gender, tribe, etc., constitutes the founding principle of race, its appeal and its discontents.

To dismiss race as myth is not to underestimate its power. Race, like religion, is immune to critiques of science and logic because it rests on belief. And people need beliefs. Although science has discredited the biological underpinnings of the notion of race, faith rushes in to seal the cracks, paper over glaring omissions in arrested explanations of human difference offered by racial ideology. Louis Till's color, the color of his son Emmett, the color of Richard Wright's fictional character Bigger Thomas, Colin Powell's color, are not problems until the myth of race and the racialized perspective it authorizes turn color into an indictment, into instant proof of innocence or guilty-as-charged. We should understand by now that race can mean anything, everything, or nothing, depending upon whom we ask.

The continuing existence of race in the United States indicates conspiracy and cover-up. An attempt to make more palatable to ourselves, and anyone watching, the not-so-secret dirty secret shared by all Americans that our country, in spite of public professions to the contrary, entertains a deeply internalized segregated vision of itself. We look at ourselves and believe we see White Americans or Black Americans. We perceive our problems as Black or White problems. The urgent task of redressing the shameful neglect of American children gets postponed by hand-wringing and finger-pointing at feckless black fathers and the damage they're inflicting upon their black offspring. Or sidetracked just as effectively by blaming society and exempting blacks because race tells us blacks are permanent victims, not agents of change. The truth of too many black boys in prison, too many black babies dying, too many hungry black youngsters being raised in dire poverty, too many terrible black schools — these truths misrepresented by discourses perpetuating the myth of separate races don't spur us to action but become an occasion for shedding crocodile tears, washing our hands of personal as well as collective responsibility. More than half a century ago James Baldwin outed this kind of hiding from the consequences of racialized thinking as *willed innocence*. At this late date, displays of surprise or ignorance about how bad things are for our children suggest dishonesty, signify complicity, conscious or unconscious, with the cover-up.

Louis Till was born fatherless in Madrid, Missouri. One could argue that the concept of race abiding today in America is a profound orphaning of all black children. Argue that any attempt to understand black fathers and to interpret their responsibilities, successes, and failures should begin right there, with a consideration of the fact that myths of race isolate children, place them at risk, disinherit and repudiate. Start by listening a moment to the roaring silence in which Louis Till is buried, the silence neither his voice nor his son's voice can break, the dark, impervious silence in which words—*good, bad, responsible, black, white*—vanish.

Daredevil

FROM *The Atlantic*

HOUR BY HOUR, day by day, Bill Buckley was just an exciting person to be around, especially when he was exhilarated by his love of sailing. He could turn any event into an adventure, a joke, a showdown. He loved risk. I saw him time after time rush his boat toward a harbor, sails flying, only to swerve and drop sail at the last moment. For some on the pier, looking up to see this large yacht bearing down on them, it was a heart-stopping moment. To add to the excitement, Bill was often standing on the helmsman's seat, his hands clutching the shrouds above his head, turning the wheel with his foot, in a swashbuckling pose. (He claimed he saw the berth better from up there.)

I once saw the importance of his swift reflexes on the boat. We had set out for a night sail on the ocean, and Bill's Yale friend Van Galbraith—later President Reagan's ambassador to France—had got tipsy from repeated shots of Tia Maria in his coffee. He fell overboard while the boat was under full sail. In a flash, Bill threw overboard a life preserver with a bright light on it, and called for us to bring the boat about. We circled back toward Galbraith, found him in the darkness, and fished him out. It was a scary moment, one that only Bill's cool rapidity kept from being a tragic one.

Bill wrote the way he sailed, taking chances. Once, he called me up to ask about some new papal pronouncement. He had got into trouble with fellow Catholics by criticizing papal encyclicals, and I had become a kind of informal adviser on Catholic matters. The statement at issue that day was obscure.

He wanted to launch an immediate attack on it. I asked why he did not wait to see what impact it would have. "Why not wait? Because I don't have *falsos testes.*" He was referring to an earlier discussion, in which he asked whether even papal defenders admit the pontiff can err. I said that medieval commentators claimed that such an error could happen if the pope was given imperfect evidence (*propter falsos testes*). He asked, "Isn't *testis* [testifier] the same word in Latin as *testicle?*" Yes. That was all the warrant he needed.

He was always ready to plunge in. Another time he called me and asked, "Have you ever heard of Joe Nuh-*math?*" This was when everybody had heard of the way Joe *Nay*-math won the 1969 Super Bowl as quarterback for the New York Jets. Bill had only just read the name in an editor's letter asking him to write about the man. I told him how Namath had beat my hero, Johnny Unitas, in the Super Bowl. There were large gaps in Bill's knowledge of popular culture, especially of popular sports. His father once wrote to Bill's future father-in-law, complaining that he had tried for years, without success, to interest his son in the ordinary games—golf or tennis or team sports. But Bill had a relish only for solo performances—sailing, skiing, horseback riding, or flying an airplane. I asked if Bill was going to write about Namath. Yes. "That should be an interesting interview." He said, "Oh, I don't have time to learn enough about football to interview him." He wrote the piece by comparing Namath's career to something he did know—the record of a famous bullfighter.

Another time, I was on Bill's boat racing to Bermuda. We saw on the horizon a huge shape like an island—it was a World War II battleship taken out of mothballs and put out for a shakedown cruise before being sent to the Vietnam War, a breathtaking sight from our lower vantage point on the water. Bill could not resist hailing it on the radio, though radioing was against racing rules except in an emergency. When we reached Bermuda, Bill was disqualified. One of the other boats had heard his conversation with the battleship and reported him. He said it was worth it. He reminded me of one of Wodehouse's blithe young men—Psmith, say, or Piccadilly Jim—who act forever on impulse.

He took risks even in routine and mundane ways. One night, after dinner at his townhouse in Manhattan, he wanted to continue our conversation, so instead of calling me a cab to take me back to my hotel, he gave me a ride on his motorbike. New York law required that bikers wear a helmet, so a policeman stopped us—neither of us was helmeted. When the cop recognized him, he let us go with just a warning, since Bill was popular with cops for opposing police review boards. Needless to say, the next time he gave me a ride, there were still no helmets.

It is amazing that Bill's risks did not end his life. At Yale he secretly learned to fly, and bought a small plane with a couple of friends, without letting his father know about it. He landed the plane on his sister's prep school campus in a spectacular visit. On the day of his college tests, he took the plane out for a celebratory flight, all by himself. He had been up the night before cramming for the exams, and he fell asleep. Fortunately, he woke in time to land the plane. A great career might have ended before it began.

For a while I was Bill's designated biographer. A shared friend of ours, Neil McCaffrey, commissioned the book for his new publishing venture, Arlington House. Bill approved the idea because, like many celebrities, he was constantly pestered by people wanting to interview him for books or magazines. With me as his chosen scribe, he could turn them down by saying he was already committed. I recorded many hours of tapes with him, his wife, his siblings, and his friends for the project, before giving it up over political disagreements. He was stunningly candid, so much so that I, like many people close to him, came to feel I should protect him from his own reckless truthfulness. He was too trusting of people he liked. He set up a former boat boy in a partnership to buy radio stations, and afterward found that his young partner had bilked him. He argued for the innocence of a prisoner who wrote him winning letters, and worked to have Edgar Smith released, only to see the man convicted again, this time of kidnapping and attempted murder.

Some of the things Bill told me on the tapes I have never repeated, except to my wife. One thing I can partly tell now that he is dead. When he entered the CIA, in 1951, he beat the polygraph test that all prospective agents have to take. (Always willing to risk.) He was determined to protect a family member from an embarrassing disclosure, and he did. I asked him how he accomplished that. "I guess that if you think you have a right to tell a lie, it will not register as one." At least it did not with him. He told me what he lied about, though I promised then to keep the secret, and I have.

*

From what I have said so far, it might be thought that Bill was self-centered. That was far from the case. He was thoughtful of others, almost to a fault. When he found that a summer intern at *National Review* was a promising young pianist who missed his practice hours back in the Midwest, he gave him the key to his townhouse (which had been UN Secretary-General Dag Hammarskjöld's) and told him he could use it, while his wife was away, to play on his splendid Bösendorfer piano.

His generosity was unfailing. He liked to do things for people, surprising them with unexpected gifts. When the writer Wilfrid Sheed was ill, Bill, who knew he was a deep student of popular song, sent him the latest books on the subject. One day in the early sixties, a large package was brought to my front door. It was the twenty-four volumes of the new edition of the *Encyclopedia Britannica*. Another time I got a package containing framed copies of two charcoal portraits by the famous British newspaper artist David Low. These were studies of G. K. Chesterton and Hilaire Belloc, men Bill knew I admired. I asked where he had got the pictures. They were a gift to him from the British broadcaster Alistair Cooke. Bill said, "They will mean more to you than to me."

He spent a lot of time thinking of what he could do for friends. When he heard that I needed a passport in a hurry, he pulled strings at the State Department to get it for me. On another occasion, when my new bride and I could not find a cheap sea liner to England for our honeymoon, he found a ship for us leaving from Canada. Bill ingeniously invented a way to institutionalize his love for giving special gifts. Because his family was so prolific, he had forty-nine of what he called "N and Ns" (nieces and nephews). He took care of the education of many of them. But supplying necessities was not enough for him. He set up a fund he called the Dear Uncle Bill Trust (DUBT, soon pronounced "Doubt"), whose administrators gave surprise treats to N and Ns—a valuable guitar to an aspiring musician, a vacation in a favorite spot—on a rotating basis.

His desire to do things for people made him an inveterate matchmaker. He did all he could to encourage his Yale friend Brent Bozell to marry his favorite sister, Patricia (Trish), which Bozell did in 1949. He hinted that another Yale undergraduate, Bill Coffin, should date another of his sisters. When I went to *National Review* in the summer of 1957, I was just two months out of a Jesuit seminary, where I had been starved for opera music, and I soon found the Sam Goody music store. But the apartment I was staying in had no phonograph. When I mentioned this to Bill's younger sister Maureen, who was working part-time at *National Review* that summer, she gave me the key to her apartment and said I could use the phonograph there any afternoon while she was working. Bill noticed that Maureen and I got along well, and when we would all go out to dinner at the end of the day, he'd put us together in one cab and take another with the rest of the party. We laughed at his matchmaking attempts. It was a family trait. Trish had met Pat Taylor at Vassar and decided Bill should marry her—as he did.

Perhaps it was his matchmaking urge that made Bill want to connect people with his church. After he learned as a child that any Christian can baptize a person in need of salvation, he and Trish would unobtrusively rub water on visitors to their home while whispering the baptism formula. In the *National Review* circle, those who were not Catholics to begin with tended to enter the fold as converts—Bozell, Russell Kirk, Willmoore Kendall, Frank Meyer, William Rusher, Jeffrey Hart, M. Joseph Sobran, Marvin Liebman, Robert Novak, Richard John Neuhaus. The major holdouts were James Burnham, a born Catholic who left the faith and never went back, and Whittaker Chambers, who was drawn to Richard Nixon's Quakerism. It was always easiest to be a Catholic around Bill. I believe Bill was so nice to me because I am what the Lutheran scholar Martin Marty called me, "incurably Catholic." There were different concentrations of people at *National Review*—Yale alumni, ex-communists (Burnham, Meyer, Chambers), ex-CIA members (Bill, Burnham, Kendall, and Priscilla Buckley, another of Bill's sisters) —but the Catholic contingent outnumbered all others.

Bill went to church on Sundays with the many Spanish-speaking house servants he had over the years. That did not fit his reputation as a snob. He was accused, at times, of being a social snob, an ideological snob, and an intellectual snob. None of these was the case in any but the most superficial sense.

Social Snob?

Bill could hardly have been a social snob when he was playing matchmaker for his sister and me. I was a penniless nobody. For that matter, Brent Bozell had no significant money or social standing when (with Bill's encouragement) he married Trish Buckley. Brent had got to Yale on a double scholarship, from the GI Bill and from an American Legion oratory award. Where his family was concerned, Bill always cared more about a person's being Catholic and conservative than about his or her being rich. I passed the Catholic test, and came close enough on the conservative point in 1957, for him to hint that Maureen and I might be made for each other.

Despite his religious and ideological preferences, Bill was basically egalitarian.

Though he always used proper titles for guests on his TV show, he was "Bill" to everyone from the moment they met him. He treated all ranks at the magazine with equal courtesy and respect. There was never any "side" to him. In this he was unlike his wife. He always dressed like a rumpled undergraduate, while she had Bill Blass and other designers dancing attendance on her. Bill and Pat were deeply in love — each called the other "Ducky," just as Spencer Tracy and Katharine Hepburn call each other "Pinky" in the movie *Adam's Rib*. But the Tracy and Hepburn characters have their differences, and so did the Buckleys. They had different (though overlapping) social circles. Bill was amused by some of her friends (like Truman Capote). But she treated some of his intellectual friends — like the literary critic Hugh Kenner — as a nuisance. Pat never finished college, and intellectual talk could make her uneasy. Once, when we were doing a night sail from Stamford, Connecticut (she never went on longer sails), I brought up the writer Donald Barthelme and she said she had no time for such pretentious stuff.

In one of his published journals, Bill described in loving detail the limousine he'd had specially redesigned as a kind of traveling office. He was widely mocked for this. But he had realized the advantage of having a chauffeur only when he ran for mayor of New York, in 1965, and needed a car and driver to get him to events where there was no time or place for parking a car himself. He saw that he could do his endless dictating of letters and columns on the move, and he kept the Irish Catholic driver who had seen him through the campaign. Before that race, he'd regularly ridden around New York on his motorbike. And he was driving his own (modest) car when I met him in 1957. After I arrived at his office in New York to talk about writing for *National Review,* he asked where I had left my suitcase. I said, "At the airport"; I thought I might be heading right back to Michigan at the end of that day. He told me to wait while he finished his editing for the day, then he drove me to LaGuardia. After I picked up my bag, he drove us out to his home in Stamford, where we talked, swam, and ate dinner. Then he drove me back into New York, put me up in his father's apartment at 80 Park Avenue, and turned around to drive back to Stamford. He was my chauffeur that day. It was the kind of thoughtfulness many people experienced from him.

Ideological Snob?

There was a better case for thinking Bill had ideological class prejudices. But when he established *National Review,* in 1955, he applied no ideological test to all those he hired or tried to hire. He wanted good writing and intellectual stimulation. That is why he printed non-right-wingers like John Leonard, Joan Didion, Renata Adler, and Arlene Croce. Later, he sailed or skied with John Kenneth Galbraith and Walter Cronkite (I sailed with both), not because they were celebrities but because he liked them and admired their minds.

The real measure of Bill was the extent to which he overcame the prejudices he began with because of his family. His mother was a southern belle from New Orleans whose grandfather had been a Confederate soldier at Shiloh. She kept the attitude toward blacks of her upbringing. One time, when we were sailing and stopped at Charleston, South Carolina, Bill took me to his father's winter home. When we arrived, we were greeted by a black retainer who had known Bill from his childhood—he called him "Master Billy." It was not surprising that Bill and I would initially disagree about the civil rights movement. In a notorious 1957 editorial called "Why the South Must Prevail," he defended segregation because whites were "the advanced race," and "the claims of civilization supersede[d] those of universal suffrage." We argued over this, and his biographer, John Judis, says that my views gradually had some effect: "Under the influence of conservative proponents of civil rights like Wills and the heated debate about civil rights taking place in the country, Buckley began to distinguish *National Review*'s and the conservative position from that of southern racists."

Another burden from Bill's early days was his father's anti-Semitism, a harder thing for him to conquer since he honored his father so profoundly. A close friend of Bill's at the *Yale Daily News* was Tom Guinzburg, later the president of Viking Press. Guinzburg and Bill's sister Jane were on the verge of being engaged, and Bill's father said that Bill, using his friendship with Guinzburg, should prevent a Jew from joining the family. Bill intervened, to his later regret. For once, he was a match breaker rather than a matchmaker. I was with him the night he finally confessed to Jane what he had done behind her back. She said it did not matter—the marriage would not have worked out. Bill said, "I wish I had known that before—I have been reproaching myself all these years." Bill did more than break *National Review* away from right-wing journals that harbored anti-Semites. When he found that a book reviewer (Revilo Oliver) and one of his editors (M. Joseph Sobran) were writing anti-Semitic stuff in other venues, he dismissed them from the magazine. Bill became so sensitive to the problem that he wrote a book on the anti-Semitic writings of right-wingers like Sobran and Patrick Buchanan.

By the time of his death, even Bill's earlier critics admitted that he had done much to make conservatism respectable by purging it of racist and fanatical traits earlier embedded in it. He distanced his followers from the southern prejudices of George Wallace, the anti-Semitism of the Liberty Lobby, the fanaticism of the John Birch Society, the glorification of selfishness by Ayn Rand (famously excoriated in *National Review* by Whittaker Chambers), the paranoia and conspiratorialism of the neocons. In each of these cases, some right-wingers tried to cut off donations to *National Review*, but Bill stood his ground. In doing so, he elevated the discourse of American politics, making civil debate possible between responsible liberals and conservatives.

Intellectual Snob?

Bill was considered an elitist because he loved to use big words. But he did it not from hauteur but from impishness. This was part of his playfulness. He liked to play games in general, and word games were especially appealing to him. He used the big words for their own sake, even when he was not secure in their meaning. One of his most famous usages poisoned the general currency, especially among young conservatives trying to imitate him. They took "oxymoron" in the sense he gave it, though that was the opposite of its true meaning. He thought it was a fancier word for "contradiction," so young imitators would say that "an intelligent liberal" was an oxymoron. But the Greek word means "something that is surprisingly *true*, a paradox," as in "a shrewd dumbness."

One time Bill's love of exotic locutions came out when he asked me for the meaning of a word I had written, "subumbrous." I said it meant "cloaked in darkness." He protested that he could not find the word in any of his dictionaries. No wonder, I said, I made it up from the Latin *sub umbra*. He loved that—it continued the word games. But his lunge toward risky words was like his other ventures into risk. He could write, for instance, that *National Review*'s "mendacity" prevented the magazine from running free advertisements, when he meant "mendicancy."

Bill was not, and did not pretend to be, a real intellectual. He gave up on the "big book" that his father and others were urging him to write. For years he tried to do a continuation of José Ortega y Gasset's *Revolt of the Masses*. This had been a sacred text for his father's guru, Albert Jay Nock. Bill took intellectual comrades like Hugh Kenner with him for his winter break in Switzerland, to help him get a grip on this ambitious project. But he told me he realized in time this was not his métier. He was not a reflective thinker. He was a quick responder. He wrote rapidly because he was quickly bored. His gifts were facility, flash, and charm, not depth or prolonged wrestling with a problem.

Bill needed people around him all the time. Frequently, when he told me he had to write a column, I would offer to withdraw from the boat cabin or hotel room where we were. He urged me not to, and as he typed (with great speed and accuracy) he would keep talking off and on, reading a sentence to me, trying out a word, saying that something he was writing would annoy old So-and-So. When I appeared on his TV show to discuss a new book of mine, it was clear to me that he had not read the book—he was given notes on each author he interviewed. Once he asked me if I had read all of Adam Smith's *Wealth of Nations*. I said yes. "Haven't you?" He had not. I suspect that was true of the other capitalist classics he referred to, by Ludwig von Mises, Wilhelm Roepke, and others. He could defend them with great panache. But he did not want to sit all by himself for a long time reading them. One of his teachers at Yale, the philosopher Paul Weiss, told me that Bill was very good at discussing books he had not read.

Bill was heatedly attacked by Catholic liberals when he dismissed papal criticism of capitalism. He dismissed John XXIII's encyclical *Mater et Magistra* for its challenge to the free market. I joked that his attitude was "*Mater sí, Magistra no,*" playing on a slogan of the time, "*Cuba sí, Castro no.*" He printed the quip in the magazine and was attacked on the assumption that the saying was his own. He questioned me about church teachings. He felt insecure because his Catholic education was so exiguous — it amounted to one year at a Jesuit prep school in England. I had been entirely educated in Catholic schools before entering graduate school at Yale, and he exaggerated what knowledge that had given me.

He wanted to know more about encyclicals. I told him I did not know much. I had read carefully the so-called social encyclicals — *Rerum Novarum* (1891) and *Quadragesimo Anno* (1931) — because Chesterton had admired their praise of medieval guilds. Bill asked if I would bone up on the subject, and I agreed to. After I had done some research on the matter, he drove up from Stamford to New Haven to spend an afternoon discussing it. He had been challenged to a debate with an editor of *Commonweal*, William Clancy. Bill suggested that each side be defended by a two-man team — Bill and I on one side, Clancy and a partner of his choosing on the other. Clancy did not like the idea. Nonetheless, when it came time for the debate, to be held across the river from Manhattan in New Jersey, Bill asked me to go along with him for some last-minute preparation in the car. We had to grab a quick dinner before the event, so we stopped at a greasy spoon in New Jersey. When Bill asked for a bottle of red wine, it came out ice cold, so he asked that it be run under hot water for a while, and we kept up our informal seminar on encyclicals.

Bill handled the debate with his customary forensic stylishness. But the Catholic attacks on him continued. By the early 1960s, they had become so voluminous that our friend Neil McCaffrey

made a collection of them, to be published with his sulfurous comments on each item. Bill asked me to write an introduction to the
collection, on the status of encyclicals. When Neil had the book
ready, Bill asked me to come out to his garage study at Stamford.
He found Neil's intemperate running commentary embarrassing.
He wanted to cancel the project—unless I was willing to expand
my introduction, incorporating some of the acidulous commentary into a calmer treatment of the matter. I said that I doubted
Neil would be amenable to having his concept taken away from
him. Bill said I should just leave that to him. Somehow, with his
smooth persuasiveness, he took the project over without losing
Neil's friendship, and I published *Politics and Catholic Freedom,* the
first of my books on the papacy.

Bill lived and wrote and lectured—and played and socialized
and exercised—at a furious pace. Partly this was because he bored
so easily. But partly it was to make money. He was commonly
thought of as a spoiled rich boy. But he had never had the kind of
money people imagined. His wife did—she came from a family far
wealthier than his. But he did not want to live on her inheritance.
Bill's oilman father had drilled many a dry hole. John Judis did the
numbers, and said that the senior Buckley's money was exaggerated. After the father's death, Bill's oldest brother, John, a heavy
drinker, ran the company without great skill.

Bill's own investments, especially in radio stations, set back
rather than advanced his financial affairs—as always, he was too in
love with risk. But he made a good living, initially from his heavy
lecture schedule and then from his profitable series of spy novels. I
remember how delighted he was, in 1960, when for the first time
he was paid a dollar a word for a magazine article (a high sum
then). He did not, of course, have to work for a living. He could
have lived, like his siblings, on a lower scale than the one he did.
But Bill wanted to maintain the swashbuckling yachts, the custom-
made limousine, the ski lodge in Switzerland, and the great generosity of his gifts to others; and he did not want to do this on his
wife's money. Thus he secretly acquired what some will consider
his least plausible identity, that of a working stiff.

For more years than I wish, Bill and I were estranged. Though
he had backed off from the southern view of black inferiority, he
thought that Martin Luther King Jr. was hurting the country in its
struggle with communism by criticizing America, and he was a

strong friend of Henry Kissinger in defending the Vietnam War. Even my own friend at the magazine, Frank Meyer, tried to have my comments against Richard Nixon killed, and Bill finally refused to publish my claim that there was no conservative rationale for our ruinous engagement in Vietnam. Later, when I moved out of my office at Northwestern and reduced my library to what would fit into my home, I gave a used-bookstore owner the pick of my volumes at the university. He went off with many titles that Bill had inscribed to me, and when irate fans of his found them in the store, they bought them and sent them back to him, calling me an ingrate for selling his gifts.

When Bill's service in the CIA under Howard Hunt came to light during the Watergate scandal, I wrote a column about Bill's CIA connections. Perhaps he thought I was using confidential knowledge he had given me on the tapes I had made for his biography, but I used nothing that was not public knowledge by then. He circulated my column to the *National Review* board of editors with the marginal notation, "I think we should smash him"—an item that Judis found in Bill's papers at Yale. For a time the magazine ran recurring "Wills Watch" features, recording the latest liberal abomination I was guilty of. Rick Brookhiser, an editor at the magazine, writes in his new memoir of working with Bill:

> It was clear to me as a reader of *National Review* that Wills had been an important figure at the magazine, if only because the magazine continued to needle him. One cover pasted Wills's head on a famous image of Black Panther Huey Newton, enthroned with spear and shotgun on his wicker chair.

John Leonard, another *"National Review* apostate," as Bill called us, told Judis:

> When Garry said what was happening to blacks was more important than what was reflected in the magazine, and it hurts me personally, morally, he spoke to that best part, that most vulnerable part of the Buckleys. It [the disagreement] went from blacks to Nixon to Vietnam.

M. Joseph Sobran, the principal Wills Watcher, said in comparing me with another "defector": "I don't think Kevin Phillips got anywhere near [Buckley's] heart the way that Garry Wills had. [Buckley] didn't covet Phillips's esteem the way he had Garry's."

When Bill went to speak at Yale, on one of his innumerable visits there, my son, Garry L. Wills, was in the line of students waiting to shake his hand. When my son gave his name as Garry Wills, Bill said, "No relation, I hope." Garry, who can be as pixieish as Bill, serenely said, "None at all"—which left Bill turning back with puzzled looks as he moved on down the line. On another occasion, Bill's son, Christopher, whom I had met years before when he was the boat boy on Bill's yacht, was a student at Yale, and he invited me to come speak at the annual *Yale Daily News* dinner. I suspected that Christopher was in one of his moments of conflict with his father, and I declined to take part in that drama.

But Bill's wonderful and selfless sister Priscilla, who always kept me in her loving circle, trusted to the real regard Bill and I still had for each other. She called me in 2005 and said it was silly for those who had been such friends not to be talking to each other. She set up a dinner at our old restaurant, Paone, where Bill and I resumed our friendship, and after that, our correspondence. Bill wrote to tell me he had given my *What Jesus Meant* as a Christmas gift to friends. It was clear that our old disagreements had been transcended. And whereas Bill had defended the Vietnam War, leading us to part company so many years before, he ended up a critic of the Iraq War.

When Bill suggested on *The Charlie Rose Show* that he was ready to die, I found his words heartbreaking, and I wrote to tell him so. When Priscilla told me that in his last days, weakened by emphysema, he could not move across the room without her pulling him up and supporting him, I thought of the figure—lithe, athletic, prompt—who brought his sailboat to rest with one deft turn of his foot on the wheel, and I grieved for one who had brought so much excitement into my life.

[handwritten annotations:] — profile; lit. crit; political; personal = conflated together
↳access or opening for non-English majors or
Orwell fan? language; images; current social crit.

[handwritten:] — best respected lit. critic

[handwritten:] — Contradictions for Orwell? privileged/argued against privilege
• idealizes but wants to improve working class

JAMES WOOD

A Fine Rage

FROM *The New Yorker*

[handwritten margin:] like Orwell / Orwell

I VIVIDLY REMEMBER when I first read George Orwell. It was at Eton, Orwell's old school. Not coming from a family with any Eton connections (a portion of my fees was paid by the school), I had refined a test: if a boy's father had gone there, then that boy's grandparents had been rich enough, in the early 1950s, to come up with the money. And, if his grandparents had been rich enough, the chances were that his great-grandparents had had enough cash to send Grandpa there in the 1920s—and back and back, in an infinite regression of privilege. There were probably hundreds of boys whose family wealth stretched so far back, into the nineteenth and eighteenth centuries, that, for all intents and purposes, the origin of their prosperity was invisible, wallpapered over in layers and layers of luck.

It seemed extraordinary to a member of the upwardly mobile bourgeoisie that these boys were incapable of answering two basic questions: How did your family make its money? And how on earth did it hold on to it for so long? They were barely aware of their enormous, unearned privilege; and this at a time of deep recession and Mrs. Thatcher, in which English fields became battlegrounds and policemen on horseback fought with armies of striking coal miners. I spent my time at that school alternately grateful for its every expensive blessing and eager to blow it up. Into those receptive hands fell Orwell's 1941 pamphlet *The Lion and the Unicorn: Socialism and the English Genius,* with its own war cry: "Probably the battle of Waterloo *was* won on the playing-fields of Eton, but the opening battles of all subsequent wars have been lost there." And also: "England is the most class-ridden country under the sun. It is a land of snobbery and privilege, ruled largely by the old and silly . . . A family with the wrong members in control."

The Lion and the Unicorn is a powerfully radical pamphlet, published at a time when Orwell thought that the only way for the British to beat the Nazis was to make the war a revolutionary one. British capitalism had been culpably inefficient, he argued. Its lords and captains had slept through the 1930s, either colluding with or appeasing Hitler. There had been a long period of stagnation and unemployment. Britain had failed to produce enough armaments; as late as August 1939, Orwell notes, British dealers were still trying to sell rubber, shellac, and tin to the Germans. By contrast, the fascists, stealing what they wanted from socialism and discarding all the noble bits, had shown how efficient a planned economy could be: "The mere *efficiency* of such a system, the elimination of waste and obstruction, is obvious . . . However horrible this system may seem to us, *it works.*" Only by shifting to a planned, nationalized economy and a "classless, ownerless" society could the British prevail. Revolution was not just desirable but necessary. And what was needed was not just a change of heart but a structural dismantling, "a fundamental shift of power. Whether it happens with or without bloodshed is largely an accident of time and place."

During the 1940s and '50s, a social revolution did take place in Britain. Though it would not be Orwell's idea of a fundamental shift of power, his writing certainly contributed to the quieter change that occurred when the Labour Party won the 1945 election, ousted Winston Churchill, and inaugurated the welfare state. After the war, Orwell became most famous as a left-baiting antitotalitarian, but he did not change his opinion that vast, systemic change was necessary in order to make Britain a decent and fair country to live in: he continued to make the case for the nationalization of major industries, tight government regulation of income disparity (he originally proposed that the highest income be no more than ten times the lowest), the winding up of the Empire, the abolition of the House of Lords, the disestablishment of the Church of England, and reform of the great English boarding schools and ancient universities. This revolution, he thought, will be a curious, ragged, English thing: "It will not be doctrinaire, nor even logical. It will abolish the House of Lords, but quite probably

will not abolish the Monarchy. It will leave anachronisms and loose
ends everywhere."

Nowadays, Orwell's imprecision about exactly *how* this revolution might come about seems telling, because, despite the fighting words ("At some point or other it may be necessary to use violence"), his vagueness seems a kind of wish fulfillment, as if a nice
muddled revolution might spontaneously emerge from the gentle
London fog. "A real shove from below will accomplish it," he writes
in *The Lion and the Unicorn.* Ah, that will do the trick.

But there is a difference between being revolutionary and being
a revolutionary, and journalists are not required to be tacticians.
More striking is that Orwell premises the economic viability of his
socialistic planned economy on the economic success of the Nazis'
planned economy, and, in turn, premises the viability of the Nazis'
planned economy only on its efficiency in wartime. Nazism *worked,*
to use Orwell's verb, because it was good at producing tanks and
guns in wartime, but how good would it be at building hospitals
and universities in peacetime? He doesn't say. So the example of
efficient fascism is what inspires the hope of efficient socialism. Orwell seems never to have realized the economic contradiction of
this, at least explicitly. Perhaps he did realize it unconsciously, because later works, such as *Animal Farm* (1945) and *1984* (1949),
worry away at the fascistic temptation inherent in the socialistic,
planned, collective economy—the "classless, ownerless" society.

This is not to suggest, as contemporary neoconservatives like
Jonah Goldberg absurdly claim, that socialism is just fascism with
a bleeding heart. Orwell never thought that. Despite the antitotalitarian books, and his reputation's later theft at the hands of
the right wing, he remained revolutionary in spirit until his death,
in 1950, at the age of forty-six. But he never really reconciled his
hatred of what he called the "power instinct" with a candid assessment of the power instinct that would have to be exercised to effect revolution. As he saw it, the English revolution would come
about precisely to dismantle power and privilege, so how could it
possibly end up replacing one kind with another? The English just
wouldn't do that. An actual revolution, in Russia, with its abuses of
power and privilege, necessarily disappointed him, because it con-
taminated the ideal. Orwell became not so much anti-revolutionary
as anti-revolution.

When I first read *The Lion and the Unicorn,* I was so blinded by superb, boiling lines like "And if the rich squeal audibly, so much the better" and "The lady in the Rolls-Royce car is more damaging to morale than a fleet of Goering's bombing planes" that I missed this incoherence. To someone surrounded by alien acres of privilege, Orwell's relentless attacks seemed a necessary, obliterating forest fire: "What is wanted is a conscious open revolt by ordinary people against inefficiency, class privilege and the rule of the old . . . We have got to fight against privilege." Now I am struck by the fact that, throughout his work, Orwell is much more vocal about the abolition of power and privilege than about equitable redistribution, let alone the means and machinery of that redistribution. There is a fine spirit of optimistic destruction in his work, a sense that if we all just work hard at that crucial, negating "shove from below," the upper-class toffs will simply fade away, and things will more or less work out in the interests of justice. In *The Lion and the Unicorn,* there is a suggestive moment when Orwell writes that collective wartime deprivation may be more necessary than political programs: "In the short run, equality of sacrifice, 'war-Communism,' is even more important than radical economic changes. It is very necessary that industry should be nationalized, but it is more urgently necessary that such monstrosities as butlers and 'private incomes' should disappear forthwith." In other words, let's agree to be vague about the economic stuff, and keep the serious rhetoric for the lady in the Rolls. This is the same Orwell who wrote in his wartime diary, "The first sign that things are really happening in England will be the disappearance of that horrible plummy voice from the radio," and the same Orwell who, dying of tuberculosis in a country nursing home, wrote in his notebook in 1949 about the sound of upper-class English voices: "And what voices! A sort of over-fedness, a fatuous self-confidence, a constant bah-bahing of laughter about nothing, above all a sort of heaviness and richness combined with a fundamental ill-will . . . No wonder everyone hates *us* so." For Orwell, getting rid of those accents was more than half the battle.

It is probably fair to say that Orwell was even more consumed by the spectacle of overweening privilege than by the spectacle of overwhelming poverty, despite the two committed books he wrote about the poor, *Down and Out in Paris and London* (1933) and *The Road to Wigan Pier* (1937). A pair of new volumes of his essays, collected as *Facing Unpleasant Facts: Narrative Essays* and *All Art Is Propaganda: Critical Essays*, allow us to experience again the strongest examples of Orwell's journalistic work. The selections, by George Packer, a journalist (and a regular contributor to this magazine), are now the best and fullest available, and a big improvement on the slightly thin Penguin collections that were in print for twenty years or more. There are useful, intelligent introductions by Packer and Keith Gessen (who writes about the critical essays). All the famous pieces are here, along with a good amount of less well-known work, like the diary that Orwell kept during the war, his account of a visit to Morocco, and the scarifying review he wrote in this magazine of Graham Greene's *The Heart of the Matter.* Again and again in these volumes, Orwell returns to the abuse of power. In his long essay on Dickens, one of the finest he wrote, he marks Dickens down for not being revolutionary enough (Dickens is "always pointing to a change of spirit rather than a change of structure"), and argues that a purely moral critique of society is not quite sufficient, since, as even Dickens recognized, the "central problem—how to prevent power from being abused—remains unsolved."

His nicely pugilistic essay on Tolstoy's hatred of *King Lear,* from 1947, is skeptical about Tolstoy's late, monkish religiosity, and sets up a binarism that is repeated two years later, in his essay on Gandhi. For Orwell, the humanist is committed to this world and its difficulties, and knows that "life is suffering." But the religious believer wagers everything on the next life, and though the two sides, secular and religious, may occasionally overlap, there can be no ultimate reconciliation between them. (Orwell was on the humanist side, of course—basically an unmetaphysical, English version of Camus' philosophy of perpetual godless struggle.) Orwell suspects that when the bullying Russian novelist became a bullying religious writer, he merely exchanged one form of egoism for another. "The distinction that really matters is not between violence and non-violence, but between having and not having the appetite for power." The example he appends is an interesting one: when a father threatens his son with "You'll get a thick ear if you do that again," coercion is palpable. But, Orwell writes, what of the mother who lovingly murmurs, "Now, darling, *is* it kind to Mummy to do that?" The mother wants to contaminate her son's brain. Tolstoy did not propose that *King Lear* be banned or censored, Orwell says; instead, when he wrote his polemic against Shakespeare, he tried to contaminate our pleasure in the play. For Orwell, "Creeds like pacifism and anarchism, which seem on the surface to imply a complete renunciation of power, rather encourage this habit of mind."

Orwell became increasingly obsessed with this kind of manipulative, insidious power; his repeated denunciations of those he thought wielded it—pacifists, anarchists, communist fellow travelers, naive leftists—reached a slightly hysterical pitch. But his terror of the tyrannical mother who lovingly murmurs at you while rearranging your brain is what makes the two books written under that shadow, *Animal Farm* and *1984*, so potent. The most appalling moments in *1984* come when the State has already read Winston Smith's mind and is committed to abolishing his interiority. A man sits in a room and thinks: we expect the traditional realist novel to indulge his free consciousness and represent its movements on the page. When we are told, in effect, that this cannot happen in the usual literary way, because this man is being watched by the State, that this man fears even to betray himself by speaking aloud in his sleep, the shock, sixty years after the book's publication, is still great. The all-seeing but benign novelist (Daddy) becomes the dreaded telescreen, or the torturer O'Brien (Mummy), who seems to know in advance what questions Winston will ask.

Eric Blair (Orwell's real name) was born in 1903, in Bengal, to a father who worked as a minor official in the Indian Civil Service; his mother was the daughter of a French teak merchant who did business in Burma. In a kind of morbid squirm, Orwell wrote that he belonged to the "lower-upper-middle class," a station with prestige but no money. Such families went to the colonies because they could afford to play there at being gentlemen. But this self-description appears in *The Road to Wigan Pier*, where it must have seemed very important to scuff his social polish a bit. In fact, "lower-upper class" would be more accurate and compact: he was the great-great-great-grandson of an earl, the grandson of a clergyman, and in later life kept up with Old Etonian chums like Cyril Connolly, Anthony Powell, and A. J. Ayer. At St. Cyprian's, a preparatory board-

—Ironies of Orwell's ire about class

ing school he was sent to at the age of eight, little Eric was inducted into a regime of violence and intimidation. According to his memoir "Such, Such Were the Joys" (which was not published in his lifetime, for fear of libel laws), he was singled out for bullying because he was a poor boy, on reduced fees. There was soft and hard power here—Mummy and Daddy were both at work. The headmaster and his wife used Blair's depressed financial status as manipulative weapons. "You are living on my bounty," the headmaster would say as he vigorously caned the boy. His wife comes across as an understudy for O'Brien; she could make young Blair snivel by saying things like "And do you think it's quite fair to *us*, the way you're behaving? After all we've done for you? You *do* know what we've done for you, don't you?"

Having crammed for an Eton scholarship, which he won, Orwell then seems to have taken the next five years off, though he read an enormous amount in his own time. Eton was enlightenment *itself* after St. Cyprian's, and he confessed to having been "relatively happy" there. But he must have been painfully aware, as he had been at St. Cyprian's, of not being able to keep up with wealthier boys. There was probably a more sophisticated version of the inquisition that he remembered from St. Cyprian's, in which "new boys of doubtful social origin" were bombarded with questions like "What part of London do you live in? Is that Knightsbridge or Kensington? How many bathrooms has your house got? How many servants do your people keep?" (I certainly remember an updated edition of this.) Unable to win a scholarship to Oxford or Cambridge, Orwell joined the Indian Imperial Police, in Burma, in 1922. It was a peculiar decision, but, like the atheist who loves churches, it perhaps represented an unconscious form of rebellious espionage.

School provided Orwell with one of his lifelong obsessions, class; his experience as a colonial policeman provided a tutorial in the other, the abuse of power. The famous essays that come out of the time in Burma are written with cool fire—a banked anger at administered cruelty. In "Shooting an Elephant," Orwell is ashamed that he must kill a magnificent elephant simply to avoid losing face, as a policeman and a white man, before a large Burmese crowd. In "A Hanging," the horror of the execution—"It is curious, but till that moment I had never realised what it means to destroy a

healthy, conscious man"—is made more trenchant by the triviality
that surrounds the event: Orwell describes a dog that bounds up
and tries to lick the face of the condemned man, and he notices, in
a celebrated moment, the prisoner swerve to avoid a puddle as he
walks toward the gallows.

Orwell claimed that in a peaceful age he might have been a
harmless, ornamental writer, oblivious of political obligation. "As
it is I have been forced into becoming a sort of pamphleteer," he
wrote in 1946. "First I spent five years in an unsuitable profession
(the Indian Imperial Police, in Burma), and then I underwent
poverty and the sense of failure." That verb, "underwent," suggests
not coercion but voluntary self-mortification. The truth is that in
1928 Orwell went to Paris, like many other poor, aspiring artists,
to see what he could produce. He ran out of money, and ended up
working as a dishwasher, or *plongeur,* in a Paris hotel. He contracted
influenza, and spent two weeks in the public ward of a hospital in
Paris, in hideous circumstances—an experience he wrote about
in "How the Poor Die." He returned to England, and tramped
around London and Kent with the down-and-out, living like the
homeless, on bread and margarine and cups of tea, and putting up
for the night at doss-houses, or "spikes." But he chose to do all this
rather than, say, go and live with his parents, because he was scout-
ing for material.

And what material! *Down and Out in Paris and London,* his first
book, which was published in 1933, is in some ways his best. There
is a young man's porousness to impressions, a marvelous ear for
speech, and a willingness to let anecdotes play themselves out. Four
years later, in *The Road to Wigan Pier,* he wrote again about the poor,
this time the miners, steelworkers, and unemployed of towns like
Wigan and Sheffield, but in that book they are hardly ever allowed
to speak. As there are no voices, so there are no *stories* in the later
book, no movement, just the tar of deprivation, which glues his
subjects into their poverty. Orwell has become a pamphleteer. The
earlier book, curiously, is a joyful, dynamic one. There is Boris, the
unemployed Russian waiter and former soldier, who likes to quote
Marshal Foch: *"Attaquez! Attaquez! Attaquez!"* There is the frighten-
ingly precise account of hunger, and the worldly tips that Orwell
enjoys passing on—such as eating bread with garlic rubbed on it,

because "the taste lingers and gives one the illusion of having fed recently." There are the vivid descriptions of the labyrinthine inferno in the bowels of the hotel where he works: "As we went along, something struck me violently in the back. It was a hundred-pound block of ice, carried by a blue-aproned porter. After him came a boy with a great slab of veal on his shoulder, his cheek pressed into the damp, spongy flesh." And there are characters like Bozo, a London pavement artist, who rattles on:

> The whole thing with cartoons is being up to date. Once a child got its head stuck in the railings of Chelsea Bridge. Well, I heard about it, and my cartoon was on the pavement before they'd got the child's head out of the railings. Prompt, I am.

And on:

> Have you ever seen a corpse burned? I have, in India. They put the old chap on the fire, and the next moment I almost jumped out of my skin, because he'd started kicking. It was only his muscles contracting in the heat—still, it give me a turn. Well, he wriggled about for a bit like a kipper on hot coals, and then his belly blew up and went off with a bang you could have heard fifty yards away. It fair put me against cremation.

Bozo, whose collar is always fraying, and who patches it with "bits cut from the tail of his shirt so that the shirt had scarcely any tail left," is both real and heightened. He is pure Dickens, and Orwell almost certainly worked up his speech like a good novelist. Who's to say that Orwell did not come up on his own with that simile, "like a kipper on hot coals"? It perfectly fulfills one of the requests he would make thirteen years later in a well-known essay, "Politics and the English Language," for "a fresh, vivid, home-made turn of speech." His own writing abounds with images of kipperlike pungency: "Even the millionaire suffers from a vague sense of guilt, like a dog eating a stolen leg of mutton." In his novel *Coming Up for Air* (1939), the old bucolic town of Lower Binfield has unattractively expanded after the First World War and has "spread like gravy over a tablecloth."

But, even if Orwell worked at his journalism like a good novelist, the strange thing is that he could not work at his novels like a good novelist. The details that pucker the journalism are rolled flat in the fiction. Orwell needed the prompt of the real to speak as a

writer. In the novel *Keep the Aspidistra Flying* (1936), the impoverished hero, about to go to a genteel tea party, ponders inking the
skin of his ankles where it peeps through his threadbare sock. It's
a marvelously evocative moment, which gives new meaning to the
phrase "down-at-heel." But it comes from something Orwell saw in
Paris, and recorded in *Down and Out*, before recycling it later in
the fiction. No one forgets the waiter in his first book, inking his
ankles, stuffing the soles of his shoes with newspaper, or squeezing
a dirty dishcloth into a patron's soup as a revenge on the bourgeoisie; no one forgets Mr. Brooker, in *The Road to Wigan Pier*, who runs
a tripe shop and has filthy fingers, and "like all people with permanently dirty hands . . . had a peculiarly intimate, lingering manner
of handling things." But there is absolutely nothing memorable in
the watery, vaudevillian description of the urban poor—"the pro-
les"—in *1984;* it is just neutered Gissing.

Orwell is famous for his frank and easy style, and for his determi-
nation that good prose should be as transparent as a windowpane.
But his style, though superbly colloquial, is much more like a lens
than like a window. His narrative journalism directs our attention
pedagogically; George Packer was right to choose the phrase "All
Art Is Propaganda" (from the essay on Dickens) as the title of one
of the new volumes. There is a cunning control of suspense. The
dog who bounds up to the prisoner in "A Hanging" is introduced
like this: "Suddenly, when we had gone ten yards, the procession
stopped short without any order or warning. A dreadful thing had
happened—a dog, come goodness knows whence, had appeared
in the yard." Whatever dreadful thing one has been made to expect
at that moment, it is unlikely to be as harmless as a dog. Likewise,
the characteristic Orwellian formulation "It is interesting that" or
"Curiously enough" generally introduces not some penny curiosity
but a gold-plated revelation: "Curiously enough he was the first
dead European I had seen," he writes in "How the Poor Die." The
man's swerving to avoid the puddle in "A Hanging" is passed off
rather similarly, as a kind of found object, a triviality noticed by
chance. But the essay is structured around two examples of irrele-
vance, each of them suggestive of an instinctive solipsism. The dog
who bounds up to the condemned man is living its own joyous, animal life, and this has nothing to do with the imminent horror; this
incursion is then "balanced"—in a formal sense—by the victim's

equally "irrelevant" swerve, which, among other things, is also an example of a body or a mind still moving at its own instinctual rhythm. The piece is highly choreographed.

Orwell almost certainly got this eye for didactic detail from Tolstoy. The man swerving around the puddle has an ancestor in the young Russian, in *War and Peace,* who, about to be executed by French soldiers, irrelevantly fiddles with his blindfold, because it is too tight. Nikolai Rostov, in the same book, finds that he cannot kill a French soldier, because instead of seeing an enemy he sees "a most simple, homelike face." In "Looking Back on the Spanish War" (usefully included in the selection of narrative essays), Orwell is about to shoot a fascist soldier, and then cannot, because "he was half-dressed and was holding up his trousers with both hands as he ran."

Orwell is wrongly thought of as the great neutral reporter, immune to the fever of judgment—the cool camera, the unbiased eyeball. He was attacked by Edward Said for propagating "the eyewitness, seemingly opinion-less politics" of Western journalism. "When they are on the rampage, you show Asiatic and African mobs rampaging: an obviously disturbing scene presented by an obviously unconcerned reporter who is beyond Left piety or right-wing cant," Said wrote about the Orwellian tradition. Almost the opposite is true. Orwell may seem cool, because he does not flinch from violence and poverty. Yet he thinks about horror coolly and watches it hotly. Henry Mayhew, whose reportage in *London Labour and the London Poor* (1861) is often compared to Orwell's, generally writes a rather detached prose. He goes around the London streets cataloguing and recording deprivation, an enlightened anthropologist. But there is nothing detached about Orwell's diction. He frequently describes the world of poverty as "loathsome," "disgusting," "fetid," "squalid." In the Paris hotel where he works, there is the "warm reek of food" and the "red glare of a fire." He labors alongside "a huge, excitable Italian" and "a hairy, uncouth animal whom we called the Magyar." Tramping around London and the English countryside with the homeless, he shares quarters in hostels with people who revolt him: "I shall never forget the reek of dirty feet . . . a stale, fetid stink . . . The passage was full of squalid, grey-shirted figures." In one doss-house, where the sheets "stank so horribly of sweat that I could not bear them near my nose," a man is lying in bed with his trousers wrapped around his head, "a thing which for some reason disgusted me very much." Orwell is woken the next morning

> by a dim impression of some large brown thing coming towards me. I opened my eyes and saw that it was one of the sailor's feet, sticking out of bed close to my face. It was dark brown, quite dark brown like an Indian's, with dirt. The walls were leprous, and the sheets, three weeks from the wash, were almost raw umber colour.

Notice, as ever, the crafty use of suspense ("some large brown thing"), and then the diction — "dark brown like an Indian's" — that borrows from a nineteenth-century sensationalist like Wilkie Collins. (The contemporary novelist Ian McEwan has in turn learned quite a lot about narrative stealth and the titration of disgust from Orwell.)

Perhaps Orwell struck Said as dangerous because, though politically didactic, he is rarely obviously sympathetic. On the contrary, he thrashes his subjects with attention. In "How the Poor Die," what stays with the reader is the description of the administration of the mustard poultice:

> I learned later that watching a patient have a mustard poultice was a favourite pastime in the ward. These things are normally applied for a quarter of an hour and certainly they are funny enough if you don't happen to be the person inside. For the first five minutes the pain is severe, but you believe you can bear it. During the second five minutes this belief evaporates, but the poultice is buckled at the back and you can't get it off. This is the period the onlookers most enjoy.

First, there is the apparent coolness ("and certainly they are funny enough if you don't happen to be the person inside"). And then the heat — the leap to that last sentence, with its combination of Grand Guignol and unverifiable self-projection: How can he really know this? Isn't it actually the moment that Orwell might most enjoy as a spectator, even while hating it?

Orwell says of Mr. Brooker, in *Wigan*, that like all men with dirty hands he handled food in a lingering way, but it is really Orwell whose eye cannot stop lingering on those dirty hands. In *Down and Out*, he cannot suppress the relish with which he tells us how many times he has seen the nasty fat pink fingers of the chef touching steak. Then he joyfully drives it home: "Whenever one pays more than, say, ten francs for a dish of meat in Paris, one may be certain that it has been fingered in this manner . . . Roughly speaking, the more one pays for food, the more sweat and spittle one is obliged to eat with it." The effect is both sadistic and masochistic, because Orwell does not exempt himself from the punishment: it is understood that at some point he, the Old Etonian, will be the patron, not the waiter, and, indeed, he seems to want to taste the sweat on the meat, as a salty political reminder. In a similar way, his rhetoric of disgust in *The Road to Wigan Pier* works so well because it involves us in his own difficult struggle to admire the working classes. If I can overcome my repulsion, he seems to say, then you can, too.

There is a long historical connection between revolution and Puritanism (with both a capital and a lowercase "P"), and Orwell sings in that stainless choir. In Paris, he exults that the only thing separating the diners from the squalor of the kitchen is a single door: "There sat the customers in all their splendour . . . and here, just a few feet away, we in our disgusting filth." This is a religious scourging. He is like Jonathan Edwards, reminding his congregation in a sermon that we are suspended over hell by "a slender thread," and that an angry God can cut it whenever it pleases Him. Throughout the 1930s and early '40s, as Orwell's radicalism grew, this politics of the slender thread became more pronounced. It provides one of the most powerful passages in *Wigan*, when he reminds us that our comfortable bourgeois existence aboveground is founded on what men do beneath, in hellish conditions:

> Whatever may be happening on the surface, the hacking and shovelling have got to continue without a pause . . . In order that Hitler may march the goosestep, that the Pope may denounce Bolshevism, that the cricket crowds may assemble at Lord's, that the Nancy poets may scratch one another's backs, coal has got to be forthcoming.

And it is the same with empire—a "stream of dividends that flows from the bodies of Indian coolies to the banking accounts of old ladies in Cheltenham."

But Orwell's radicalism was also conservative. He was a socialist artist but utterly anti-bohemian; a cosmopolitan who had lived in Paris and fought alongside Trotskyists in Spain but who was glad to get back home to lamb and mint sauce and "beer made with veritable hops." He wanted England to change but stay the same, and he became a great popular journalist in part because he was so good at defending the ordinary virtues of English life, as he saw them, against the menace of change; even when he is attacking something politically disagreeable—like the popular boys' weekly the *Magnet*, featuring Billy Bunter, whose tales were set at a posh, Eton-like boarding school—he sounds as if he wanted it to last forever. In the '40s, he wrote a column for the weekly left-wing paper the *Tribune*, as well as squibs for the *Evening Standard* (some of them included in Packer's selection), in which he praised the ideal cup of tea, the ideal London pub, the solid English food he liked (Yorkshire pudding, kippers, Stilton—"I fancy that Stilton is the best cheese of its type in the world"); attacked women's makeup ("It is very unusual to meet a man who does not think painting your fingernails scarlet is a disgusting habit"); asked why people use foreign phrases when "in nearly every case an English equivalent already exists"; and lamented the disappearance of the warming pan and the rise of the hot-water bottle ("clammy, unsatisfying").

What makes his essays about Donald McGill's seaside postcards, and Dickens, and the decline of the English murder, and Billy Bunter so acute is his talent for describing closed worlds and for adumbrating their conventions. If he pioneered what became cultural studies, it is because he could see that these worlds were both real (in that they were produced by a living culture) and unreal (in that they subsisted on their own peculiar codes). He transferred to the description of these existent fictional worlds the talent he lacked as a novelist of nonexistent worlds; he needed a drystone wall already up, so that he could bring his mortar to it and lovingly fill in the gaps. And he did the same with the closed world of English life, reading the country's narrative conventions. This semifictional England, beautifully described in *The Lion and the Unicorn*, was a rather shabby, stoical, anti-American, ideally classless place, devoted to small English pleasures like marmalade and suet pudding and fishing in country ponds, puritanical about large luxuries like the Ritz Hotel and Rolls-Royces, and suspicious of modern conveniences like aspirins, shiny American apples, cars, and radios. There is an undoubted comedy in Orwell's never having realized that what was obviously Utopia to him might strike at least half the population as a chaste nightmare.

The biggest convention in this semifictional world is the working class. In *The Road to Wigan Pier*, Orwell says that he knows too much about working-class life to idealize it, and then proceeds to idealize it, like some moral-moistened Victorian genre painter. In the best kind of proletarian home, he says, "you breathe a warm, decent, deeply human atmosphere," and a working man has a better chance of being happy than an "educated" one. Life is good there: "Especially on winter evenings after tea, when the fire glows in the open range and dances mirrored in the steel fender, when Father, in shirt-sleeves, sits in the rocking chair at one side of the fire reading the racing finals, and Mother sits on the other with her sewing, and the children are happy with a pennorth of mint humbugs, and the dog lolls roasting himself on the rag mat." What will that scene be like in two hundred years' time, he asks, in that Utopia where there is no manual labor and everyone is "educated"? There will be no coal fire, he answers, and no racing news, and the furniture will be made of rubber, glass, and steel.

Like many radicals, Orwell had strong Rousseauian tendencies: the simpler, apparently more organic life of the countryside seemed a tempting birdsong compared with London's mechanized squawks. He could see that, with or without a revolution, postwar British society would be very different from the bucolic pre-1914 world in which he grew up, and, uneasily, he returns repeatedly to what lies ahead. For millions of people, he laments, the sound of the radio is more normal than the sound of birds. (In his nursing-home diary, he noted with pleasure that the chief sound was of birds.) Modern life should be simpler and harder, he argues in this vein, not softer and more complex, and "in a healthy world there would be no demand for tinned foods, aspirins, gramophones, gaspipe chairs, machine guns, daily newspapers, telephones, motor-cars, etc., etc." Note that "etc."—there speaks the puritan, reserving the right to stretch his prohibitions, at cranky whim. In his novel *Coming Up for Air* (1939), the hero returns to the country town not far from London that he remembers from childhood (based on Orwell's own childhood memories of the Thames Valley) to find that it has become an overdeveloped horror, full of flimsy new houses and orbital roads; it looks just like "these new towns that have suddenly swelled up like balloons in the last few years, Hayes, Slough, Dagenham . . . The kind of chilliness, the bright red brick everywhere, the temporary-looking shop-windows full of cut-price chocolates and radio parts." The same new towns recur in *The Lion and the Unicorn,* when Orwell admits that life has improved for the working classes since 1918, and that people of an "indeterminate social class" have emerged, in new towns and suburbs around London, places like "Slough, Dagenham, Barnet, Letchworth, Hayes." He acknowledges that this is the future; indeed, he says that this puzzling nonclass will provide the "directing brains" for the postwar socialist revolution. But he cannot really admire these people:

> It is a rather restless, cultureless life, centring round tinned food, *Picture Post,* the radio and the internal combustion engine . . . To that civilization belong the people who are most at home in and most definitely *of* the modern world, the technicians and the higher-paid skilled workers, the airmen and their mechanics, the radio experts, film producers, popular journalists and industrial chemists.

Lest one be in any doubt as to what Orwell feels about this "indeterminate class," it is just such people who, in *1984,* have emerged after the wars and now run the totalitarian apparatus: "The new aristocracy was made up for the most part of bureaucrats, scientists, technicians, trade-union organizers . . . These people, whose origins lay in the salaried middle class and the upper grades of the working class, had been shaped and brought together by the barren world of monopoly industry and centralized government."

"Monopoly industry" and "centralized government" sound pretty much like capitalism and socialism, respectively. And perhaps Orwell had, by the late 1940s, soured on socialism, along with capitalism. On the one hand, capitalism produced unemployment and monopoly and injustice (i.e., England in the 1920s and '30s); and, on the other hand, socialist collectivism produced totalitarianism and barren machine-progress (i.e., Soviet Russia). And both political economies seemed to point to the loathsome postwar world of rubber and industrial chemists and hot-water bottles. During the mid- to late 1940s, when Orwell was writing his two most famous books, he remained faithful to an ideal English revolution, while losing faith in actual socialism, because, for all his powers of political prophecy, and his general approval of what the Labour Party stood for, he could not envisage a *realistic* English postwar future. (In *1984*, when Winston and Julia meet for their first illicit lovemaking, they travel outside soulless London into the unspoiled rural world that Orwell grew up in.)

I sat up when I encountered Orwell's two references to the bleak East London suburb of Dagenham, because that was where my father was born, in 1928, into exactly the "indeterminate class" that Orwell cannot bring himself to admire. My grandfather ended up as a quality-control checker at the Ford factory that came to Dagenham in 1931, and my father's passage out of and up from that indeed rather "cultureless" world was the traditional one for bright working-class boys: he went to the Royal Liberty School, in East London, established in 1921 by the local council, to aid boys like him, and then to Queen Mary College, at the University of London, a product of late-Victorian charity, established to educate workingmen. (An equivalent social movement occurred in America with the passage of the GI Bill in 1944.) He was good at science, and went on to become a professor of zoology. Theoretically, Orwell had to approve of men like him; practically, he could not, and in *The Road to Wigan Pier,* in perhaps the most scandalous paragraph he ever wrote, he announces that the working class's attitude toward education is much sounder than the middle class's, because they see through the nonsense of education: "Working-people often have a vague reverence for learning in others, but where education touches their own lives they see through it and reject it by a healthy instinct." The working-class teenager sensibly wants to leave school as soon as possible, and "to be doing real work, not wasting his time on ridiculous rubbish like history and geography." He should be bringing home a pound a week for his parents, Orwell says, not stuffing himself into silly uniforms and being caned for neglecting his homework.

"It's a good British feeling to try and raise your family a little," Mr. Vincy says in *Middlemarch*. George Eliot, an estate manager's daughter who ended up living on Cheyne Walk in grand Chelsea, knew that "good British feeling" very well. But Orwell was suspicious of this indeterminate, petit-bourgeois class, because it wanted to change itself first and society second, if at all. Margaret Thatcher, born in 1925 to a small-town shopkeeper, is the model of this kind of conservative class mobility. Orwell suspected Dickens of the same impulse, noting with displeasure that the successful novelist sent his eldest son to Eton. That is why the great Dickens novels want to change things but in fact leave everything in place: "However much Dickens may admire the working classes, he does not wish to resemble them." Orwell means this as a judgment against Dickens, but it is unwittingly comic. Why on earth should Dickens have wanted to resemble the working classes? Why would anyone want to, least of all the working classes themselves? But Orwell did—at least, up to a point. The upper-class masochist lived frugally, dressed down, and for most of his life, until *Animal Farm* and *1984* sold well, earned relatively little. His sister said after his death that the kind of person he most admired was a working-class mother of ten children. But if the problem with wanting to get out of the working class is that someone is always left behind, then the problem with "admiring" the working class is that admiration doesn't, on its own, help anyone to get out of it at all. (Notice that Orwell, who reported so vividly on extreme poverty, brought none of his documentary rigor to the kind of ordinary working-class life he was happy to idealize.)

So the question hangs over Orwell, as it does over so many well-heeled revolutionaries: Did he want to level up society or level it down? The evidence points to the latter. The real struggle for this puritan masochist, the one that was personal—the one that was, ironically enough, *inherited*—was the struggle to obliterate privilege, and thus, in some sense, to obliterate himself. This was, at bottom, a religious self-mortification, and was not always politically coherent. In *Down and Out in Paris and London,* he pauses to consider the plight of the *plongeur,* slaving in hotels so that wealthier people can stay in them. How is this bad situation to be mitigated? Well, Orwell says, hotels are just needless luxuries, so if people stopped going to them, there would be less hard work to do. "Nearly everyone hates hotels. Some restaurants are better than others, but it is impossible to get as good a meal in a restaurant as one can get, for the same expense, in a private house." As Philip Larkin puts it in a poem, "useful to get that learnt." A similarly telling moment appears in Orwell's review of Friedrich Hayek's *The Road to Serfdom* (1944). There was much in the book to agree with, Orwell said. (It was also admired by the young Margaret Thatcher.) But Hayek's faith in capitalist competition was overzealous: "The trouble with competitions is that somebody wins them." Not, you notice, that somebody loses them—which would mean raising those people up. Somebody wins them, and that cannot be allowed.

It is hardly fair to claim that Orwell did not earnestly long for the emancipation of the working classes; he did. But, for all his desire to abolish class distinctions, he could barely credit actual class mobility. For although it may be true that the upwardly mobile working classes do not want fundamentally to change society, their very ascension does change it. (Orwell is sometimes criticized for ignoring the American example, but, closer to home, if he had taken any interest in Scotland, he would have seen a relatively dynamic social culture propelled by a serious stake in education.) Actual class mobility was unappealing to Orwell—unconsciously, of course—because he believed in a mystical revolution, a revolution in which England changed and stayed the same; and, for him, what seems to have guaranteed England's preservation was the idea of a static, semifictional working-class world of decency and good-tempered bus conductors and bad teeth. Change that, and you change England. Thus it is, I think, that Orwell stresses, throughout his work, "equality of sacrifice" rather than equality of benefit. The former could be controlled—indeed, is control itself. The latter might lead to the Ritz and the Rolls-Royce.

Orwell feared what he most desired: the future. But it is too easy to gloat over his contradictions—to point out that he wrote so well about the drabness and the horror of totalitarianism because he himself had a tendency toward drab omnipotence; or that the great proponent of socialist collectivity liked rustic isolation (he wrote most of *1984* on the Hebridean island of Jura); or, more simply, that the hater of private schools put his adopted son down for Westminster, one of the grandest London academies. So Orwell was contradictory: contradictions are what make writers interesting; consistency is for cooking. Instead, one is gratefully struck by how prescient Orwell was, and by how much he got right. He was right about how capitalism had failed British society; he was right about education (private institutions eventually opened themselves to state-aided students, as he had demanded, and the Butler Act of 1944 universalized free secondary school education);

Whitman : " Do I contradict myself? Yes,
I contradict myself, So be it. I contain
multitudes. "

about colonialism (that he so disliked Gandhi seems to me only to strengthen Orwell's position, by making it disinterested); about to-talitarianism. If his novelistic imagining of totalitarian horror now looks a bit dated, it is partly because his fiction provided the dusty epitaph on a dustier tombstone that he himself helped to carve; and, anyway, his coinages, like "doublethink" and "Newspeak" and "Big Brother," now live an unexpectedly acute second life in the supposedly free West. (To see Fox News go after Jeremiah Wright or Bill Ayers for days on end during the last presidential election was to think, simply, "Hate Week.")

And Orwell's revolutionary mysticism turned out to be curiously precise: he was right not in spite of but because of his contradic-tions. Although an Orwellian revolution never quite came about, an Orwellian victory did. In part, Hitler was defeated by the exer-cise of a peculiarly English—peculiarly Orwellian—combination of collectivity and individualism. (He marveled, in the summer of 1945, that Britain had come through the war without becoming either socialist or fascist, and with civil liberties almost intact.) This combination of conservatism and radicalism, of political sleepiness and insomnia, this centuries-long brotherhood of gamekeeper and poacher, which Orwell called "the English genius," was also Or-well's genius, finding in English life its own ideological brother-hood. For good and ill, those English contradictions have lasted. If Orwell hammered so noisily at privilege that at times he couldn't hear the working classes eagerly knocking at the door to be admit-ted, it is because he knew the immense size of the obstacle they would face. To level an Orwellian emphasis, what is remarkable about British society today is not how much bigger the middle class is but how little the upper classes have given up. The working classes got richer, but the rich got much richer. Next year, it seems likely, Britain will elect its nineteenth Old Etonian prime minister —a Conservative, of course. The Orwell who wrote about the play-ing fields of Eton would be shocked to discover that, for all the transformations that Britain has undergone, the lofty old school is still there, much as it always was, educating the upper classes to govern the country, wreck the City, and have lovely house parties.

Contributors' Notes

ELIF BATUMAN is the author of *The Possessed: Adventures with Russian Books and the People Who Read Them*. She has written for *The New Yorker*, *Harper's Magazine*, the *New York Times*, the *Guardian*, the *London Review of Books*, the *Nation*, and *n+1*. Her blog, My Life and Thoughts, can be found at www.elifbatuman.net. She lives in San Francisco.

TONI BENTLEY was born in Perth, Western Australia. She attended the School of American Ballet and danced with Balanchine's New York City Ballet for ten years. She published her first book, *Winter Season: A Dancer's Journal*, while still dancing, at the age of twenty-two. She is the author of five books—all named Notable Books of the Year by the *New York Times*—including *Sisters of Salome* and *The Surrender: An Erotic Memoir*, which has been translated into eighteen languages. She writes for the *New York Times Book Review*, the *New York Review of Books*, and *Playboy* and is the recipient of a 2008 Guggenheim fellowship.

JANE CHURCHON studied at California State University, Sacramento, and UC Berkeley, where she won the Shrout Short Story Prize. She is a frequent contributor to the *Sun*, and her work has also appeared in *Something to Declare: Good Lesbian Travel Writing* and the *Berkeley Fiction Review*. Jane lives in Sacramento with her partner, MK, her two children, and an embarrassing number of cats. She is a registered nurse and nursing supervisor at a large northern California medical center and is working on a collection of essays about nursing and life.

BRIAN DOYLE is the editor of *Portland* magazine, at the University of Portland, in Oregon. He is the author of five collections of essays, two nonfiction books (*The Grail*, about a year in an Oregon vineyard, and

The Wet Engine, about how hearts work and don't), and two collections of "proems," most recently *Thirsty for the Joy: Australian and American Voices*. His novel *Mink River* will be published in October 2010.

JOHN GAMEL is professor emeritus of ophthalmology at the University of Louisville School of Medicine. He has published ninety articles in scientific journals on topics ranging from fingerprints to breast cancer. He has also published sixteen personal essays in a variety of literary journals, including the *Alaska Quarterly Review, Boulevard, Epoch,* and the *Antioch Review*. These have been assembled into a memoir, *Spinal Beauty, Pendulous Love, and the Man Who Lived in an Eggcup: A Medical Odyssey*.

WALTER ISAACSON, a graduate of Harvard College and of Pembroke College of Oxford University, is the president and CEO of the Aspen Institute and has been the chairman and CEO of CNN and the editor of *Time* magazine. His books include *American Sketches, Einstein: His Life and Universe, Benjamin Franklin: An American Life,* and *Kissinger: A Biography*. He lives with his wife and daughter in Washington, D.C.

STEVEN L. ISENBERG is the executive director of the PEN American Center, the largest branch of the world's oldest human rights organization, devoted to free expression and the promotion of literature through an international literary fellowship. Isenberg has also been a visiting professor of humanities at the University of Texas at Austin, the chairman of the board and president ad interim of Adelphi University, the publisher of *New York Newsday*, the executive vice president of the *Los Angeles Times*, and the chief of staff to New York's Mayor John V. Lindsay. He holds degrees from the University of California at Berkeley, Worcester College of Oxford University, and Yale Law School. He lives in New York City.

JANE KRAMER has written *The New Yorker*'s "Letter from Europe" for more than twenty years. She is the author of nine books, among them *The Last Cowboy, Europeans, The Politics of Memory,* and, most recently, *Lone Patriot,* and has been the recipient of many awards, including a National Book Award and a National Magazine Award. With *Europeans,* she became the first woman—as well as the first American—to win the Prix Européen de l'Essai Charles Veillon, Europe's most important award for nonfiction. In 2005 she was made a Chevalier de la Légion d'honneur. She divides her time between Europe and New York.

ARTHUR KRYSTAL is the author of two essay collections: *Agitations* and *The Half-Life of an American Essayist*. A longer version of "When Writers Speak" will appear in *Except When I Write,* to be published in 2011.

MATT LABASH is a senior writer at the *Weekly Standard* and the author of *Fly Fishing with Darth Vader: And Other Adventures with Evangelical Wrestlers, Political Hitmen, and Jewish Cowboys*. The *Columbia Journalism Review* named him one of "ten young writers on the rise." *Esquire* has called him "one of the absolute greatest magazine writers in America." In 2007 and 2009 he won a "Sidney Award" from the *New York Times* columnist David Brooks, who lists each December what he considers the best essays and articles of the year. He lives in Owings, Maryland, with his wife and two sons.

PHILLIP LOPATE is the author of a dozen books, most recently *Two Marriages* (a pair of novellas) and *Notes on Sontag*. A book of his selected poems, *At the End of the Day*, is forthcoming. He is a professor at Columbia University and lives with his wife and daughter in Brooklyn.

IAN MCEWAN is the author of two collections of short stories—*First Love, Last Rites* and *In Between the Sheets*—as well as the following novels: *The Cement Garden, The Comfort of Strangers, The Child in Time, The Innocent, Black Dogs, The Daydreamer, Enduring Love, Amsterdam* (winner of the 1998 Booker Prize), *Atonement, Saturday*, and *On Chesil Beach*. His most recent novel is *Solar*.

STEVEN PINKER is Harvard College Professor and Johnstone Family Professor in the Department of Psychology at Harvard University. He conducts research in cognition, psycholinguistics, and evolutionary psychology, and has written seven books, including *The Language Instinct, How the Mind Works, The Blank Slate*, and *The Stuff of Thought*. He has won many prizes for his books, research, and teaching, and is the chair of the Usage Panel of *The American Heritage Dictionary*.

RON RINDO, a professor of English at the University of Wisconsin in Oshkosh, has published three short story collections, most recently *Love in an Expanding Universe*. The Wisconsin Library Association cited his previous books, *Suburban Metaphysics* and *Secrets Men Keep*, on its list of the top ten books published by Wisconsin writers in 1990 and 1995. He has also twice received artists' fellowships from the Wisconsin Arts Board. His recent short fiction has appeared in the *Bellevue Literary Review* and Terrain.org. "Gyromancy" is his first published essay. Rindo lives with his wife, Jenna, and their five children on a hobby farm in rural Pickett, Wisconsin.

DAVID SEDARIS is the author of the books *Dress Your Family in Corduroy and Denim, Me Talk Pretty One Day, Naked, Holidays on Ice, Barrel Fever*, and *When You Are Engulfed in Flames*. He is a regular contributor to *The New Yorker* and National Public Radio's *This American Life*. His latest collection, *Squirrel Seeks Chipmunk: A Modest Bestiary*, will be published in October 2010.

ZADIE SMITH is the author of three novels: *White Teeth*, *The Autograph Man*, and *On Beauty*, which won the 2006 Orange Prize for fiction. She is also the author of *Changing My Mind: Occasional Essays* and the editor of a story collection, *The Book of Other People*.

S. FREDERICK STARR is chairman of the Central Asia–Caucasus Institute at Johns Hopkins University's School of Advanced International Studies. He was founding chairman of the Woodrow Wilson Center's Kennan Institute and president of Oberlin College and the Aspen Institute. He began his career doing archaeological work in Turkey and teaching intellectual history at Princeton and has picked up those threads in the present article, which is based on a book he is writing.

JOHN H. SUMMERS is the author of *Every Fury on Earth* and editor of *The Politics of Truth: Selected Writings of C. Wright Mills*. He is a frequent contributor to magazines and newspapers, and his essays have appeared in the *New Republic*, the *Nation*, the *New York Times Book Review*, *Boston Review*, and the *Baffler*, as well as in leading academic periodicals. Born and raised in Gettysburg, Pennsylvania, Summers received his Ph.D. in history from the University of Rochester in 2006 and taught at Harvard University from 2000 to 2007. Since then he has been a lecturer in American studies at Columbia University and given courses at Cooper Union and Boston College, where he is a visiting scholar. He lives with his wife and daughter in Cambridge, Massachusetts.

JOHN EDGAR WIDEMAN is a two-time winner of the PEN/Faulkner Award and has been a nominee for the National Book Critics Circle Award. He has also received a MacArthur grant, and in 1998 he won the Rea Award for the short story. His novels include *A Glance Away*, *The Lynchers*, *Sent for You Yesterday*, *Reuben*, *Philadelphia Fire*, *The Cattle Killing*, *Two Cities*, and *Fanon*. Along with several short story collections, most recently *God's Gym* and *Briefs*, Wideman has written four memoirs: *Brothers and Keepers*, *Fatheralong*, *Hoop Roots*, and *The Island: Martinique*. He teaches at Brown University.

GARRY WILLS, an emeritus professor of history at Northwestern University, has published nearly forty books on a wide variety of subjects that include history, biography, criticism, politics, and religion. His most recent publications include *What Jesus Meant*, *Head and Heart: American Christianities*, *What the Gospels Meant*, *Bomb Power*, and *Outside Looking In*. He received the Pulitzer Prize in general nonfiction for *Lincoln at Gettysburg: The Words That Remade America*. He was also the recipient of the

National Book Critics Circle Award (twice) and the Presidential Medal of the National Endowment for the Humanities.

JAMES WOOD is a staff writer at *The New Yorker* and Professor of the Practice of Literary Criticism at Harvard University. He has written two books of essays, *The Broken Estate* and *The Irresponsible Self,* as well as a novel, *The Book Against God.* His most recent book is *How Fiction Works.*

Notable Essays of 2009

SELECTED BY ROBERT ATWAN

CHRIS ABANI
Ethics and Narrative: The Human
and Other, *Witness,* vol. 22

RAYMOND ABBOTT
The Haverhill Journal, *Journal of
Kentucky Studies,* Fall

KIM ADRIAN
How to Buy Peaches, *Tin House,*
vol. 10, no. 3

AMIN AHMAD
205 Lower Circular Road, *Harvard
Review,* no. 37

MARCIA ALDRICH
The Dead Dog Essay, *Florida Review,*
vol. 34, no. 1

BETH ALVARADO
Clarity, *Cimarron Review,* Winter

ROBYN ANSPACH
Three Hooks, *New Letters,* vol. 75,
nos. 2 & 3

JULIANNA BAGGOT
For All the Ladies in My Mother's
Book Group, *Hayden's Ferry Review,*
Spring/Summer

POE BALLANTINE
The Fine Art of Quitting, *Sun,* April

PHYLLIS BARBER
Sweetgrass, *Upstreet,* vol. 5

JULIAN BARNES
Such, Such Was Eric Blair, *New York
Review of Books,* March 12

HELEN BAROLINI
The Curio Cabinet, *Southwest Review,*
vol. 94, no. 4

JOCELYN BARTKEVICIUS
Crossroads, *Fourth Genre,* vol. 11,
no. 1

RICK BASS
The Rains in September, *TriQuarterly,*
133

KIRSTEN EVE BEACHY
Selling the Farm, *Shenandoah,*
Spring/Summer

DAN BEACHY-QUICK
Of Verdant Themes: Toward One
Sentence in Proust, *Puerto del Sol,*
Summer

MARY BEARD
Scrolling Down the Ages, *New York
Times Book Review,* April 19

PAUL BECKMAN
Another One of His Punishments,
New Haven Review, Summer

BRIAN BEDARD
Aisle 22, *South Dakota Review,*
Summer

LEE ZACHARIAS
The Bride Beneath My Bed, *Pleiades*,
vol. 29, no. 1

PAUL ZIMMER
Four Cats and the Pathetic Fallacy,
Georgia Review, Fall

Notable Special Issues of 2009

Bidoun, Flowers, ed. Negar Azimi and
Michael C. Vazquez, Spring

Conjunctions, Not Even Past, ed.
Bradford Morrow, no. 53

Critical Inquiry, The Fate of Disciplines,
ed. James Chandler and Arnold I.
Davidson, vol. 35, no. 4

Daedalus, The Merging Voices, ed.
Steven Marcus, Spring

Essence, President Barack Obama:
Celebrating the Dream, ed. Angela
Burt-Murray, January

Georgia Review, Culture and the
Environment, ed. Stephen Corey,
Spring

Health Affairs, Celebrating a Decade of
Narrative Matters, ed. Ell Ficklen,
July/August

Hedgehog Review, Youth Culture, ed.
James Davison Hunter and Jennifer
L. Geddes, Spring

Hunger Mountain, Journeys, ed. Miciah
Bay Gault, no. 14

Iowa Review, The River, ed. David
Hamilton, Fall

Lapham's Quarterly, Travel, ed. Lewis H.
Lapham, vol. 2, no. 3

Massachusetts Review, Celebrating Fifty
Years, ed. Thomas L. Dumm, David
Lenson, and Ellen Dore Watson, vol.
50, nos. 1 & 2

McSweeney's, San Francisco Panorama,
ed. staff of *McSweeney's*, no. 33

Michigan Quarterly Review, Bookishness:
The New Fate of Reading, ed. John
Freedman, Fall

New England Review, Remembering Ted

Solotaroff, ed. Stephen Donadio,
vol. 30, no. 3

New Literary History, Play, ed. Rita Felski,
vol. 40, no. 1

Oxford American, Race, ed. Mark
Smirnoff, no. 64

Prairie Schooner, Baby Boomer Issue, ed.
Grace Bauer, Fall

River Teeth, Best of *River Teeth* (2 vol.
compendium), ed. Joe Mackall and
Daniel W. Lehman, vol. 10, nos. 1
& 2

Smithsonian, Special Issue: Dream
Destinations, ed. Carey Winfrey,
September

Sonora Review, Thank You, David Foster
Wallace, ed. Michael Sheehan, nos.
55 & 56

Tikkun, Remaking America, ed.
Michael Lerner, March/April

Tin House, Dread/Hope, ed. Rob
Spillman, vol. 11, no. 1

Western Humanities Review, Nature,
Culture, Technology, ed. Anne-Marie
Feenberg-Dibon and Reginald
McGinnis, vol. 63, no. 3

Wired, The Mystery Issue, ed. J. J.
Abrams, May

Witness, Dismissing Africa, ed. Amber
Withycombe, no. 22

Correction

The following author's name was
misspelled in Notable Essays of 2008:
"The Empty House," from *Under the
Sun*, was written by Sue Eisenfeld.